Reshaping Rural England

A social history 1850–1925

Reshaping Rural England

A social history 1850–1925

ALUN HOWKINS

London and New York

First published 1991 by HarperCollins*Academic*

Reprinted 1992 by Routledge
11 New Fetter Lane, London EC4P 4EE

Simultaneously published in the USA and Canada
by Routledge
a division of Routledge, Chapman and Hall, Inc.
29 West 35th Street, New York, NY 10001

Printed in Great Britain by Billing and Sons Ltd.,
London and Worcester

British Library Cataloguing in Publication Data

Howkins, Alun.
Reshaping Rural England 1850–1925: a Social History
1. England. Rural regions. Social conditions, history
I. Title
942.009734

Library of Congress Cataloging in Publication Data

Howkins, Alun.
Reshaping Rural England: a social history 1850–1925 /
Alun Howkins.
p. cm.
Includes bibliographical references and index.
1. England–Rural conditions. 2. England–Social conditions–19th century. 3. England–Social conditions–20th century. I. Title.
HN 398.E5H69 1991
307.72′0942–dc20
90–21857

ISBN 0–415–09066–0

Contents

For Linda

Preface and acknowledgements

During the writing of this book I have incurred many debts to those who have helped me and provided me with access to records and materials. I would like to thank the staffs of the East Sussex Record Office; the Kent County Record Office; the Norwich and Norfolk Record Office; the Northumberland Record Office; the Oxfordshire Record Office and the Devon Record Office [Exeter]. Most of the staff will not remember me, and I know only a few names, but I was always treated with unfailing courtesy and helpfulness. I would also like again to thank Brenda Corti and Mary Girling at the University of Essex for helping me when I was working on the Essex Oral History Archive, and Paul Thompson for letting me have access to the material held there. As always with any work of British history I owe an enormous debt to the staff of one of our most sacred and constantly threatened institutions, the British Library, both in its grand form in Bloomsbury and its suburban cousin at Colindale. Finally I would like to thank my own institution, the University of Sussex: the School of Cultural and Community Studies for helping me with research expenses and a term's sabbatical leave, and the library and its staff who even now send me references to obscure and rural works.

There is always a different kind of debt, to friends, colleagues and students who have knowingly or unknowingly shaped one's own thought and work. I owe a huge amount to the undergraduate students I have taught over the last ten years especially on my special subject 'The Remaking of Rural England, 1875–1914'. Here for them is the book of the course which they have helped make. Next there is a group of graduate students and colleagues at Sussex who have listened, argued and given of their time. Thanks then to Brian Short, Maggie Morgan, Mick Reed, Sue Wright, John Lowerson, John Barrell, Lesley Wallace and Judy Gielguid. Finally there are personal thanks. To Stuart Laing for being a good mate and a supportive and stimulating colleague during the writing of this; to Raphael Samuel for lots of ideas; to Anna Davin for good talk and an insistence on feminism and, above all, to Linda Merricks, to whom the book is dedicated, for more than putting up with it. In the end though, and as always, the fault is my own.

Abbreviations

AHR	*Agricultural History Review*
Bod L.	Bodleian Library, Oxford
DRO	Devon Record Office, Exeter
EcHR	*Economic History Review*
ENRC	*East and North Riding Chronicle*
EOHC	Essex Oral History Collection, University of Essex
ESRO	East Sussex Record Office, Lewes
EWL	*Eastern Weekly Leader*
EWP	*Eastern Weekly Press*
HJ	*Historical Journal*
HWJ	*History Workshop Journal*
JOJ	*Jackson's Oxford Journal*
JRASE	*Journal of the Royal Agricultural Society of England*
KCRO	Kent County Records Office, Maidstone
LG	*Labour Gazette*
MC	*Morning Chronicle*
MLE	*Mark Lane Express*
NN	*Norfolk News*
NNRO	Norwich and Norfolk Record Office, Norwich
NRO	Northumberland Record Office, Newcastle-upon-Tyne
OC	*Oxford Chronicle*
ORO	Oxfordshire Record Office, Oxford
OT	*Oxford Times*
P&P	*Past and Present*
PP	*Parliamentary Papers*
PRO	Public Record Office
SAC	*Sussex Archeological Collections*
SAE	Sussex Agricultural Express

Introduction

The social history of rural England in the years from 1850 until after the Great War is complex. To begin with we must recognize that the notion of 'one' rural England is in itself problematic. Although we have been accustomed to seeing the United Kingdom as the first 'modern' economy with a unified market and productive system, it is clear from even the most cursory examination that this was simply not so for all of the nineteenth century and much of the twentieth. Rather England was an amalgam of regional economies each with its own often distinctive social and economic structures. This idea is central to some recent historical work. In an economic sense C. H. Lee has stressed the regional diversity of England's growth during the nineteenth century and talked about 'a number of quite distinct regional structures'.[1] For the social historian, current work in anthropology associated with Anthony Cohen and others raises probably more important questions. Cohen writes of:

> a populist tendency to cultural 'localism' which has forced us to revise our over-simple view of the homogeneous nature of British culture, a caricature much exploited by politicians and the mass media, although thoroughly misleading and reviled by the members of localities, who see in it a gross misrepresentation of their special circumstances and their distinctive cultures.[2]

Although much of this anthropology of rural Britain has looked at 'marginal' communities its implications are important for all rural structures. Finally, Hugh Kearney in his stimulating and important book, *The British Isles. A History of Four Nations*, throws the net wider still.

> Upon closer examination what seem to be 'national' units dissolve into a number of distinctive cultures with their own perceptions of the past, of social status ('class' is here seen as subordinate to culture), of religion and of many other aspects of life.[3]

As well as these regions there are what the historian perceives as the continuities and the discontinuities of English social life and social structure in the past. Throughout the period covered by this book there are central continuities apart from that of region. The family, the sexual division of labour, aspects of the church and other institutional structures, for example, are continuous presences. Equally, although it is currently unfashionable to recognize them, there were discontinuities. Rural depopulation, agricultural depression, new farming techniques or ideological shifts do not have the causal clarity of a single variable change but certainly altered the world in which men and women lived, and, perhaps more importantly, were seen by those who experienced them as being decisive changes.

However, these changes existed within an all-pervasive regionality, not as determined by them or determining of them but in a relationship of mutual influence. This meant that the development of, for example, an unproblematically capitalist social and economic order in rural England, did not follow a 'national' timetable, nor did all aspects of that system emerge at the same time and in the same place. Rather capitalism in rural England developed unevenly depending on pre-existing economic, social and even cultural structures for the precise form in which it finally emerged.

All this leads to problems for the writer of the 'general survey'. For example Harold Perkin's brilliant and in some ways persuasive book *The Rise of Professional Society. England since 1880* gives a unitary experience to England which effectively ignores the rural. At one level this is hardly surprising since his definition of a 'professional society' as one based on 'career hierarchies of specialized occupations, selected on merit and based on trained expertise' hardly fits any aspect of rural social or economic life for most of the period before 1945.[4] That is not to say that elements of 'professionalization' are not present in rural society – indeed they are an important part of socio-cultural change especially after 1890 – rather that they coexist with other 'definitions' of the social order, some of them older, some simply different, from that distinguished by Professor Perkin.

A way round this, the traditional one, is to impose periods, and to some extent that is done in this book. What follows is divided into three main 'sub-periods' within the overall combined and uneven development of a broadly agrarian capitalist social and economic system. However across these periods continuities and above all regional experience remain.

The first sub-period, covered by Chapters 1 to 5, runs from approximately 1850 to 1875. This, it is argued, was a time when rural society and its productive systems entered a state of calm in which the rural order functioned by and large successfully after a period from the 1790s which had been dominated by endemic unrest and economic uncertainty. This is *not* to argue that it was free from contradictions and problems, rather that these contradictions were controlled, in most situations. The mixture of 'carrot and stick' which is at the heart of the new paternalism of the period after 1850 is the subject matter of Chapter 3, while the problems of the system, economic and cultural, are looked at in Chapters 4 and 5.

The first sub-period also looks at some of the continuities of home, work, family, gender and community. These form the subject matter of Chapters 1 and 2. Although this material is placed here, aspects of it stretch well beyond the 1870s. Farm structure and family employment, differences between north and south, for example, remain in many ways the same until after the Great War. In these areas simple chronology breaks down and we need different time scales which are not easy to find and which exist outside the narrow determinisms of the political or even the economic.

The second sub-period runs from approximately 1872 to 1895. The overlap is a result of an argument that this is a time in which the established and apparently 'permanent' society of the years after 1850 entered a series of crises. These came partly from contradictions within the system itself, for example the growth of education, or rural depopulation, and partly from factors outside the system and over which it had no control, particularly the import of food stuffs. The outcome of these problems was a period of flux and readjustment in which some long-term factors, the growth of religious nonconformity for instance, came together with the problems caused by economic depression to present a challenge to the models of paternalism whose economic base had anyway been weakened. These problems are looked at in Chapters 6 and 7 which are 'divided' on loosely class/status lines.

The third sub-period runs from 1895 to 1925. Here we see the emergence of a 'new' farming system based on a much more diverse cropping combined with an undermining of some of the traditional regional farming patterns as transport improved and urban incomes, especially among the working class, rose. The problems of control and order which emerged again in the 1870s and 1880s in the new form of trades unionism and even radical politics continued to develop, bringing country districts more 'in line' with an overwhelmingly 'urban' society. It is during this sub-period that we see the first serious erosion of regional cultural patterns. The period is in some senses dominated by the Great War, but it is difficult to distinguish between what effect the war had and what was happening anyway. For instance the 'decline' of the traditional elites, especially sections of the aristocracy and gentry, was clearly happening before the war but was also, at the very least, speeded up by the conflict.

Even within the England of 1925 there remained elements which would have been familiar 100 years earlier. Despite modifications the great regional farming divisions remained the same. Even if contemporaries like S. L. Bensusan – who toured the rural districts in 1927 – thought everything had changed, the modern reader finds a good deal in common between his account and that of A. D. Hall in 1911–13, or Sir Henry Rider Haggard in 1902, or even James Caird in 1851.[5] There are also changes, only glimpsed in these accounts, which are so slow as to be almost continuities. The long-term relationship between town and country was, for most of our period, unproblematically one way, with the city drawing young men and women from the countryside, demanding ever more and ever different food and imposing its view of progress on the whole nation. By the 1900s, with only just over 6 per cent of national income coming from agriculture and about 6 per cent of the population employed in it, the town seemed triumphant.[6] Yet at precisely that moment there were those, in growing numbers who believed the town had 'failed' and that only in the countryside was truth and beauty and 'real Englishness' to be found. They started a revolution, the flight from the cities by the affluent, which still seeks a proper history and which we are still living with today.

There were other slow but vital changes which are perhaps clearer but which span the whole period from 1850 to 1925. Of great importance was a gradual move, from the 1870s onwards, to a smaller and more regularly employed workforce which was largely male, with women, though still vital, pushed more and more into the position of a reserve army of casual labour. Also from the 1870s there seems to have been a gradual erosion of gentry and aristocratic power and status, in which their former positions were taken over by the tenant farmers so that employment/power relationships became increasingly centred on farmer/labourer without the 'outside' influence of the landlord. This went hand in hand with the gradual growth of owner occupancy.

All this means that the coverage in this book is uneven and probably idiosyncratic. Its structure is perhaps over-determined by its materials yet I believe it can be defended. Ultimately 'rural England' was reshaped between 1850 and 1925 though not by cataclysmic forces. Rather, with the exception of the agricultural depression of the 1870s and 1880s and the Great War, it was a process of attrition, of gradual nibbling away – of endless, almost meaningless local change. Only when we try to aggregate that change, with all its contradictions and problems, do we get any sense of that reshaping.

NOTES

1 C. H. Lee, *The British Economy Since 1700. A macroeconomic perspective* (Cambridge, 1986), p. 135.
2 Anthony P. Cohen, (ed.) *Belonging: Identity and Social Organisation in British Rural Cultures* (Manchester, 1982), p. 1.
3 Hugh Kearney, *The British Isles. A History of Four Nations* (Cambridge, 1989), p. 7.
4 Harold Perkin, *The Rise of Professional Society. England since 1880* (London, 1989), p. 2.
5 S. L. Bensusan, *Latter Day Rural England* (Edinburgh, 1927); A. D. Hall, *A Pilgrimage of British Farming* (London, 1913); Sir Henry Rider Haggard, *Rural England* (London, 1902); James Caird, *English Agriculture in 1850–51* (London, 1852).
6 Whenever figures for population or labour force are given in this text they refer, unless stated otherwise, to both men and women.

1

The Rural World: Nation and Community

Our school histories, and still more so our popular historical sense, sees the nineteenth century as the century of industrialization. We inherit, almost in our blood, images of urban poverty, of factories and child labour. It was the age, in this view, which produced the first urban/industrial conurbations in Bradford and Manchester, the age of industrial progress and of 'dark Satanic mills'. While there is truth in this view, for much of the nineteenth century England remained an agricultural country physically and an agricultural economy.

When the census enumerators in 1851 had finished their work they found that the majority of England's population was still physically situated in the countryside. The returns showed that the population was divided almost exactly equally between 'urban' and 'rural' areas, but, since an administrative definition of 'town' was used rather than one based on size, the 'urban population' included many people in towns like Lewes in Sussex or Aylesbury in Buckinghamshire which were predominantly rural in character.[1] Even ten years later when the census report proclaimed with great pride, 'The English nation . . . without losing its hold on the country . . . has assumed the character of a predominating city population'[2] the figures suggest a very different story.

Table 1.1 Population spread, England and Wales, 1851–81

	Rural areas	Urban areas
1851	8,936,800	8,990,809
1861	9,132,990	10,993,234
1871	9,801,619	12,910,647
1881	10,529,143	15,445,296

In addition there were, and are, enormous regional differences in the spread of population between the urban and the rural areas. Most obviously there is the urbanized and industrial 'axial belt' 'following an axis aligned from south-east or north-west, and broadening as it gets further from greater London.'[4] Although this region is perhaps not so precise as was once argued it certainly stands in marked contrast to the areas to the east and west of it which retained a much more rural character. The spread of suburban areas, of which more later, heightened this division with the growth of cheap public transport after the 1880s.[5]

The rural nature of English society in the third quarter of the nineteenth century is further emphasized if we look at those who worked in the countryside and the wealth they produced. In 1851, and indeed at every census until 1901 agriculture was the largest single employer in England. Again it is necessary to modify what is perhaps the conventional wisdom of British social history. In 1851 particularly, England was far from an industrial nation even in terms of those employed. In that year there were nearly twice as many people employed in agriculture as in the mills and factories of the industrial revolution and nearly three times as many as there were miners.[7] Even in terms of wealth produced, agriculture was holding its own until the mid-century, although it shows gradual decline after 1811. Percentages also hide the fact that the value of agricultural production at current prices increased from £75.5 million in 1801 to £104.6 million in 1901. All figures like this conceal as much as they reveal except as the most general indicators. They propose, for example, a unified and equally developed industry with similar and comparable units, sizes, and levels of technology. In terms of people they are probably worse still. They obviously exclude the large numbers living in rural

Table 1.2 Numbers[a] employed in agriculture, 1851–81[6]

	In agriculture	Total employed population	Per cent in agriculture
1851	2,017,000	9,373,000	21.5%
1861	1,942,000	10,523,000	18.5%
1871	1,769,000	11,752,000	15%
1881	1,633,000	12,731,000	12.8%

[a] Men and women, to the nearest thousand, based on 1911 census categories.

Table 1.3 Percentage main industrial distribution of national income (Great Britain) 1801–1901[8]

	Agriculture	Mining, Manufacturing Building	Trade/Transport	Rents
1801	32.5	23.4	17.4	5.2
1811	35.7	20.7	16.6	5.7
1821	29.1	31.9	15.9	6.1
1831	23.3	34.4	17.3	6.4
1841	22.0	34.3	18.4	8.1
1851	20.3	34.3	18.6	8.1
1861	17.7	36.4	19.5	7.5
1871	11.2	38.0	21.9	7.5
1881	10.3	37.6	23.0	8.4
1891	8.6	38.2	22.4	8.0
1901	6.3	40.2	23.3	8.1

areas who did not work directly in agriculture. Even in the 1850s there were considerable numbers of professionals, tradesmen and artisans whose individual skills had nothing directly to do with agriculture but who relied upon it almost totally for their living. They also hide, in the form presented here, the divisions within agriculture and agricultural society in that the basis used for classification is all those employed in the industry, ranging from the greatest 'landed proprietor' to the meanest day labourer. Finally, they certainly underestimate the numbers of women involved at all levels of agriculture.

Agricultural society was – ignoring for now those who lived in the country but did not work the land – divided conventionally into three ranks: the landowners, who lived largely by rent although some might farm; the farmers, who lived by working the land usually, but not always, with the labour of others; and finally the labourers, who had nothing to sell but their labour power. This is what James Caird called in 1851 'the three great interests connected with agriculture – the landlord, the tenant and the labourer . . . '[9] At all these levels there were both men and women: the farmer, the labourer or the landlord was likely to be a man but this was not always the case. In 1851 almost 9 per cent of farmers were women, often though not always widows. Among the labouring poor there were more women 'indoor' servants in agriculture than men, and women made up about 8 per cent of full-time outdoor farm labourers. At the other end of the scale there were 13,268 women landed proprietors in 1851 as against 17,047 men, although there were many more landlords than this since, as the census of 1861 put it, 'as the land proprietors of the country fill many public offices under which they are returned, the tabular numbers are defective.'[10]

There are similar problems with the description of a man or a woman as an 'agricultural labourer.' Even the census takers, who tended to reduce what were real and complex differences in occupation within a community to the lowest common denominator, that is, labourer, had problems. For example the 1881 census noted 'the confusion between agricultural and other labourers on the schedule'.[11] The 1891 census was more specific still.

> There is no doubt that a considerable number of agricultural labourers return themselves simply as 'labourers' without anything to indicate they are employed on farms, and these would be classified as general labourers. Similarly there is good reason to believe that many agricultural carters and waggoners . . . get transferred to the carters, carriers and hauliers of general traffic.[12]

There are also problems of comparing over time, since the figures given from census to census do not match. However, with all these problems in mind the following table gives some basic idea of the relative size of these groups in the third quarter of the nineteenth century.

Looking at each of these groups in turn a number of factors appear. One is the fairly constant size of the landowners as a group. The 'new Domesday' of 1876 which was the only serious attempt during the nineteenth century to quantify landholdings suggests that there were about 43,000 people who owned more than 100 acres of land. However, as *The Spectator* said, 'this 43,000 is in practice influenced by a much smaller number of great territorialists'. Some weeks later the same paper produced a list of 710 people who held more than 5,000 acres in any one county.[13] A true and, as the nineteenth century papers put it 'political', definition of landownership produces a figure somewhere between. If we take owners of more than 300 acres we get a rural landowning class of 13,800[14] but in many areas owning less than this could take one into the elite so a figure of about 28,000 seems reasonable

Table 1.4 The 'Agricultural Orders', England and Wales, 1851–81

Year	Landowners[a]	Farmers[b]	Labourers[c]	Total
1851[1]	30,315	630,900	1,253,786	1,915,001
1861[1]	30,766	589,651[2]	1,188,768	1,799,342
1871[3]	14,191[4]	605,589	980,166	1,611,096[5]
1881[6]		325,104	870,798	
		575,434[7]		1,472,555[8]

[a] This is obviously a difficult category. The census of 1851–71 (thereafter the category goes) refers to these as those who do not return any other occupation. On this basis it is clearly an underestimate. See page 10.

[b] Again, not straightforward. It includes both male and female relatives of farmers – it is an attempt at a social/class classification.

[c] Includes shepherds, horsemen and 'ordinary' labourers.

[1] 1861 census. England and Wales including wives and daughters etc. over 15 in farmers. Men and women, indoor and outdoor servants.

[2] This drop seems to be almost entirely in the relatives' category of both sexes.

[3] 1871 census.

[4] This is male only. Adjusted in proportion with 1851/61 it would give a total of 25,341.

[5] This total includes the estimate [note 4] for landed proprietors.

[6] 1881 census.

[7] From now on women relatives of farmers (crucially wives and daughters) do not appear as employed. This I believe to seriously misrepresent the position on the *majority* of English farms in this period, an opinion shared by the census office before 1881. I have therefore added another figure underneath the census one which is an estimate of the number of women 'relatives' assuming a constant ratio based on earlier figures of 56 per cent male and 44 per cent female within the farming category but also assuming women relatives are leaving the land at the same rate as men, for example, 2 per cent in 1881 but 10 per cent in 1891. A problem here is that as women were more prone to migration than men this is probably an underestimate of decline. Women farmers were still included.

[8] This includes the estimate for farmers' female relatives but does not include a figure for 'landed proprietors'. Assuming a constant figure of about 28,000 based on earlier census categories this gives 1,500,555.

although of course a small proportion of these landowners would not be rural.

The material also suggests a fairly constant decline in the number of farmers (or more accurately farm family members) over the period. In addition, it indicates that if the kind of proportions of male/female, married/unmarried that we see present in 1871 remain roughly constant the contribution of women to the product of the farm is very much larger than census figures suggest. The drop in the number of farmers between 1851 and 1861 is probably the result of changes in census-taking which seems to have shifted out of the category a number of farmers' relatives, especially sons and daughters. This is a much more serious problem after 1881 when this category is removed altogether for women, causing an apparently huge drop in the number of women employed. We shall return to this point below.[15] More striking, if concealed by this change, is the drop in male farmers after 1871, a decline put at 10.39 per cent by the 1881 census.[16] Related to this change, but directly outside the 'great' agricultural orders, there is an increase in farm bailiffs from 10,561 in 1851 to 19,377 in 1881. Much of this increase seems to have occurred because landowners took farms 'in hand' as a result of the agricultural depression after 1875.[17]

The decline in the number of labourers was again noted by contemporaries and an attempt was made in 1901 to see this movement in the longer term. It was suggested then that a general decline in purely rural areas in 'in the ten years 1851–61 continued at an accelerated rate until the last decennium' [that is, 1891–1901].[18] However, changes which at local level probably seemed almost cataclysmic were often concealed by these national aggregates. The loss of one or two families from a hamlet whose total population might only be a dozen families loomed large as an indicator of change and even decay – and such experiences, especially in the smaller settlements were increasingly common as the 1860s became the 1870s. That such movement was usually two-stage, that is, small village to large village to town, and that many such migrants simply never left their native counties, was not obvious to those left behind, nor, often to those receiving the influx, especially given the possible variety of population change.

For example, the villages of an area of East Sussex show how different, even within a small area, the experience of different communities could be. The Rotherbridge Hundred which contains both the large, but controlled town of Petworth and the large but more open parish of Kirdford, saw ten out of twelve parishes lose population in the years between 1851 and 1881 including both these large settlements as well as some of the smallest. However, in the adjoining Hundred of West Easwrith only five out of twelve parishes lost population in the same period and both Amberley and Billingshurst, the largest settlements in the Hundred, gained substantially.

More surprisingly in view of most explanations, the smallest village in the Hundred, Parham, an estate village, also grew in the same period.[19] Individual village explanations could be advanced for these changes but the important thing is the diversity of experience. Indeed, it might be that beyond the most broad explanations of the lure of the city or the poverty of country life, no general or regional explanations are possible before the onset of the depression in the 1870s.

By the late 1860s, though, the movement of male workers from the rural districts was beginning to cause concern among farmers and landowners. As Mr William Climenson of Welney in the Fens told the 1867 Children's Employment Commission, 'labourers, ie (*sic*), the good ones are getting scarcer every year. The best leave. Emigration is the first drain; then manufactures come to Peterborough, Whittlesea, and all parts of the country, and sweep away whole families.'[20] However, it was not only or mainly men who left, for the first to go from many a remote rural settlement would have been a young woman entering service. From the 1850s the growth of domestic service and the demand for rural and, thus it was argued, more reliable girls, meant that few villages of rural, and especially southern England, had not sent someone into service. The sheer size of this grouping was noted by the 1881 census. 'Out of every 22 persons in the population at all ages one was an indoor *Domestic Servant* (*sic*).' In proportion their numbers were 'lowest in the mining and manufacturing parts, higher in the agricultural districts, and highest in towns, especially in such towns as are the habitual resorts of the wealthier classes.'[21] In 1881 for example there were 57,602 Norfolk-born women in London and the south-east, the vast majority of them in the wealthy areas of Westminster and Kensington, and the new bourgeois suburbs like Wandsworth and Lambeth.[22]

But these changes were still relatively minor. After all, as the Victorian census-takers reassured themselves, the population of rural districts as a whole had not really fallen. Indeed, in terms of absolute numbers no county of England showed an absolute decline in population before 1871 and the decline in Rutland, Huntingdon and even Cornwall in 1881 was sufficiently small to be swallowed in the general optimism of the 1881 census.

Nor had the distribution among different classes altered much, not before 1871 at least. There was gradual attenuation of numbers among the poorest group, the labourers and their families, but not to a sufficient extent to cause alarm before the very late 1860s. If hindsight suggested that 'rural depopulation', that favourite fear of the 1890s and 1900s, had begun in the 1850s nobody then seemed to notice it. The agricultural nation gave every sign of stability.

If England remained more rural in the third quarter of the nineteenth century than we often think, it was certainly not an homogeneous rural world. Enormous differences existed in landscape, farming and settlement patterns. Although there are great regional divisions, to which we shall come shortly, it is important to remember that even within small areas there could be great differences. Northumberland, for instance, is divided internally as much by a highland/lowland line as it is separated from Scotland by a county border. Northumberland and Scottish shepherds moved back and forward across the border, hiring in England or Scotland but seldom moving down to the lowland zones of either – their world was defined by farming and hiring not by any administrative notions of place.[23] Similarly, in the very different landscape of Sussex, the division between the High Weald in the north of the county and the Downlands and especially the coastal plain was very marked. In the Weald farms were small, almost peasant in character; on the coastal plain they were larger and partook more of the style of capitalist agricultural production.[24]

These local divisions retained an enormous importance in how people viewed their world and how they lived their lives, and we shall return to them, but they tended to be subsumed, by contemporaries at least, into the larger divisions of the English regions. When James Caird toured England for *The Times* in 1850–1 he divided rural England into two great areas, the 'corn' counties and the 'grazing' counties, basically an east/west division. 'The chief commodity of the western farmer is the produce of his diary, his cattle and his flock. The large eastern farmer looks principally to his wheat and barley.'[25] However, even without the kinds of intra-regional distinctions, like those mentioned above, this is clearly too simplistic a model even if it holds true at the most basic level. Ultimately both Caird and the Royal Agricultural Society used a system which divided rural England into five types of region, the sandlands, the fens, the south-east chalk and limestone areas, the claylands and the uplands.[26]

Although none of these regions was actually a precise geographical entity – that is, many if not most counties contained a number of soils types and hence potential agricultural 'sub regions' – we can think of main areas which had common elements.

The sand districts of eastern England were the apogee of high farming – the intensive use of labour and capital guided by scientific principle which characterised much that was best in mid-century agriculture, Here, on the light lands, the great gains of the 'golden age' were at their most obvious. In Norfolk, Suffolk, and parts of Cambridgeshire the optimism of eighteenth century agricultural improvement still dominated. Even in the 1890s, when the depression had taken its toll in many of the eastern counties, Clare Sewell Read, the epitome of the Norfolk farmer, could write,

> Norfolk has long been celebrated for the superiority of its agriculture. It was certainly the first county to adopt practical and theoretical improvements which have recently raised the pursuit of farming in the eyes of the world . . . From the middle of the last century Norfolk has stood foremost in everything which tends to elevate this important branch of our national wealth . . . [27]

This was overwhelmingly arable land. Sixty-three per cent of the land of Norfolk was under the plough and wherever the light soils dominated, as in the Bagshot Heath area of Surrey, the proportion was similar. The light soils also extended northwards and included areas of East Nottinghamshire and crucially Northumberland where it formed the basis of the Norfolk-style of farming on a five-course rotation rather than a four.[28] The fens were also arable and like the light soil wheatlands did well during the long periods of high prices between the late 1830s and the mid-1870s. However, although at one level the fens can be 'taken in' to the 'lowland districts where men could look back on a period of remarkable progress',[29] the structure of these wild and often very remote areas was very different from that of adjoining light soil areas.

The chalk and limestone areas of the south-east were essentially the downlands and high chalk plateaux of Sussex, Hampshire, Dorset and Wiltshire. Again this was arable county, although in the 'unimproved' areas especially in Wiltshire there was still a good deal of rough grazing for sheep.

Frederick Law Olmsted, an American farmer who visited England in the early 1850s, described Salisbury Plain as a

> strange weary waste of elevated land, undulating like a prairie, sparsely greened over its gray (*sic*) surface with short grass; uninhabited and treeless; only, at some miles asunder, broken by charming vales of rich meadows and clusters of farm-houses and shepherd's cottages, darkly bowered about with the concentrated foliage of the whole country.[30]

This is the mixed landscape familiar to the reader of Thomas Hardy's *Tess of the Durbevilles* where Tess moved from the low and sheltered valley agriculture of her youth, through the dairy farms of slightly higher ground, to the open chalk downland with its mixture of poor arable land and sheep.

Lying further west and north, stretching in a band from the South Hams in Devon to Durham, were the main areas of the claylands. Here was the beginning of Caird's second England, the England of horn as against corn. It was a landscape of small field and hedgerows.

> the whole . . . ,' wrote Edward Little in 1844, 'consists of enclosures, some of which are very small; and in many places the hedgerows are so thickly stocked with trees as to give the appearance of an extensive plantation when viewed from a distance.[31]

Although this land was still agriculturally backward in the 1850s, two aspects of clay land farming were still doing well in the third quarter of the nineteenth century. On the pasture land, especially in the west and north west, dairying was well established, particularly cheese production. 'The graziers of the west make cheese, which, for the most part, is very much esteemed', wrote the Frenchman de Lavergne.[32] Additionally, in these areas there was some emphasis on rearing and feeding beef cattle. Also, some of these heavy soil areas maintained their old position as granary counties producing a mixed farming system, especially in the midlands and the southern clay areas like the Weald of Surrey and Sussex. Oxfordshire was a county like this which, as de Lavergne said, 'affords an example of every kind of crop, every sort of land, all grades of rent, and every method of cultivation . . . '[33]

The fifth of the basic soil regions were the uplands. Here cultivation was limited by altitude. In the softer southern climate of Somerset it was thought possible to cultivate up to 800-900 feet but in the north 600 feet was thought to be the upper limit of cultivation for wheat. Much northern land was also unstinted rough grazing as above Allendale in Northumberland. Here the co-existence of lead mining, coal mining down the valley and subsistence farming enabled peasant agriculture to survive well into the twentieth century. Even where there were high sheep farms there was often small-scale production, usually by the women of the unit, for exchange and barter.[34] The most prosperous areas of hill farming were the rich grazing valleys of the North Riding of Yorkshire. In Wensleydale and Swaledale good pasture supported a dairying economy which fed into the industrial areas to the west and south. What C. Webster wrote of Westmorland in 1868 could well apply to all these areas. 'So long as the tall chimneys of Yorkshire and Lancashire smoke, so long will the Westmorland farmer have a never-failing demand for all his produce – beef, mutton, butter, cheese, and wool.[35]

These kinds of geographical division make sense at one level, but there were other divisions which often came from the physical differences of region but which are less easy to tie down. There were for instance great differences in settlement types within rural England. In the south and east the nucleated village tended to be the norm which, while it may well have effectively been an occupational community during the nineteenth century, still saw a separation between home and workplace. At the other extreme are the areas of the north where settlement developed around an individual farmhouse. Here the space for work and for living was not so clearly divided. Between these two extremes are a huge number of possible variations.

This was also reflected in the physical appearance of the areas. Obviously there are differences between the open and rolling country of the south-eastern chalk downland and the close hedgerows of the midland clays. But it was not only that. The style of vernacular architecture reflected regional differences both in usage and in appearance. The long houses of Dartmoor and to a lesser extent Exmoor, were the products of a particular farming system but also of local materials. Again a north/south divide is the one most often pointed to.[36]

> As a broad generalisation we can say that buildings in the highland areas are likely to be built of hard intractable stone

> and those in lowland areas of softer more easily worked stone, of timber or of brick . . . In addition, in most valley areas, whether in the lowland or highland zones, we can expect traditional buildings of timber to predominate.[36]

There are still problems though. Economic demand, agricultural usage and simple poverty or prosperity can modify these patterns but it is important to stress just how unusual is the half timbered and thatched 'country cottage'.

As well as the physical divisions and boundaries of the world there were other non or semi-physical boundaries usually dealt with under the broad term 'community'. 'The community' is a nebulous concept. It suggests both a physical world and a social one; boundaries drawn by settlement or land type and use, but also drawn by *mentalitié*. As Cohen says 'such boundaries are not "natural" phenomena: they are relational, they may be contrived and their very existence is called into being partly by the purpose for which one group distinguishes itself from another.'[37]

Initially, though, certain distinctions can be made, beginning with the physical 'types' of community. Broadly speaking the south and east were areas of village settlement, those of the north and west farm-based. 'Village England', writes Christopher Taylor, 'is really a broad zone stretching from the south coast through the Midlands to the north-west.'[38] The rest of England is either based on hamlets or 'clachans' to use the term of historical geography, or a complex mixture of village and other settlement types. As Taylor points out, ' . . . it might be said that nucleated villages, far from being a normal form of settlement, are an aberration, especially in view of their late development and limited distribution.'[39] These different settlement types obviously produce quite different social structures and hence social relations. To talk, for instance as many have done, as if the village was somehow the basic unit of English rural society, is clearly nonsensical – community could, even in physical terms, mean very different things in different places.

I want to look at community then in three ways: to begin with, those communities as defined by the farm or hamlet – the clachan – where the centre of the settlement is a farm and its associated buildings, the dominant structure in 'upland' Britain; next the nucleated village settlement which was most common in the lowland areas; and finally, and briefly, at the market town, a 'community' common to both forms and in a different way defining each. This inevitably simplifies what is a complex question. Clearly in many areas different settlements existed side by side, yet it is necessary as in this way the differing social structures can be pointed to, and certain ideas about different social structures examined.

The farm as community was very much a product of those areas of the north and west of England where a combination of remoteness, farming system, and labour costs made living in, or near, the farm house the logical method of organization. Here 'hamlets and farmsteads predominate, reflecting a pattern of settlement which has been established for millenia.'[40] This is not to say that these were the only reasons for a rural settlement pattern based on the usually isolated farmstead. Indeed Taylor suggests that the clachan was the original form of settlement.[41] However, it was often these reasons which ensured the system remained operative well into the twentieth century.

An extreme example of the farm as community is provided by the agricultural system in parts of the Glendale area of northern Northumberland. In 1894 the assiduous investigator Arthur Wilson Fox, visited this area for the *Royal Commission on Labour*. He wrote at the beginning of his report that, 'owing to the concentration of cottages on the farms, the scarcity of villages, and the large area of the (area) my enquiry was more protracted than either of my previous ones.' He continued that Glendale's farming was of relatively recent date, 'even 100 years ago large portions were covered with broom and gorse.'[42] In fact much of Glendale was 'improved' eighteenth and early nineteenth century farming set down on an older pattern of hamlets and lone farms. One of these was the 950-acre Castle Heaton Farm near Coldstream.

The 1881 census shows it to have been almost a hamlet of the kind that was noted by Mr John Coleman who investigated the area for the 'Richmond' Commission in 1881. 'Each large farm', he wrote, 'represents a small colony in itself, with accommodation provided for labour requirements for all but extraordinary occasions, such as hay and corn harvest . . . '[43] Around the farm house at Castle Heaton were 14 cottages which housed families employed on the farm. This was characteristic of all the larger farms in this area and in many areas of the north where 'owing to the scarcity of villages' the farmers had 'all their labourers living in cottages on the farms.'[44] In 1889 the cottages at Castle Heaton provided 14 men and 10 women who were regular workers plus between 4 and 6 casuals of both sexes.[45]

The workforce at Castle Heaton who lived on the farm all hired by the year and by the family. We have no hiring agreements from the farm but it is unlikely they were very different from those elsewhere in north Northumberland. These guaranteed [or demanded] family employment, and gave cottages and wages in kind. Isaac Atkinson, hired in 1865 with Sir Edward Blackett at Hexham hirings as a hind for one year,

> . . . and to have the following wages viz. 16/6d per week in money, House and garden rent free & coals led. – My wife to work when wanted and to have 10d per day except in Harvest when she is to be at liberty to look to others for what she can make.[46]

As well as wages, coals and house it was usual on many farms to encourage the keeping of animals by allowing cow pasture and making payments in kind to enable pigs to be kept.[47] Payment in kind remained a central feature of the Northumberland system as it did elsewhere where hamlet settlement predominated, well into the 1920s. As Wilson Fox wrote, 'owing to the scarcity of villages and the difficulty of spending money the system of payment in kind long survived among the hinds, and still survives among the shepherds.'[48] In 1855 George Morton hired at Middleton Hall and got, 'a Cow Grassed throughout Summer, and Wintered upon Straw. One ton of hay from the Banks'. He was allowed to keep a pig 'shut up or tethered', to plant 1,200 yards of potatoes and was given 6 boles of Oats, 4 of barley, 13 of corn, 1 bole 2 measures of peas or beans, 1 bole 4 measures of wheat and 4 measures of rye.[49]

By southern standards these were excellent conditions. Wages in the south and east in the 1850s and 1860s were nearer 10s to 11s per week and this seldom included a cottage or any regular wages in kind. Accommodation was, by southern standards again, often very good. Cottages were stone built and usually had pig sties and, although there were bad ones, Wilson Fox thought in the 1890s that they were generally much better in Northumberland than in the south and east. This should be treated with caution as the minimum standard was very low but there is little doubt that, relatively speaking, conditions were decent in the north-east compared with elsewhere.[50]

This workforce was bound together by ties of kinship and close physical proximity as a brief examination of Castle Heaton Farm shows. In 1881 Alexander Mckay lived in 'Castle Heaton Farm Hind's Cottages No. 1', he had three daughters aged 19, 18, and 15 all of whom are described as farm labourers. At No. 2 lived James Harrington a domestic coachman and his family while at No. 3., as in other cases, the 'head of household' was a widow Mary Sprat who is described as 'housekeeper', a full-time job as she had two daughters and three sons all described as 'agricultural labourers.' At No. 4 the head of household was also a woman, Sarah Tully, who again was a 'housekeeper' with two sons and a daughter described as 'agricultural labourers'. These women were what Wilson Fox called 'cottars', 'a single woman or widow who is hired direct by the farmer and lives in a cottage by herself on the farm.'[51] There were women on these kind of agreements also at Nos. 5 and 6. At No. 7 was Ralph Jackson, a hind with two sons and two daughters, all labourers, and at No. 8 lived the farm steward and his family. His wife did not work and his children were too young to hire. A little way away were two other cottages. In one lived the shepherd and his family, all of whom were employed on the farm, in the other another cottar with two sons and a daughter working on the farm.[52]

This general situation continued on Castle Heaton up to the Great War although there were probably changes which are not obvious to this kind of comparison. In 1890 there were 11 'family' groups employed on the farm, only one apparently headed by a woman. In 1913 there were 10 groups, none headed by a woman. Whether there actually was a decline in the numbers of women on 'cottar' hirings is difficult to judge but it seems unlikely. More probable is that the brothers Smith in 1890, for example, had a mother or sister looking after them as 'housekeeper' although she did not actually work regularly on the farm and therefore does not appear in farm records.[53] Similarly there is no way of telling, from farm records, what the relationship between men and women of the same name is, although wages can give some idea. What is certain is that the group around a farm changed regularly. In 1889 there was not a single family employed on Castle Heaton Farm that was there on the 1881 census. By 1913 the entire workforce has changed again.

This 'migratory habit', as Wilson Fox called it, was certainly contributed to by the isolation of many of these hamlets. Looking back to the thirty years or so before his report of the 1890s Wilson Fox wrote of the changes brought by the railways and the gradual [and very early] introduction of half day on Saturdays as breaking the 'somewhat monotonous routine of the distant farm'. He also wrote approvingly of the lack of drunkenness due again to the 'scarcity of villages' although the other side of that was to deny to the labourers one of the crucial sites of sociability.[54] Bob Hepple of Cowpen talked about this isolation which was felt especially by the young, who tended either to remain with their own families until marriage or live in with a steward or hind. 'Oh twas quiet, there was no road for two mile to Greenlea and I walked to Haltwhistle every Saturday night, seven miles and seven back . . . for company, for other lads'.[55]

This situation was very different in areas where, as in Yorkshire, or classically the north-east of Scotland, the young farm workers lived together on the farms. Here although the settlement pattern was still non-village, family hiring was unusual. In the East Riding of Yorkshire in the 1860s it was said,

> Boys generally go into farm service from 13 to 14 years of age. They hire for the year . . . Farmhouses are so scattered and farm servants so separated from rest of the world that early neglect cannot be overcome later in life . . . Where as in the East Riding of Yorkshire the farms are large and very detached, the farmer's house is like a barrack with a long chamber full of beds, one of which the foreman commonly occupies to keep order.[56]

Here, where living on the farm was part of the life cycle rather than a permanent state, the isolation seems to have been much less and elements exist of a youth culture of the kind associated with Aberdeenshire.[57] This was based on a masculine community defined by living in with other lads and represented through the rough culture of the plough-plays and the notorious carnival of the annual hirings.[58]

The hamlet or the farm as community produced a particular kind of social relations. In those areas, like Northumberland, where living on or close to the farm was the pattern throughout the individual's working life, a particular closeness often grew up between master and man, reinforced by the wide use of payment in kind up to the 1880s. 'The labourer shared with his master in vicissitudes of seasons as affecting the quality of the produce.'[59] This was especially true of shepherding where it was usual to pay a substantial part of a shepherd's wages in the form of sheep of his own to run with the flock. At the end of the 1870s Coleman gave many examples of shepherds getting no money wages at all as in the case of a hill farm shepherd who was 'paid' in 53 cheviot sheep, 1 cow kept, 60 stones of oatmeal, potatoes supplied and a house and 3 tons of coal.[60] In cases like this the identification of the worker with his 'master' and his master's fortune could be total.

> The shepherd has a personal interest in the well-being of the flock, and the testimony as to the good conduct and high character of these men was universal . . . Not only does the system ensure personal interest, but the shepherd's sons are brought up to the business from the cradle, and are, as it were, to the matter born . . .[61]

Payment in kind was merely part of the cement of a social structure which was much more solid. Again Coleman saw it, as did Wilson Fox fifteen years later, in particular when it came to relations between master and man. Coleman referred to what he called the 'centralization' of Northumberland farming, and went on that,

> the men were willing and able to do a fair day's work, that they had not been injuriously affected by unions and above all, that the system of centralization did, to a considerable extent, promote a feeling of interest in the work, which would be naturally strengthened according to the influenced radiation (*sic*) from the centre of the colony. An influence for good or evil of so momentous a character as to throw a grave responsibility upon both the master and mistress who are the head of such a community.[62]

This is not to say relationships on a Northumberland farm were free from antagonism – they certainly were not. However, there can be little doubt that relationships on the farm – the isolation and payment in kind – meant that the farm as community was as an important a factor in ensuring harmony, and particularly the lack of unionization in the north of

England, as the bargaining power of the hinds at hirings.[63] It created a set of social relations which were close and 'clannish', to quote Coleman again, anyway up to the 1880s when things appear to change in the north-east, as elsewhere.

However, relationships do not seem to have been so smooth on those cranach-type settlements where living-in was age specific and related to the youth phase of the life cycle. Here, for example in the East Riding of Yorkshire and parts of Lincolnshire, groups of young, single men lived together on farms. On these large eastern farms,

> . . . there is large kitchen . . . in which they have their meals and can sit in the evening. From this a staircase, or more commonly a broad tread ladder with handrail, leads to a large room, neat as a barrack room and having no communication with the rest of the house.[64]

In this situation conflicts between the young horsemen and their employers were more frequent and the closeness of relationship, especially on big farms, does not seem to have developed in the way it did in Northumberland.[65]

In parts of Lancashire and elsewhere in the north-west a kind of intermediate situation existed. Here, although living-in was restricted to the young and living on the farm where you worked does not seem to have been normal at marriage, the smaller size of farms seems to have promoted close relationships. As a Lancashire farmer told Wilson Fox in 1894, 'I go to work with my men and show them how. My wife and I dine with the servants. They have the same food as we have.'[66] There was also a good deal of mobility between farms in Lancashire and in Cumberland. Here though, unlike Lincolnshire or Yorkshire, the fact that the hired men were often the sons of farmers themselves, and frequently went on to be farmers, tended to create a situation of stability and social harmony.

The farm as community then produced a number of different sets of social relations but most tended to be relatively stable with conflict between master and man reduced although not totally eradicated. In village England a similarly complex situation existed. The simple word village covers a huge range of settlement types, from a carefully planned group of model cottages clustered around a great house, to a straggling mix of houses, pubs and shops of settlements like Castle Acre in

Norfolk which, in the 1870s, was larger than many market towns. For simplicity's sake, by village I mean 'a settlement of twenty or more individual homesteads' which is 'nucleated', that is, centred on or 'clustered round a focal point'.[67]

In this sense a village as a community is less problematic than the farm in that it accords both with our common sense views of social organization as well as with the views of many contemporaries. However, apart from size, it has been conventional, since at least the 1840s to divide parishes into 'open' and 'close'. At the most basic this definition refers to land ownership, open parishes having many landowners and thus being open to settlement, close having few or only one landowner, and those closed to settlement. However, as Sarah Banks has pointed out, this simple dichotomy conceals as much as it reveals.

> For 'open' and 'close' were used to refer to parishes with any of a number of characteristics including all or some of; many owners [open] or few [close]; unrestrained or restricted settlement; high or low rates or poor expenditure; expanding or contracting population. The terms also might or might not have various connotations, especially pejorative ones such as the demolition of cottages for economic ends and the creation of problems in neighbouring parishes.[68]

However, simply to dismiss any such classification is clearly counter-productive if for no other reason than that contemporaries, even if their definitions were seldom precise, used the category frequently. What we should begin by stating though is that there were few ideals of either 'close' or 'open' parishes or villages. Rather we might, initially at least think of a continuum of 'openess>closeness'. The most extreme close type was the specially-built (or rebuilt) estate village. Here all housing and secular and religious institutions were under the control and eye of the landlord. In this situation, as for instance on the Prince of Wales's estate at Sandringham in Norfolk, church and chapel building, shop provisions as well as housing were absolutely controlled. As his agent told the *Royal Commission on the Housing of the Working Classes* in 1884;

> He (the Prince) selects his own tenantry, and he knows exactly the condition of, I may say, every hole and corner of his own estate . . . and certainly no cottage tenant or labourer is ever forgotten in this general knowledge by the Prince.[69]

Such a comment may have been praise from a land agent but the poor did not always see it in the same way. Flora Thompson's radical father said sarcastically of such a village, 'only good people were allowed to live there. That was why so many were going to church.'[70] Control, in the interests of making the villagers 'good', often extended to pub building. There were, in 1884, no pubs at all on the Sandringham estate, perhaps strange given the behaviour of Edward, Prince of Wales. 'Anyone', said his admiring agent, 'who now goes to a public house from Sandringham would have to walk two miles.'[71]

The other end of the continuum is less easy to define. Again Flora Thompson's father's description of her native Lark Rise contains many elements of the ideal, 'the spot God made with the leftovers when he'd finished creating the rest of the earth.'[72] More precise is Raphael Samuel's superb picture of Headington Quarry in Oxfordshire. The basis of this village was squatting on the old quarry sites and rough wasteland around. It had no resident gentry until the influx of the academic middle class in the 1960s, no church until the 1850s, and certainly no dominant landowner. In contrast to Sandringham and its estate village it had two enormously popular pubs and a reputation for toughness that lasted well into the 1930s.

> Quarry was a village which had grown up singularly free of gentlemen. For centuries it enjoyed what was virtually an extra-parochial existence, a kind of anarchy, in which the villagers were responsible to nobody but themselves.[73]

This points to the moral aspect of the problem. 'Open' and 'close' were not, to the Victorians at least, simply physical or sociological categories, they were moral entities which influenced a whole range of attitudes and behaviour and from which moral absolutes and social predictions could be drawn. A striking example occurs in relation to the reports made between 1867 and 1872 on the employment of children, young persons, and women in agriculture. The 'model' of open and close parishes presides over these reports as the main, perhaps even only, category of analysis. A good example comes from the Rev. James Fraser's report on Norfolk, Suffolk, Essex, Sussex and Gloucestershire. He writes;

> It is impossible to exaggerate the ill-effects of such a state of things in every aspect – physical, social economical, moral, intellectual ... Socially nothing can be more wretched than the condition of 'open' parishes like Docking in Norfolk, and South Cerney in Gloucestershire.[74]

Whether or not the pattern of landownership and the consequent distribution and condition of cottages was to 'blame' is at one level irrelevant since contemporaries, especially in the period up to the 1880s, tended to see the problems of village England in these terms.[75] This moral aspect was usually related to the presence or lack of resident gentry rather than directly to landownership patterns. For example it was said of Horstead in Norfolk in 1867,

> Though the non-residence of the landowners must affect the condition of the parish, yet this parish suffers less from this cause than might be expected, in consequence of the interest taken by several residents in the condition of the poor.[76]

Time and again it appears in the open/close dichotomy that it is not merely landownership but the social effects and duties attendant on landownership which is the important question. Nor do these need to be carried out by a landowner, any 'gentry' will do. In written evidence to the 1867 reports from 'principal inhabitants' of investigated villages we see this time and again. From Ringland in Norfolk they wrote: 'Neither landowner or clergyman are resident which operates much to the disadvantage of the parish', and from Sprowston in the same country, 'the parish is found to suffer from the non-residence of the landowners.'[77]

The presence of a powerful or interventionist elite was seen to have the opposite effect and to give a village its 'correct' or ideal structure as at Honingham in Norfolk where the meeting reported in 1867, 'the landowner is resident, and takes an active interest in the parish and people. Ill-conducted people would not be allowed to remain in the parish.'[78] 'Ill conducted' could mean many things apart from being chargeable to the rates as a pauper. As we shall see below, those who sought to form trades unions, or like Michael Home's father in the close village of Hockham in Norfolk, simply held radical opinions, could lose job and home in these paternalist ideal worlds. As Home wrote years later, 'considering my father's political views, it might have been uncomfortable and even hazardous' had his father not rented one of the few holdings in the village not owned by the squire.[79] Even the advance of an alternative godliness in the form of religious nonconformity could have the same effect. The memoirs of Jane and William Inskip talk about Hatfield in Hertfordshire in the 1860s.

> (the Methodists) were anxious to buy a piece of ground for a chapel, but word went round from Hatfield House and the High Church party, that no ground was to be sold to Methodists. *That* (sic) class of people were not wanted in aristocratic Hatfield . . .[80]

An element which this kind of moral category with its stress on order ignored, as indeed it had to, was the actual interdependence of village types, or rather the total dependence of the ideal model and close village on the lawless open one. At Sandringham for instance the agriculture of the estate would simply not have functioned without the supply, particularly of casual labour, from 'the adjoining large parish of Dersingham.'[81] Here 'many of the cottages were overcrowded' and many of the labourers worked 'out of the parish'. As distinct from one great owner in the Prince of Wales, there were 'at least 20'. For all their problems at least the labourers had half-a-dozen pubs.[82]

Between the extremes, between Sandringham and Dersingham, almost all possible variations of village type existed, and one begins to wonder if these 'models' are any more than a moral category. The answer must be that they are. Although overlaid with ideology the material basis for such an analysis is to be found even if the material base is often within the realm of *mentalitié* rather than pure social structure. Also locality and elements operating from outside a particular village were of vital importance. As Sarah Banks points out 'extra-parochial' constraints, 'such as geographical location, government policy . . . the economic climate . . . demographic trends . . . as well as conditions in the parish itself' were vital in creating conditions in a particular village. 'Precisely what happened', she continues, 'and in what situations would depend on the particular configuration of local conditions.'[83]

In both farm and village England the markets and towns associated with them created areas around them which represented, on occasion, real administrative districts and, probably as importantly, areas of loyalty and belonging. This is in some ways the area that the peasant man or woman of France knows as their *pays* – the area to which they belong. Curiously this is recognized by the 1851 census's attempt at working out population density where the results accord fairly clearly with other kinds of definitions of world boundaries.

> To the 21 preceding 'villages' there is on average a town, which stands in the midst of 110 square miles of country, equivalent to a square of 10 1/2 miles to the side, a circle having a radius of nearly 6 miles; so that the population of the country around is, on average, about 4 miles from the centre.[84]

If we look at local directories this kind of world appears clearly. East Dereham, in West Norfolk is described in Kelly's Directory for 1896 as follows: ' . . . in the centre of a fertile and highly cultivated district, and its distance from any other market of any consequence, cause Dereham to rank among the best markets in the county'.[85] There were markets at Norwich [15 miles east], Swaffam [12 miles west], and Wymondham [11 miles south-west]; in other words Dereham's *pays* was almost exactly the same size as the national optimum suggested by the 1851 census. In other parts of rural England where population was less dense the distance might have been greater, but the principle would remain the same.

What lies at the heart of our *pays*? In Dereham an impressive range of services, at least by the 1890s. In administrative terms it was the head of a county court district, the base of the petty sessional and Poor Law Union of Mitford and Launditch, the rural deanery of Higham, and the circuit town for both the Wesleyan and Primitive Methodists. It provided for those around an enviable array of religious and secular institutions including churches and chapels, a Corn Hall [for balls], an Assembly Rooms [for all kinds of public functions], a Volunteer Battalion, a Liberal Club, a Unionist Club, a Working Men's Unionist Club, and a Reading Room and Athenaeum. Above all, market towns, like Dereham provided an array of shops and services. To list them here would make little sense, but certainly by the end of the 1880s our *paysan* did not have to travel far to buy the goods of the industrial revolution.

Market towns and markets created and defined not only economic and administrative areas but social and cultural ones. In North Oxfordshire people thought of themselves as being in 'Banburyshire', in central Northumberland as being of 'Hexhamshire'. In Northumberland and elsewhere hiring fairs had their areas which defined the boundaries of a world centred again on the market town. Richard Olney writes of the importance of these boundaries to a Lincolnshire farmer.

> When T. M. Richardson of Hibaldstow decided to attend the newly revived market at Kirton-in-Lindsey, the change of allegiance from Brigg was not undertaken lightly. 'He left kindred spirits . . . friends of his childhood and his youth, and therefore it could not be surprising that he should be found clinging to home with its endearing recollections and associations.'[86]

The growth of the local press, usually seen as a 'modernizing' influence which brought the outside world into the country, was in fact contradictory in effect and often added to a sense of locality. Certainly these 'penny-papers' which appeared in large numbers after the 1860s opened up perceptions of a wider world but these were always mediated through the local. All local papers were dominated by local news and advertising and, with no headlines, local events had the same structural significance as national or international ones. There was even, in many areas, a conscious revival of localism through the use of dialect stories and poems in which the local sees through the shams of urban or non-local life. 'Giles's Trip to London' and 'Giles Meets the Grand Old Man' (that is Gladstone) were Norfolk examples of the 1880s. Written in 'dialect' they showed the superiority of the regional culture of the 'stupid' countryman by his triumphs in the shallow world of London. Virtually identical but in the Sussex 'dialect' are 'Tom Cladpole's Trip to America' and 'John Cladpole's Trip to London' from roughly the same period.

The market town though was not one thing. All had their rough streets and their grand ones and the different classes of rural society drew different things from them. To the county gentry these towns provided social centres. Nathaniel Paine Blaker wrote of Lewes in Sussex in the 1850s:[87]

> Lewes was then not only the County Town but a very gay and busy place, though it had ceased to be the winter residence of

> the nobility and gentry of, at all events, the eastern part of the County, whose residences, with the remains of their former grandeur . . . still remain.

Lewes, like most market towns was the social and cultural centre of its *pays*, 'a festive place. Balls and parties were frequent.'[88] What Richard Olney writes of Lincolnshire was probably true of village England at least.

> In the market towns of Lincolnshire . . . the favourite amusements were assemblies, theatre going and (where they existed) race meetings . . . the county assemblies varied in social character with the towns in which they were held, but they were in the main middle class affairs.[89]

To these came the minor gentry and larger farmers and their families, creating a middle rank of county society which, much more than the great landowners, really ran the rural area. The county town for them was a key centre not only in the economic sense of its marketing function but also in terms of social and political contacts. Here marriages were made and alliances formed. Here the Poor Law Guardians met, and often the Bench of Magistrates, the two groups which effectively made up county government before 1889.

> The rural middle class of clergy and farmers was thinly scattered over the country, but the market towns provided centres where they could transact business, meet friends and discuss current affairs. The clergy assembled officially at archdiaconal visitations, but the farmers came regularly to the weekly corn markets.[90]

The English countryman or country woman of the second half of the nineteenth century inhabited a world structured by their relationship to economic and social power. The landlord, who owned the land, the farmer who used his capital and sometimes his labour to exploit it, and the labourer who worked the land, all had precise relations to social and economic power.

Yet this power was mediated through their locality – it looked, and indeed was different in different areas of England. Crucially it was different in the way in which people experienced and thus interpreted their world. The great Norfolk tenant farmer, like Clare Sewell Read with thousands of acres, a workforce bigger than many factories in the 1860s, his place on the bench, in the Chamber of Agriculture and in the Royal Agricultural Society was, in all but the most formal of senses totally different from the family producers of the Weald of Sussex or the lead miner/farmers of Allendale. Nor was it simply a matter of farm size and wealth, although that certainly had a lot to do with it; it was the whole culture in which people lived, their local world, which created or influenced these differences.

The parameters of this world are both clear and almost impossible to trace. Contemporaries often saw them clearly. The Northumberland shepherd had a world, as we have said, that was defined clearly by the lines of the hills which marked the sheep walks.[91] Here the fens are a good example. Even Norfolk fenmen looked west to Cambridge and Wisbeach rather than east to Norwich for the centre of their *pays*. There were certainly differences in the productive system between the high farming of West Norfolk and the often small-scale farming of the fens. However, it was outside this narrow economic division that the real division existed. It was culture that created the idea of the 'fen-tiger', the hard working, hard drinking, and hard fighting man, who was beholden to no one and quite distinct from the tied and hired farm labourers of west Norfolk.

In some areas of England though the local world was yet smaller, defined perhaps by a farmhouse or farm settlement in the first instance. Mr John Coleman, who was Commissioner charged with investigating Northumberland for the Royal Commission of 1881, explained the farms of the county for an audience raised in village England. Here was a very small local world.

> The whole management of a Northumberland farm must appear very peculiar to a southern farmer. Each farm is, to a large extent, a colony in itself. No doubt, owing to the scarcity of the population, and to the absence of villages, this was a necessity in the original laying out of the land . . . but there is a sort of clannish feeling between the labourer and his employer, from their living together on the farm . . .[92]

These worlds, though they defined much of people's experience, were not closed, rather the wider world was seen through them and their institutions. But there were other boundaries which had some of the qualities of continuity that characterized regional and local differences – those of the more internal world – the 'communities' of farm and family. It is to them we shall now turn.

NOTES

1 *PP 1852–53, LXXXV*, 'Census of Great Britain, 1851, Population Tables I. Report', p. 182.
2 *PP 1863, LIII*, 'Census of England and Wales for the Year 1861', p. 11.
3 *PP 1883, LXXX*, 'Census of England and Wales, Vol. IV. General Report', p. 9.
4 E. G. R. Taylor, 'Discussion on the Geographical Distribution of Industry', *Geographical Journal*, vol. 92 (1938) p. 23.
5 See the discussion in Peter Hall, Harry Gracey, Roy Dewett and Ray Thomas, *The Containment of Urban England*, (London, 1973) Vol. 1 pp. 76ff.
6 This table is constructed from B. R. Mitchell and Phyllis Dean, *Abstract of British Historical Statistics*, (Cambridge, 1962) p. 60.
7 ibid.
8 Derived from ibid., p. 366.
9 Caird, op. cit., p. 520.
10 *PP 1863*, op. cit., p. 35.
11 *PP 1883*, op. cit., p. 23.
12 *PP 1893–4, CVI*, 'Census of England and Wales, Vol. IV. General Report', p. 43.
13 *The Spectator*, 12th Feb. 1876 and 4th March 1876 quoted in Introduction by David Spring to John Bateman, *The Great Landowners of Great Britain and Ireland*, (new edn, Leicester, 1971) p. 12.
14 ibid., p. 515.
15 For a discussion of this problem see Edward Higgs, 'Women, Occupation and Work in the Nineteenth Century Censuses,' *HWJ* no. 23, Spring 1987, pp. 59–80.
16 *PP 1883*, op. cit., p. 36.
17 ibid.
18 *PP 1904, CVIII pt. 1.*, 'Census of England and Wales, General Report', p. 25.
19 Figures from *The Victorian County History of Sussex*, Vol. 1. General discussion in R. Lawton, 'Rural Depopulation in Nineteenth Century England' in D. R. Mills, (ed.) *English Rural Communities: the Impact of a Specialized Economy*, (London, 1973).
20 *PP 1867, XVII*, 'Royal Commission on the Employment of Children in Trades and Manufactures not Regulated by Law, Sixth Report', p. 187.
21 *PP 1883*, op. cit., p. 47.
22 *PP 1881, LXXX*, 'Census of England and Wales: London', p. 71.

23 NRO., T/62. Interview with Mr Murray, shepherd, Kielder. See Cohen, op. cit., pp. 1–18 for a general discussion of these ideas.
24 For a discussion of the differences in the agriculture structure of Sussex see Brian Short, 'Agriculture in the High Weald of Kent and Sussex', Unpublished PhD thesis, University of London, 1973.
25 Caird, op. cit., p. 482.
26 For this and parts of what follows see, J. B. Harley, 'England circa 1850', in H. C. Darby (ed.), *A New Historical Geography of England after 1600*, (Cambridge, 1976).
27 Clare Sewell Read, 'Agriculture', in *White's History, Gazetteer and Directory of Norfolk*, (London, 1890), p. 84.
28 Leonce de Lavergne, *The Rural Economy of England, Scotland and Ireland*, (Edinburgh and London, 1855) p. 272.
29 Harley, op. cit., p. 242.
30 Frederick Law Olmsted, *Walks and Talks of an American Farmer in England, 1852* (new edn., Ann Arbor, 1967), p. 272.
31 Edward Little, 'Farming of Wiltshire', *JRASE*, vol. 5. 1844, p. 172.
32 de Lavergne, op. cit., p. 236.
33 ibid., p. 247.
34 NRO., T/62, op. cit.
35 Quoted in Harley, op. cit., p. 252.
36 John and Jane Penoye, *Houses in the Landscape. A Regional Study of Vernacular Building Styles in England and Wales*, (London, 1978) pp. 21–2.
37 Cohen, op. cit., p. 3; but see also Colin Bell and Howard Newby, *Community Studies*, (London, 1971).
38 Christopher Taylor, *Villages and Farmstead. A History of Rural Settlement in England*, (London, 1983), p. 125.
39 ibid.
40 ibid., p. 175.
41 ibid., Chs 7–8.
42 *PP 1893–4, XXXV*, 'Royal Commission on Labour. The Agricultural Labourer. England. Report by Mr Arthur Wilson Fox . . . upon the Poor Law Union of Glendale (Northumberland)', p. 101.
43 See Chapter 4.
44 *PP 1893–4, XXXV*, op. cit., p. 102.
45 NRO, Wood MS, op. cit., NRO 302/24.
46 NRO, Hiring Agreements, Hatton Hall Estate, NRO ZBL/78.
47 *PP 1893–4, XXXV*, op. cit., pp. 105–6.
48 ibid., p. 105.
49 NRO, Simpson MS, NRO Z51/72, Misc. Hiring Agreements Middleton Hall, nr. Wooler.
50 *PP 1893–4, XXXV*, op. cit., p. 106.

51 ibid., p. 102.
52 NRO, Enumerators Books, 1881 Census, Berwick on Tweed Union, Cornhill District.
53 NRO, Woods MS, op. cit., NRO 302/26.
54 *PP 1893–4, XXXV*, op. cit., p. 110.
55 NRO, T/70, Interview with Mr. Bob Hepple.
56 *PP 1867–68, XVII*, 'Commission on the Employment of Children, Young Persons, and Women in Agriculture, First Report', p. 363.
57 On Aberdeenshire see the fine study by Ian Carter, *Farm Life in North East Scotland 1840–1914. A Poor Man's Country*, [Edinburgh, 1979].
58 This is dealt with in Alun Howkins, 'Ploughboy Lads and Horsemen. The culture of labouring men north and south', unpublished paper given at the British Agricultural History Society Conference, Kings Lynn, 1988.
59 *PP 1882, XVI*, 'Royal Commission on the Depressed Condition of the Agricultural Interest . . . Northumberland', p. 6.
60 ibid., p. 7.
61 *PP 1893–4, XXXV*, op. cit., p. 104.
62 *PP 1882, XVI*, op. cit., p. 7.
63 For a general discussion of this problem see, J. P. D. Dunbabin, *Rural Discontent in Nineteenth Century Britain*, (London, 1974) Chs VI and IX. For the Scottish end see the very important discussion in Ian Carter, op. cit.
64 *PP 1893–94, XXXV*, 'Royal Commission on Labour. The Agricultural Labourer . . . Report by Mr. Edward Wilkinson . . . upon the Poor Law Union of Driffield', p. 57.
65 See Howkins, 'Ploughboys', op. çit.
66 *PP 1893–94, XXXV*, 'Royal Commission on Labour. The Agricultural Labourer . . . Report by Mr. Arthur Wilson Fox upon the Poor Law Union of Garstang', p. 167.
67 Taylor, op. cit., p. 125.
68 Sarah J. Banks, 'Open and Close Parishes in Nineteenth Century England'. Unpublished PhD Thesis, University of Reading, 1982, p. 114.
69 *PP 1884–5, XXX*, 'First Report of Her Majesty's Commissioners for Inquiring into the Housing of the Working Classes', p. 594.
70 Flora Thompson, *Lark Rise to Candleford*, (pb. edn., Harmondsworth, 1973) p. 302.
71 *PP 1884–5, XXX*, op. cit., p. 595.
72 Thompson, op. cit., p. 254.
73 Raphael Samuel, 'Quarry Roughs' in Raphael Samuel, (ed.) *Village Life and Labour*, (London, 1975) p. 155.
74 *PP 1867–68, XXVII*, 'Royal Commission on the Employment of Children, Young Persons and Women in Agriculture. Report

of . . . Rev. James Fraser', p. 95.

75 There is a vast literature on 'open' and 'close' parishes. The most recent, and in some ways best contribution, is in Banks, op. cit.. The 'standard' account is probably Dennis R. Mills, *Lord and Peasant in Nineteenth Century Britain*, (London, 1980).

76 *PP 1867–8 XXVII*, op. cit., p. 29.

77 ibid., p. 29 (Ringland); p. 29 (Sprowston).

78 ibid., p. 30.

79 Michael Home, *Winter Harvest* (London, CBC edn. 1967) p. 47.

80 Yvonne Nicholls and Sylvia Woods (eds), 'The Memoirs of Jane and William Inskip' in *Miscellanea*, The Publications of the Bedfordshire Historical Records Society, vol. 59, (Bedford, 1980) p. 105.

81 *PP 1884–5, XXX*, op. cit., p. 595.

82 *PP 1867–68, XXVII*, op. cit., p. 49.

83 Banks, op. cit., p. 426.

84 *PP 1852–53, LXXXV*, op. cit., p. xlvi.

85 *Kelly's Directory of Norfolk, 1896*, (London, 1896) p. 100.

86 R. J. Olney, *Rural Society and Government in Nineteenth Century Lincolnshire*, (Lincoln, 1979) p. 68.

87 Nathaniel Paine Blaker, *Sussex in Bygone Days. Reminiscences of . . .* (Hove, 1919) p. 115.

88 ibid., p. 121.

89 Olney, op. cit., pp. 14–15.

90 ibid., p. 68.

91 NRO, T/62, op. cit.

92 *PP 1881, XIV*, 'Royal Commission on the Depressed Condition of the Agricultural Interest. Final Report', p. 392.

2

Farm and Family

We said at the end of the last chapter that the local world constructed the experience of those who lived and worked in rural England. But it is clear that different groups within the rural world must have had different experiences of it. Centrally, class and gender vitally affected the individual's relationship to the wider world. It also depends on what perspective one wishes to take. For example, if we were to argue that work was the determinant and vital experience of the majority of people in our period then the basic unit of rural society would be the farm, however constructed. If, on the other hand, we took social life or non-work life as the most important then the home, family or perhaps the village would be central. In reality most people see the world through both home and work, in our case the farm and the village. However, there are obvious differences. Women, or the majority of them who married, spent a greater part of their lives in the home. Their work was domestic labour, and their rural world was probably very different from that of their menfolk. The larger farmers, and especially the gentry and aristocracy, were able to move out of the local world completely and move into relationships with their equals at a county, national and even international level. Yet, as we shall argue below, they remained essential parts of the local world.

What we shall do then is take these units in turn, remembering all the time that they do not exist in isolation [for example, farm and home] and that the relationships between them are not necessarily determinant ones, but ones of flux and movement.

In 1875 there were 470,000 agricultural holdings in England and Wales. About 20,000 of these were less than one acre so certainly would not qualify as a farm. Apart from that the question as to what a farm is, and hence what a farmer is, is enormously difficult.[1] As B. A. Holderness has put it,

> . . . the census category (of farmer) included capitalists occupying 2,000 acres and small holders with but 5 or 10 acres . . . By 1851 farmers were readily differentiated only by the size of their holdings, but the diversity of agriculture was such that mere acreage was an inadequate indicator of social status.[2]

A few straightforward examples will serve to illustrate the point. A 100-acre farm in East Norfolk, on some of the best land in England, would certainly be a capitalist unit employing a number of full and part-time workers and producing enough profit for a farmer to live well. In parts of the Midlands 100 acres would be a family unit with the farmer and his wife both working and usually employing workers only when needed at hay time or harvest. Yet Mick Reed, in a very important article, has suggested that a 100-acre farm may be a 'peasant' unit employing only family labour and producing substantially for subsistence.[3]

The problem is one we already know well – regional differences and the nature of the farming system such differences produced. A huge Norfolk wheat farm was classically the most intensive user of labour in the 1850s and 1860s yet market gardening obviously employed more workers 'per acre', while sheep farming, which probably had the largest acreage per unit, employed hardly any workers. Less obvious were the complexities of regional farming and working patterns. A 150-acre farm in Dinnington, Northumberland, which was a mixed but basically arable farm, employed in 1907 three 'hinds' regularly and a variety of other workers on a casual basis usually for harvesting[4] whereas in Norfolk in 1892 a 'high' arable farm of 130 acres employed seven full-time 'hands'.[5] In Devon in the same year a mixed farm of 158 acres employed six men more or less regularly plus others at harvest.[6]

Can we draw lines at all? To some extent yes. If we take forty acres we see that there were, in 1851, on a 'sample' of seventeen counties, 25,688 farm units of less than that size, which is remarkably close to the 23,540 farmers in the same sample who employed no labour that year. It also works very roughly with the notion that you needed one man to every thirty-five to fifty acres of mixed farmland which is implicit in a good deal of writing about farming in the period. Given this size, whatever regional variations we point to, it is clear that there were, throughout the years between 1850 and 1875, a very large number of small farms all over England. In 1871 there were 22,679 farmers in the same sample holding fewer than 40 acres, about 37 per cent of all farmers, which fits accurately with the figures given in 1875 by the agricultural census.

These small farmers though were not a unified group. At the bottom of the scale were those who held land who would not have appeared on the census as farmers at all but who had farming 'functions' and possibly status within a community.[7] For example, rural tradesmen often held a little land. William Hubbard of Swanton Morley in Norfolk who was betimes a labourer, cockle-seller and higgler as well as 'farmer' is shown in the 1873 'Domesday' as owning an estate of 2 acres 1 rod 11 polls in his native village.[8] In Surrey, George Sturt's grandfather William Smith was a potter who acquired land on his second marriage and became the 'potter and farmer' of the title of his grandson's book. Later on his daughter opened her 'shop' selling bacon produced on the farm.[9]

Even in larger villages and small towns 'farm' landholding was widespread. Samuel Hayes of the large open village of Ingham in North Lincolnshire had in 1871 a small shop and bakery. By the 1900s he owned two shops including a drapery but also had his own land on which he, like William Smith, kept pigs that were slaughtered for bacon and lard which was then sold in the shop.[10] Even a small town shopkeeper, like Charlie Clifton of Bicester in Oxfordshire, had a little land.

> Every week end he bought a pig or a sheep and had it killed and sold the joints see . . . he'd to to market perhaps and buy three . . . pigs or three sheep . . . [he kept them] in a little corner meadow . . . and round Bonner's Gardens he had pig sties.[11]

Most tiny 'farmers' combined this with some other manual occupation. There is simply no way beyond very detailed local study by which the extent of landholdings and 'farms' of this size can be estimated. Certainly at the mid-century they were present in some form in most areas of England. However, they tended to be most numerous where the particular development of more capitalist agriculture left them physical space, that is on agriculturally or geographically marginal lands, or on the outskirts of industrial and urban areas where there was a ready market for cash or barter crops. In both these types of area there needed to be other forms of (usually) waged employment which subsidized the agricultural holding at lean times.

To begin with the marginal lands. It is important to stress that 'marginal' here is not a definition based only on distance from centres of population. Rather it refers to those lands which, usually for agricultural reasons, were not taken into larger farming units. A good example is the Sussex Weald where poor soil and a complex mesh of ownership and customary relationships prevented, or at least discouraged, capitalist farming. In the Weald, as in areas of Oxfordshire or the edges of Dartmoor and Exmoor, the survival of some kinds of common rights was essential. Crucially these areas existed in a kind of symbiotic relationship with capitalist farming or even industry which provided casual and piece-work for cash. The much vaunted 'independence' of the small farmers of Ashdown Forest in north-east Sussex rested as much on their ability to get work in the Downlands, the coastal plains or even London, as on their common rights and tiny family holdings. Henry Heaseman worked with his father as a sawyer for large farmers and contractors in the summer as well as cutting turf and peat and selling it. In winter he cut litter in the Forest. Later in life he 'worked about' in the summer and cut litter in the winter.[12] William Young, who was born in the Forest in 1834, had to go away to Woolwich Arsenal for seven years until he was 24 years old and inherited his father's tiny farm.[13]

This group was probably declining nationally even in the 1850s. They relied heavily on casual employment in agriculture and industry which was becoming (albeit very gradually) a thing of the past after the 1850s and especially, as we shall see below, after the 1880s. Equally importantly their holdings were not easily 'improved', at least where the land was agriculturally marginal, which meant that productivity remained very low. This prevented them taking advantage of new crops and methods which saved small producers elsewhere.

This leads directly to the second group of worker/labourer/farmers – those who relied on the nearness of an urban market. In the 1850s these were, to an extent, a new group, but they were growing and were to continue to grow, especially after 1880. This kind of farming had been in existence since at least the early seventeenth century but the increased scale and spread of urban growth in the nineteenth century made it more viable. In East Lancashire, as Alistair Mutch's work shows, small dairy farmers supported themselves by working in the cotton mills when the urban milk trade was slack, a double reason for the survival of small farming on the edge of a town.[14] The hill farmers of Northumberland and Durham had a similar double support system with a ready market for farm produce and the pits and lead mines should farming temporarily fail.

> Some went to Consett district, followed the pits . . . down on Tyneside . . . I know two or three went to Newcastle. (My father) went to Ryton, he was five or six years there; then he came back to the farm . . . course he was bred to the farm . . . and he came back to it.[15]

Whether they were 'new' market gardeners or old peasant/labourers these small family producers lived little differently from the labourers around them. As William Little's report on Sussex for the Richmond Commission of 1881 said, ' . . . he lives harder and works harder than the ordinary labourer.'[16] Or, as de Lavergne said of the small farmers of Co. Durham, 'the average extent of the farms is sixty acres, and the farmers, generally speaking are common labourers who do everything for themselves.'[17]

For these small farmers the workplace and the home were the same place, the family and the workforce the same thing. Women and men worked the farm. Mrs Martha Barker from the Ashdown Forest area of East Sussex, told W. E. Raper in 1877, 'the first year we were at Colemans Hatch my mother and I and the other children cut 9 load of brakes on the forest.'[18] Susannah Rice, who was a widow from the same area, said she 'always turned out stock and sheep and cut brakes, myself and my husband cut litter and underwood.'[19] More telling than Raper's cryptic notes is an account, again from the Weald of Sussex, which could almost be from a French peasant autobiography.

> There was a young woman servant at my employer's house. I married her, and then my prosperity began. She was poor – if you reckon having no money to be poor – but indeed, she was anything but poor to me. She was strong, active, industrious and a good manager. She would do all kinds of work . . . What a wife mine was![20]

And from the opposite end of England the daughter of a small farmer remembered her childhood in the Kielder area of Northumberland.

> In those days the cows were out on the hill and they had to be brought in and milked up the dyke back in the summer, and the milk carried back. We helped with whatever farm work was going on, setting potatoes, or taking up potatoes, and hoeing and weeding potatoes . . . we made our own butter . . . then the water was to carry (sic) . . . there was always plenty work on a farm, never time to be early (sic).[21]

Social differentiation between these small farmers and labourers was unclear, especially in areas like Ashdown Forest where some holdings were little more than gardens and those who held them worked the vast majority of their time as wage labourers. The boundary between the two groups was also in constant flux particularly in places like the Garstang area of Lancashire where small farms dominated.

> At Hambleton there are a number of small farms occupied by men (who) have risen from the ranks of labourers . . . Some of the labourers on Mr Fitzherbert-Brockholes' estate have every facility for thus rising to a better position. Five of them rent land from the employer varying in amount from 5 to 30 acres . . . They sell butter at Preston and Garstang, and their wives and children do the necessary work. Their wages vary from 15s and 18s a week, and they can have regular employment all the year round, but they may stop away whenever they want to in order to work on their own land.[22]

If the farming ladder went up, it also went down, although obviously the nineteenth century agricultural writers were less keen to stress this aspect. This made the thankless and often unthanked toil of the small farmer's son or daughter especially important and especially hard to bear. As the *Agricultural Gazette* put it in 1894 writing of Lancashire; 'the sons and daughters receive no wages . . . but they have "expectations" which are sadly too often not realised.'[23] In the Isle of Axholme this was made worse by the custom of leaving land to grandchildren rather than children, making the intervening generation merely tenants for life. As one farmer said in 1892, 'parents are often suspicious of their children'.[24]

Once a farm started employing men and women the nature of the farmer's relationship to them and the wider society began to change. Even if he himself worked, even if, as was certainly the case in many middle sized farms throughout England, he ate with his men who may well have lived in the farmhouse, 'master and man' appeared as different categories. James Rogers of Rotherfield in Sussex talked in the 1920s of entering farm service at Huggett's Furnace Farm in 1853. 'I . . . lived indoors with three others who all shared the same bedroom . . . (there was a) very long table in the farmhouse kitchen . . . We all sat down together at it, Master, Missus, maids, and men.'[25] However, at another farm of roughly the same size, at the same period and only a few miles away, subtle changes had taken place. 'About the meals, we did not sit down together. The Master and Missus were served at their table and cut of my dinner from the same as they ate. The three men had their dinner at the same time but at their own table.'[26]

This gradual separation of master and man and of missus and maid increased both as the century progressed and as one moved up the scale of farms. Where living-in continued, as it did in areas of the north until after the Great War, it seems to have been increasingly separate except on the very smallest holdings. William Wood, for example, grew up in the 1850s and early 1860s just north of Brighton. As a child he visited his uncle's farm in Twineham where his uncle and his aunt still ate at the head of the table with their servants. When his uncle died in 1874 and Wood's father took the farm all that changed. The old house was sold, so was the pewter service that all had eaten from and eventually the great common table and benches. One assumes that long before this date the men had left the 'house' for good.[27]

But it was not only the passing of time but of a culture. The farm labourers' songs from the 1800s to the 1850s are full of scathing references to the 'new fashioned farmer' who abandoned the old ways. One of the most popular, 'When this Old Hat was New', put it clearly.

At the board's head stood the farmer, the table for to grace,
And welcomed all as they came in, each knew his proper place.
The farmer's wife was there, to give each man his due,
Oh happy were my youthful days, when this old hat was new.

But the times are greatly changed, the poor are quite done o'er,
They give to them their wages now, like beggars at the door.
In the house we must not go, allthough we are but few.
'Twas not the way, when Bess did reign, and this old hat was new.[28]

The farmers, so the labourers thought at least, sought gentility by separating themselves from their men and women servants. Richard Olney notes this separation taking place in Lincolnshire in the twenty-five years after 1850. 'Large farmers left more of the day-to-day supervision to foremen, and the foreman's wife in many cases took over the lodging of the confined (living-in) men.'[29]

Farmers' wives and daughters were the particular butt of accusations of 'over gentility'. In Lancashire the *Barrow Herald* wrote in 1875 of the 'improvement of manners' among the farmers of the area and especially among their children.

> . . . a respectable farmer's daughter would be thought ignorant if she could not treat you to a selection of operatic airs on her neat instrument. In place of the village school, the sons go to boarding school or college.[30]

James Rogers of Rotherfield in Sussex made the same point, but with different conclusions, 'No! there are no indoor farm servants nowadays, and I tell you for why – farmer's wives are too "ladyfied" to look after the men'.[31] Nevertheless, living-in did persist in some areas and we shall have occasion to return to both the system and its social effects later.

At the other extreme, at the top end of the farming ladder the difference between a farmer and landlord or minor gentry was almost imperceptible, at least in economic terms. The great hill farming 'flockmasters' of Sussex were, according to William Wood, 'the aristocrats of the farming community',[32]

> and lived in corresponding style. Only a few months ago I was talking to large farmer who came up to Sussex from the West of England in 1879 or thereabouts. He told me that one evening he rode over the Hill to see Mr T. Cooper at Norton; to his surprise Mr. Cooper came out to see him dressed in evening dinner dress; he had never seen in his own county any farmer so attired.

To these farmers institutions like county balls, agricultural societies and the increasingly class structured hunts enabled them to move out of their purely local world into a county and class based society. The diary of John Simpson Calvertt, who farmed 1,190 acres in West Oxfordshire, gives a fine picture of this kind of affluent farmer. His social world was based around visiting, shooting and the Heythrop Hunt. The entry for 30 October 1876 recounts his first 'public' meet with the Heythrop Hounds after arriving from Lincolnshire.

> Drove Alice and Eliz. to the grand annual 'Meet' at Heythrop Hall – we Champagned – saw over part of the House – the stables – the Gardens – &c. They killed a Fox near the Ovens Gorse . . . We Luncheoned again at Mr. Blake's.[33]

Calvertt's world stretched across West and North Oxfordshire and beyond. He visited the Royal Show most years as well as the Oxfordshire Show and was a member of the Royal Agricultural Society, sitting on its council. Each winter he visited London usually for the annual shows at the Agricultural Hall in Islington where he often met old friends from Lincolnshire, went to the theatre and 'witnessed the sights' of the capital.

At home in Oxfordshire his friends were from the upper ranks of county society – men like himself of more than modest wealth and gentlemanly leisure. At Moreton-in-Marsh Steeplechases in 1878 he took champagne with two large local farmers and one of the Brassey family, the railway magnates turned gentry and the owner of Heythrop House, 'home' of the hunt. Later in the day he took claret with Sir Morgan Crofton, absentee landlord of some 11,000 Irish acres.[34] More usually he visited the farmers of the area, although he was certainly on speaking terms with most of the West Oxfordshire gentry.

A farmer like Calvertt was totally separated from his workers physically, economically and socially. Their points of contact were few, if any, and often only ritualistic as when the farm workforces attended harvest festival at Church or were there as 'supporters' and observers at the Hunt Meets. Even the minimal contacts of capital seem to have been avoided. For example Calvertt didn't pay his men, his steward did that for him, and although he certainly took an active part in the farms he worked, it was firmly as a manager.

If the farm was one basic unit of economic and social organization the family was another. For women in particular the home was the site not simply of leisure or the 'joys of the hearth' but of work. If the farm produced value and profit, the home reproduced it, literally reproducing the workforce by feeding and clothing it and rearing children. To the elites it was also the defining system of inheritance – familial relationships dictated who should inherit what and how, although this was not always as straightforward as the law would have liked.

The basic form of the family in rural England in our period is an apparently unproblematic one. Most people lived in a nuclear family, that is, a two generational unit of parents and children. Usually, on the surface at least, these units were based on legally married couples. If we look at the manuscript census returns we see house after house in village after village which conforms to this norm. Yet there are problems even where the nuclear family seems to dominate. Firstly, we do not know, or cannot simply adduce from the bald description 'nuclear family' anything about the relationships within it or how it came into being. It is now obvious that, for example, relations between parents and children altered enormously between *c.*1600–*c.*1850 although throughout that period the nuclear family/household was the dominant form in England. Secondly, simply to describe a family as nuclear is to miss out whole ranges of informal support of an extended kind. Thirdly, roles, in a productive sense, within the family are obviously different at different times. Again this is often concealed not only by the common usage of family to suggest father=bread winner; mother=housewife and so on, but by the census itself. Fourthly, each family itself passes through a number of stages – its life cycle which is the composite life cycle of the individuals in it. Finally, detailed work on the census, with all its problems, shows that there were in fact a wide variety of 'alternatives' to the nuclear family.

'Marriage' as a standard form of religious service and civil contract, binding for life and with a range of real and implied obligations dates from Hardwickes's 'Act for the better preventing of clandestine marriage' of 1753. Under this Act, from Lady Day 1754 the Anglican marriage service, proceeded by the calling of banns or the purchase of a special licence from a bishop, was the only form of legally recognized marriage in England and Wales. From 1837 what were essentially the same constraints were enshrined in 'civil' marriage by a registrar.[35] However, these Acts could not change the huge range of custom and belief which were associated with 'marriage' and which were based on a firmer sense of economic and social reality than the essentially imposed ideas in either piece of legislation.

This was especially true of the long-established practice of regarding betrothal as the most important ceremony, and the one which marked the beginning of sexual relations. The origins of this are simple enough. For a small farmer or even tradesman children were an essential part of the family workforce. No man would marry a barren woman and conversely (though one suspects rarely) no woman would marry an impotent husband. Enshrined in custom and bolstered by a complex system of popular beliefs, betrothal survived even into the urban areas of the industrial revolution as more important than marriage in church among the poor. As a result, in many rural areas betrothal customs continued to be recognized by the poor themselves as having the same (or greater) legitimacy as marriage in church. As the 'Special Correspondent' of the *Morning Chronicle* wrote in January 1850,

> . . . I have reason to believe that in an immense number of cases young people come to a distinct understanding with each other to cohabit illicitly, until the woman becomes pregnant, the man promising to 'make an honest woman of her' as soon as that takes place . . . This they find more convenient than marrying at once, inasmuch, as the girl may be of service for herself, and the man elsewhere employed all the time.[36]

In many rural areas marriage did not follow. In Ash-next-Sandwich in Kent some 30 years earlier it was estimated as many as 15 per cent of couples simply never married.[37]

By 1850 this was beginning to change. The New Poor Law of 1834, with its insistence on 'bastard bearing' women being incarcerated in the workhouse, had succeeded in combining moral stigma with a harsh economic reality so that the old ways withered before it. Equally importantly, the basis of the old betrothal customs and relationships was rapidly vanishing even in the rural areas as their economic base, small farmers and rural artisans, began to decline, especially after the 1870s. Finally the new evangelical spirit in the Church of England, which we shall look at in the next chapter, as well as the growth of religious nonconformity among a section of the poor themselves, led to the gradual acceptance of 'new' moral standards. As a result Gillis has estimated that the extent of 'common-law' marriage dropped from a peak of between 15 to 20 per cent in the 1820s to about 5 per cent by 1900. In the same period the proportion of illegitimate births fell rapidly.[38]

Even this needs to be treated with some caution. The pre-nuptial pregnancy rate remained high at around 30 per cent until the 1900s showing that, even if marriage was the outcome of sexual activity resulting in pregnancy, sexual activity outside marriage remained far from abnormal. In rural areas the indications are that the old ways lasted longer than in the towns. Although a good deal of the material is difficult and has to be treated with some caution the reports on the employment of women and children in agriculture from 1867–72 all suggest that sexual standards were much more 'lax', especially in southern and eastern England, than conventional pictures of 'Victorian values' would suggest. One, albeit extreme, example will illustrate the point.

> I have frequently observed whilst there (Castle Acre, Norfolk) that it was next to impossible to visit a cottage where there happened to be one or two grown up daughters without finding one or more illegitimate children. The young women were utterly shameless; all female delicacy of character utterly gone. I have sometimes when taking my walks had the misfortune to have a gang of 12 or 20 young women following at my heels, and the obscenity of their conversation and the lewdness of the songs they sang were such as needed to be heard in order to be believed.[39]

Norfolk certainly had a well above average illegitimacy rate and Castle Acre was a large open village well outside control of vicar or squire but it is nevertheless clear that the campaigns to moralize the poor, which we shall look at in the next chapter, left many untouched.

This is also true of the nuclear family which, while it was certainly the dominant 'type' of household relationship, was not the only one. The census enumerator's books for the village of Wheatley in Oxfordshire, a large parish of just over 1,000 inhabitants in 1871, and Leafield, a scattered woodland settlement in the same county, show the range of possibilities within family and household types.[40] The majority of family and household types in both villages conform to the nuclear model – that is father, mother, children living in the same house with father as breadwinner. However, it is equally clear that as well as domestic work a large number of women worked at wage labour which seriously modified the internal structure of the household even if its external appearance remained the same.

In Leafield, in particular, a combination of outwork and woodland trades produced a range of family and household structures. Central here was outwork gloving which employed most of the women as outworkers, with mother and daughter(s) in many families employed on this basis. The possibility of work of this kind produced real modification to the 'nuclear' model on occasions. At 'the Row' in Leafield for example lived Elizabeth Eeles, a spinster, Martha Eeles, her niece, John Eeles, her nephew, and another niece, aged 5, Mary Anne Hopkins. Martha worked at the gloving and John, aged 18, was a farm labourer. Gloving also kept 19 year old Maryanne Pratley, an unmarried mother and her 1 year old son out of the workhouse and enabled Jane Shayler, a widow of 31, to support her 10 year old and 3 year old daughters. The woodlands which surrounded Leafield [known locally as Field Town until the 1900s] also provided a variety of family employments. Several women worked at chairmaking which enabled Phoebe Dadd to raise her family although she was a widow.

In Wheatley there was no dominant occupation for women although laundry work and seamstressing seem to be the main sources of employment. Here, one assumes, the relative nearness of Oxford with its University-generated demand was important. In both villages, the census reveals the extent to which children at home contributed to the family economy. In Wheatley, Mary Judge, aged 13, was an 'agricultural labourer'; John Tonks, aged 13, was an 'agricultural labourer'; Emily Freeman, 16, was a 'general servant' still living with her mother Elizabeth who was a farm labourer and a widow; while Jesse East, at 13, had the grand title of 'gentleman's servant' though he was still living at home. In Leafield gloving again enabled (or forced) daughters to work and contribute to family income from 12 or 13 years of age. Informally children probably contributed even more. School log books show constant involvement of children in agriculture throughout the year. In Sussex in the 1860s and 1870s they went hop pole shaving, flint picking, beating, shepherding, hop pole tying, barking, flower selling, hay making, weeding, picking hops, harvesting and gathering acorns, as well as endless versions of 'helping father'.[41]

This points to another aspect of the nuclear family concealed by the description – the family as workforce. We have talked of the farm as the site of employment for most of rural England but the family remained an important element. In Dorset in the late 1860s it was noted,[42]

> When a labourer is engaged by the year, the size of the family and the vigour of his wife and sons, becomes an important element for consideration as they are expected to go out to work when required. If the wife cannot go, she must send a daughter or [as I found in at least one parish] she must provide a substitute.

This insistence on family labour persisted in many counties of southern and eastern England in an informal way into the twentieth century as an elderly labourer remembered in the 1970s: ' . . . (a boy) had to go sometimes, they'd even compel them to. Boys have got a job at, like a builders at Stalham, and they've had to leave and come on the farm or they'd turn them out of their house.'[43]

The system of family hiring was at its most advanced and firmly entrenched in Northumberland and other northern counties. Here again well into the twentieth century hiring contracts specify what was effectively family hiring.

> I James Nixon do hereby agree to serve Sir Edward Blackett Bt. as Hind at Hatton for one year from the 13th day of May next . . . My boy James to have constant employment for the Summer half year . . . and my two daughters to work when wanted and to be paid at the discretion of the farm steward.[44]

The best known aspect of this family hiring was the notorious [in the nineteenth century] and over-romanticized [in the twentieth] 'bondager' system. At its most basic this simply meant that every hired hind [living-in regular worker] had to provide a female worker to work with him. As Mrs Brown, who was born in 1876 near Wooler in Northumberland, said, 'Anybody that hadn't a woman it was hard to get hired . . . and if they had no woman workers, well they could hire one and take her to live with them.'[45] Francis and Christopher Storey hired with Sir Edward Blackett in March 1865 as hinds, 'House and garden rent free and coals led [ie brought to house]'. However, these two brothers were unmarried and so had 'no woman' and so turned to the extended family – 'our niece to work when wanted and to have 10d per day in summer and 1/6 a day during harvest.'[46]

Women hired in this way were sometimes known as 'bondagers' although the term seems to have been less frequently used in Northumberland than later writings, and indeed contemporary outsiders, would suggest. In 1881 Mr Coleman's report to the Richmond Commission went as far as to say that women workers were 'formerly styled a bondager, a term which is now most strongly objected to because it was supposed to denote a degraded condition of servitude'.[47] This is borne out by the fact that out of ten agreements spread over the period from 1853–1904 in the Northumberland Country Record Office which mention the provision of a worker, only one, the earliest, uses the word bondager. Nor do farm accounts use the term.

These farm accounts of Northumberland farms, especially those on the low lands in Glendale to the north and east of the Cheviots show the family as a working unit up until the Great War. Not only were these workers hired as families they were paid as a group. For example, the account books from Castle Heaton Farm which we looked at in the last chapter, record each worker's earnings individually but also show that they were paid monthly as a group to the 'head' of the household, usually the father. For example, the entry for October 1889 for the family of Robert Waugh reads,[48]

Oct, 26 Waugh.	£	s	d
Robt. 4 w. @ 14/-	2	16	0
James 4 w. @ 15/-	3	0	0
Thomas 4 w. @ 14/-	2	16	0
Margt Anne 18 1/2 days @ 1/4	1	4	8
	9	16	8

The money is then recorded as paid to Robert Waugh. This practice continued until the Great War. After then, although families continued to be hired as a family, the money was recorded as paid to each member as an individual.

The complex relationships between family, workplace and household shown on the large Northumberland farms cast real doubts on the ideal of a nuclear family as a simple category in this, and other northern areas. Family hiring enabled widows to exist as wage earners with independent status as cottar tenants, nieces and nephews were hired by and lived with uncles, the family remains undivided by generation since sons and daughters are a real economic asset. The home and the workplace also remain almost the same place and strong bonds grow up between families, and between master and workers on the same farm.

Northumberland provides perhaps an extreme example of the variety of social structure concealed behind the term 'nuclear family' but even Wheatley in Oxfordshire, de Lavergne's 'most' representative county, provides a range of complexities. Most obviously, still in 1871, was the problem of the relationship between family structures and living-in service of various kinds. We have looked at some aspects of this earlier, mainly seeing it in terms of employer/worker, but it must also be seen in the family context, especially when the role of servant is confused with that of relation.

George Rose, for instance, appears on the 1871 census of Wheatley as a 'Butcher and Farmer of 55 acres'. He was unmarried but Richard Rose, his nephew, an assistant butcher, and Eliza Cooper, a 'general servant', lived in his house. John Froud was a master carpenter. In his house, as well as himself, his wife and daughter, lived two sons-in-law who were also his journeymen. John Mott, a master shoemaker, also accommodated two journeymen, one his son and one, Richard Holden, who was no relation. In Leafield we see similar situations where relationships between family/servant/generation produce complex households of a non-nucleated type. At Witney Lane, Leafield, lived John Empson and his wife. He was a cattle dealer and his two eldest daughters, aged 16 and 13, had no occupation so it seems likely they were relatively well off. They had four other children at school. Also living in the house was a 'farm servant' aged 20 called Robert Empson, probably a relative and possibly the son of an elderly couple called Empson who lived nearby. This kind of pattern, where a 'wealthy' family member takes the child of a less wealthy one is seen clearly elsewhere, for instance in the Kent and Sussex Weald.[49]

Although by the 1850s, let alone the 1870s living-in had long ceased to have the importance and significance it had in the seventeenth century it remained an important part of both family and individual life cycles. The chronology of decline, which sees living-in service as a thing of the past or at best a regional anachronism by the middle years of the nineteenth century, has now been radically altered. At the most basic level the 1851 census says 'the practice of taking the young labourer or servant into the house may be traced through every county'.[50] In 1851 there were 109,452 male indoor servants over the age of twenty and 126,491 under twenty. Twelve per cent of male labourers over the age of twenty and 39 per cent of those under twenty were indoor servants. Of women labourers 53 per cent over the age of twenty were indoor servants while under twenty the figure is much larger at 81 per cent.[51] Although at a national level these numbers declined absolutely as the century progressed, living-in continued to be vital in many areas, particularly in the north where the numbers of indoor servants as a proportion of the workforce actually increased up to 1871.[52]

This opens up important questions as to the nature of farm service. It is often assumed that 'indoor farm servant' was an immutable category, that somehow the farm servant of the 1850s was identical with his or her forebear of the 1750s or 1650s. This is clearly nonsensical if looked at in any detail. We saw above the subtle differences of eating, and social gradations concealed by the term 'living-in' within a distance of a few miles in Sussex in the 1850s. There was also a world of difference between the small scale 'living-in' of the Sussex or Kent Weald, where a farmhouse might have one or two indoor servants, and where the status difference between a small farmer and his wife, and the maid or man employed was not great, and a great Northumberland or Lincolnshire farm where living-in simply meant living on the same site but in separate buildings. Yet there were continuities and similarities over long periods and across different regions. The living-in servant was almost inevitably young and unmarried and hired for a long period. This was usually a year but could be six months or sometimes even less. These shorter hiring periods tended to become more common as the nineteenth century progressed and the institution of living-in came under pressure from a variety of sources.[53] Living-in service was part of the life cycle for many young workers well into the 1870s. Even in southern England, where the institution had all but vanished according to most sources, Reed's work on the manuscript census returns shows a much higher survival rate especially in the marginal areas of the Weald, than is usually argued.[54]

Workers like these left home in their early teens to go into service where they remained often up to their mid-twenties. Michael Maynard, who was born in 1809 in Ashdown Forest, left home at fourteen to go into service. At the age of thirty he returned to inherit his mother's small farm.[55] John Heaver, also of Ashdown, worked for his father until he was fourteen 'then went to work for William Payne at Leggs Heath for a year . . . ' Between then and his marriage at the age of twenty-six he lived-in for various periods [including as little as a month] at no fewer than ten 'places'.[56] In Norfolk, a county where living-in farm service for men was practically non-existent by the 1870s, as late as the 1890s young farm workers went away to Yorkshire to hire by the year and save enough money to get married.

> In Yorkshire they used to go to what they called a hiring you know, and the farmers used to hire them for . . . a year . . . and you used to go there and live in, you got £18 or £20 a year and your food . . . and come back and marry.[57]

Young women seem to have left home slightly earlier. Mrs Lambert from Great Bentley in Essex went into service at twelve living-in with a local farmer/butcher. Seventy years earlier Martha Barker of Fletching in Sussex 'went away to service to East Grinstead' at thirteen.[58] Girls went earlier because their home earnings were less regular and predictable than those of boys – a situation which got worse as living-in farm service vanished almost totally in the south. In Flora Thompson's Lark Rise, 'there was no girl over twelve or thirteen living permanently at home . . . The girls, while at home, could earn nothing.'[59] The difference here between the north, where the family hiring system encouraged girls to stay at home, and much of the south, where it had all but disappeared, is striking.

The family as workforce, as receiving institution for workers or as almost a work unit in itself, all of which are present among the rural poor, were much less significant among the elites. Similarly, inheritance, which had been an overwhelming concern in earlier periods, was less of a problem as the century went on. Primogeniture had become all but universally established in England by the 1850s, creating, along with entail, a mainly smooth passage from one generation of nuclear households to another. Where there were problems of inheritance they concerned younger sons and unmarried [or unsuitably married] daughters. Nevertheless the elite obsession with 'family' remained although it is clear that the social restrictions on marriage into 'trade', if they had ever been a serious problem, were rapidly vanishing by the 1870s. The demand for Walford's series of books called *County*

Families, which first appeared in the 1860s, and the later county 'Who's Who's' and 'Leaders Social and Political' testify to a desire to place oneself absolutely in an age of change but also, by including 'new' wealth, these elite directories testify to the at least partially open nature of the county ruling class.[60]

However, problems could, and did occur which would not disgrace the pages of a sensational novel. The papers of the Rolfe family, middle ranking and old established gentry from Norfolk, show just how badly wrong things could go. A contested will, brought about in classic fashion by an unwise marriage, and which spent years in Chancery, drained the modest fortune of the family. The 'senior' branch was forced to let the family house and live abroad to save expense while the younger sons were bought commissions in the navy or 'set-up' overseas with varying degrees of success. As we shall see below the agricultural depression was the final blow to this family's fortunes.[61]

To people between the level of the poor and that of the gentry and aristocracy family was vital even to those better off than the peasant farmers of a few acres mentioned earlier. As Davidoff and Hall show in their brilliant study of the family and business [which unfortunately ends in 1850] 'well into the nineteenth century the family remained the basis for most economic activity . . . Most production for profit was through the family enterprise.'[62] Marriage provided both capital and labour on a small farm, and kinship did the same. A woman who had been in living-in service on a farm brought to her marriage skills and capital. The children she produced and reared were cheap or even free labour. Davidoff and Hall quote the example of an Essex family where a woman who had been in service returned to marry 'a man from a farming family who had descended to being a wage-paid team man'. Her skills as a dressmaker as well as her help with running the farm 'restored the family to independent farming.'[63] The labour of the wife and daughter was especially crucial in the dairying districts. In Cheshire, cheese was 'almost invariably made by the farmer's wife or his daughters' well into the 1870s although 'factory production' was beginning to appear. This labour, the 1881 report said, 'is not much considered because it is done by the farmer's family and not paid for out of pocket.'[64]

Even in districts where dairying was a secondary concern family labour, though often hidden, was equally vital to the survival of the family farm. George Ewart Evans interviewed a Suffolk woman who had grown up on a family farm in the 1890s. 'I did some work on the farm. I have milked and I used to warm the milk from the farm for the calves . . . My main job was to go by pony and trap to Halesworth every week with fowls, butter and cheese.'[65] As well as these jobs this young woman was effectively an unpaid servant since as soon as she reached 13 years of age the one living-in servant was dismissed and she took over all the household work including brewing, butchering and curing meat. As another woman, who grew up in Cornwall, put it, 'I was the cook, washer, maid and all, dairy maid and all . . . '[66]

Nor was it only girls. A boy's labour, whether or not he expected to inherit, was vital on all family farms. What H. St. George Cramp wrote of growing up in Leicester in the 1920s has a universality.

> Yeoman farmers down the ages have managed their farms with mainly family labour. We did likewise and rarely employed more than one outside labourer . . . Nor did father need more, with nine lusty children . . . Between the ages of five and eighteen I graduated in every task a graziers farm throws up . . .[67]

The life of a son or daughter of a family farm is often romanticized in autobiography but in many respects it was harsh. Such work was effectively unpaid. As Mrs Robinson, daughter of a small farmer from Nottinghamshire, said, 'I just had pocket money . . . I got what father and mother could spare.'[68] It also restricted choice and opportunity. The Leicestershire farmer H. St. G. Cramp felt that he was not disadvantaged although his older brothers were.[69]

> When in later years I searched the primary school records there seemed an all-to-obvious liaison between the local school headmaster and my father . . . and it showed in the absences of my brothers . . .[69]

A Devon farmer's son suffered in the same way, although he, as eldest, inherited the farm. 'Being the older members of the family we were expected to go onto the farm and help the family. Whereas, the next son had an opportunity to go away to a boarding school and had a better education . . . [70] Mrs Cheeseman, a small farmer's daughter from Co. Durham, was told by the local doctor that she should go for nursing training, and wanted to go, 'but I – I never got . . . no. Me mother had too much work.'[71]

The family, then, remained as a constant and vitally important factor of social and economic organization throughout our period. It was a site of work as well as leisure and as such intersected with the farm as a unit of social organization. It also varied over time and over area. Although marriage legally and for life was the experience of a majority of men and women, by the 1870s there were still important distinctions within that institution. Similarly, if the nuclear family dominated, as at one level it did, as the most common form of family organization it concealed enormous differences of function.

However, what was probably the family's most important function in some ways remains obscured. The family was a primary site of socialization. Here were learnt the virtues that were to guide through life. As we shall see in the next chapter the ethics of paternalism placed a very high value on the family and family life, and the attack on women's work in agriculture after 1865–70 was centrally based on notions of the role of women as wives and mothers. Indeed the decline in importance of the family unit as a workforce, among the labourers at least, saw a rise in its importance as a unit of socialization.

NOTES

1 Ministry of Agriculture, *A Century of Agricultural Statistics. Great Britain 1866–1966*, (London, 1968), p. 19.
2 B. A. Holderness, 'The Victorian Farmer', in G. E. Mingay (ed), *The Victorian Countryside*, 2 Vols (London, 1981), Vol. I. p. 227.
3 Mick Reed, 'The Peasantry of Nineteenth Century England: A Neglected Class?', *HWJ*, no. 18, Autumn 1984, pp. 5–6.
4 NRO, NRO 479, Farm Diaries of J. W. and J. C. Rutherford, North Masons Farm, Dinnington, Northumberland.
5 *PP 1895, XVII*, 'Royal Commission on Agricultural Depression. Report by Mr. Henry Rew . . . on the County of Norfolk, p. 40.
6 DRO, DRO 1021 M/E, Clovelly Court Estate Papers.
7 Reed, op. cit., pp. 56–7.
8 *PP 1874, LXXII pt. 1*, 'Return of Owners of Land (1873). Vol. I, Counties, England', p. 34.

9 George Sturt, *William Smith: Potter and Farmer*, 1919, (new edn., West Firle, 1978).
10 Thea Vigne and Alun Howkins, 'The Small Shopkeeper in Industrial and Market Towns,' in Geoffrey Crossick (ed), *The Lower Middle Class in Britain*, (London, 1977), p. 204–5.
11 ibid., p. 200.
12 ESRO, Transcript of evidence collected by W. E. Raper, Book II, f. 20.
13 ibid., Book III, f. 7.
14 Alistair Mutch, 'Rural Society in Lancashire, 1840–1914', Unpublished PhD thesis, Manchester University, 1980, p. 160.
15 NRO., T/30, Interview with Mr. J. R. Armstrong, Allendale.
16 *PP 1881, XV*, 'Royal Commission on the Depressed Condition of the Agricultural Interest', p. 407.
17 de Lavergne, op. cit., p. 267.
18 ESRO, Raper transcripts, op. cit., Book I, f. 13.
19 ibid.
20 Alice Catherine Day, *Glimpses of Rural Life in Sussex During the Last Hundred Years* (Kingham, n.d. but c. 1928), p. 10.
21 NRO, T/63, Interview with Mrs Murray.
22 *PP 1894, XVI pt. 1*, 'Royal Commission on Agricultural Depression. Reports by Mr. Wilson Fox on the Garstang District of Lancashire and the Glendale District of Northumberland', p. 16.
23 Quoted in Mutch, op. cit., p. 163.
24 *PP 1894, XVI pt. 1*, 'Royal Commission on Agricultural Depression. Report of Mr. R. Hunter Pringle on the Isle of Axholme', p. 6.
25 Day, op. cit., pp. 12–13.
26 ibid., Mrs Wren of Mayfield, in Day, op. cit., p. 17.
27 William Wood, *A Sussex Farmer*, (London, 1938), pp. 21–2.
28 For a discussion of this song, and others, see Alun Howkins and C. Ian Dyck, '"The Times Alteration"; Popular Ballads, Rural Radicalism and William Cobbett', *HWJ* no. 23, Spring 1987.
29 Olney, op. cit., p. 62.
30 Mutch, op. cit., p. 167.
31 Day, op. cit., p. 14.
32 Wood, op. cit., pp. 71–2.
33 Celia Miller (ed), *Rain and Ruin. The Diary of an Oxfordshire Farmer, John Simpson Calvertt, 1876–1900*, pp. 29–30.
34 John Bateman, op. cit., p. 112.
35 For much of what follows see John R. Gillis, *For Better, for Worse. British Marriages, 1600 to the Present*, (New York and Oxford, 1985). For a general introduction to the family in history see Michael Anderson, *Approaches to the History of the Western Family 1500–1914*, (London, 1980). For a discussion

which centres more on the rural poor see K. D. M. Snell, *Annals of the Labouring Poor*, (Cambridge, 1985) Ch. 7.

36 *MC*, 18th January 1850.
37 Gillis, op. cit., p. 117.
38 ibid., p. 111.
39 *PP 1867, XVI*, op. cit., 'Evidence on Agriculture Gangs Collected by Mr. J. E. White', p. 181. The evidence being quoted is a letter from the Rev. M. S. Jackson, formerly curate of Castleacre in Norfolk, then (1865) Rector of Wickham Market, Suffolk.
40 PRO, R.G.9/899 (Wheatley) and PRO R.G.9/889 (Leafield).
41 Extracted from the School Log Books of Bishopstone, Falmer and Stanmer, Laughton, Udimore, and Waldron Schools held in the ESRO. I am grateful to Diana Hitchen for this material from her own work.
42 *PP 1867–68, XVII*, 'Royal Commission on the Employment of Children, Young Persons and Women in Agriculture, Report by the Hon. E. Stanhope', p. 4.
43 Interview AJH/Jack Leeder, Happisburgh, Norfolk, Tape in author's possession.
44 NRO ZBL/78, Hiring Agreements, Hatton Hall Estate. April 1865.
45 NRO T/98, NRO 1208, Interview with Mrs J. Brown.
46 NRO ZBL/78, op. cit.
47 *PP 1882, XIV*, op. cit., p. 6.
48 NRO, Wood MS, op. cit.
49 PRO R.G.9/889 and R.G.9/889, op. cit.
50 *PP 1852–53, LXXXVIII pt. 1*, op. cit., p. xci.
51 ibid.
52 J. P. D. Dunbabin, 'The incidence and Organization of Agricultural Trades Unionism in the 1870s', *Agricultural History Review*, XVI (1968), pp. 123–4.
53 This is a long and complicated argument but see Snell, op. cit., Ch 2, and Anne Kussmaul, *Servants in Husbandry in Early Modern England*, (Cambridge, 1981).
54 Mick Reed, 'Indoor Farm Service in Nineteenth-Century Sussex: Some Criticisms of a Critique,' *SAC*, Vol. 123, 1985, p. 228. See also Brian Short 'The Decline of Living-in Servants in the Transition to Capitalist Farming: a Critique of the Sussex Evidence,' *SAC*, 122, (1984).
55 ESRO, Raper transcripts, op. cit., Book IV, f. 20.
56 ibid., Book II. p. 18.
57 Interview, AJH/Mrs Moy, Yaxham, Norfolk. Mrs Moy's father went to Yorkshire. Tape in Author's possession.
58 EOHC, University of Essex, Tape no. 15. ESRO, op. cit., Raper transcripts Book I, p. 13.
59 Thompson, op. cit., pp. 155–6.

60 For a brief discussion of this see John Lowerson, 'Breakdown or Reinforcement? The Social and Political Role of the Late Victorian Gentry in the South-East' in M. D. G. Wanklyn (ed), *Landownership and Power in the Regions*, (Wolverhampton, 1978).

61 Veronica Berry, *The Rolfe Family Papers. The Chronicle of a Norfolk Family, 1559–1908*, (Brentwood, 1979).

62 Leonore Davidoff and Catherine Hall, *Family Fortunes. Men and Women of the English Middle Class 1780–1850*, (London, 1987).

63 ibid., p. 280.

64 *PP 1881, XVII*, 'Royal Commission on the Depressed Condition of the Agricultural Interest', pp. 918-19.

65 George Ewart Evans, *Spoken History*, (London, 1987), p. 18.

66 EOHC, Tape no. 442.

67 H. St. G. Cramp, *A Yeoman Farmer's Son. A Leicestershire Childhood*, (London, 1985), p. 38.

68 EOHC, Tape no. 182.

69 Cramp, op. cit., p. 38.

70 EOHC, Tape no. 352.

71 ibid., Tape no. 256.

3

The Sources of Stability and Harmony

To many people, especially those 'outside', the rural world of the twenty or so years after 1850 presented a picture of stability and harmony unequalled in recent history. Although the 'dark side of the landscape' was a continuing reality, compared with the 1830s and 1840s, the years after 1850 were calm indeed. For example rick burning and machine breaking, although both continued, ceased to have their almost endemic character after the outbreaks in East Anglia in the late 1840s.[1]

The reasons for this 'calm' are many. David Jones talks about 'the spirit of exhausted desperation' which characterizes many memoirs of the late 1840s.[2] In one sense this was simply a result of defeat. This is not the place to talk in detail about the 1830s and 1840s but it does seem that the repression which followed the Swing rising made its mark. If the poor needed further proof of the harshness of the new world it was provided in 1838 by the 'Battle of Bossenden Wood'. Here a group of Kent labourers, the followers of a self-styled Messiah, clashed with the army and more were killed than at the more famous 'Peterloo Massacre' of fifteen years earlier.[3]

The repression of Swing and the other protests of the 1830s was not only a physical act but an ideological one. At one level those who protested before the 1850s [and even in some places after] acted within an understood framework of what Thompson has called 'moral economy'.[4] In the rural areas the 'moral economy' was closely linked to the 'rights of poor men': to work or maintenance, fair wages and fixed prices. No matter how illusory these may have been in reality – and there is good evidence that in many areas they were not – they controlled the poor's view of social structure and social relations.[5] When these were given they were half of a reciprocity. In his dedication, 'To the Ploughboys of England', which was to preface his planned autobiography, William Cobbett, the theorist of this social order, bade them be 'sober, industrious, early rising, merciful to the horse and oxen; [and] to be obedient to their masters in all their lawful commands.' But if their masters failed them, if they broke the reciprocal agreement, these same ploughboys were to 'perish if necessary, rather than live upon POTATOES, SALT AND WATER.'[6]

The protests, of the 1830s especially, sought not to overturn the social order, rather to put it back the right way up. The processions, face blacking, ritual cacophony and public display which accompanied many such actions were an open assertion of right and an equally public 'reminder' to those in authority to 'do their duty' to the poor. In the past such protest had been accepted, indeed condoned; by the 1830s they were not.[7] Instead of reacting by at least accepting that the poor had rights the elite turned to a brutal legal repression. The law, an alien instrument at the best of times, was brought in to replace custom – it was as if the rules of the game had been changed half-way through the match without one side being told. As James Obelkevich has put it;

> there was thus a disjuncture between the class conscious gentry and farmers on the one hand and the labourers on the other, with their lingering if unreciprocated 'communal' expectations.[8]

Or, in the words of a ballad of the 1830s.

> So now my bold companions,
> The world seems upside down,
> They scorn the poor man as a thief,
> In country and in town.[9]

Hand in hand with the denial of the right to work and fair wages went the attack on the right to maintenance. The 'reform' of the Poor Law between 1834 and 1840 was a rural matter. It was not to the urban areas of industralization that Chadwick looked for problems but to the backward and the rural. The reforms were directed ultimately against payments in wages and kind, the roundsman system, and parish support of wages and prices, which were overwhelmingly rural phenomenon. Chadwick's harshest criticisms were directed against the rural areas and their administration, but often the witnesses called in 1834 and again in 1837, when the Act was first reviewed, stress the independence that the old law gave the poor and their belief in their rights, as the main cause of the problem. As Keith Snell has argued, parish settlement was prized by the poor as a birthright entitling them to relief and support as well as 'the generous and widely encompassing nature of relief' under the old law.[10]

When the first years of the workings of the new system were looked at in 1837–38 both the notion held by the poor that they had 'rights' and the behaviour this produced was widely noted. Mr Hawley, an assistant-commissioner, described to the commissioners in 1837 the 'indolent and tattered parish bird, who leaning on his hoe, with insolence and suspicion in his eye made it a practice, either by word or gesture, to insult every respectable person who passes him.'[11] The Reverend William Watkins of Sussex also referred to the 'insolence' of the poor before 1834 and their threatening 'to go to the magistrates' to get a relieving order over the heads of the vestry.'[12]

However, also by this date, witnesses constantly told the same commissioners that things were changing in the countryside. Mr John Lattman Ellis, vice-chairman of the Board of Guardians at Petworth in Sussex, said, 'the introduction of the law has certainly produced a good effect upon the moral character, because, I think that I see less drunkenness, and I hear less noise in the streets at night.'[13] The assistant commissioner, Mr Hawley was also convinced that the bad old days' were passed. The 'vicious characters . . . steeped in vice and habitual pauperism.' Had vanished, an 'almost magical change of system is perceptible.'[14] Relations between master and man were also better; according to the Rev. Watkins, 'there is a better feeling towards their masters than there was before . . . '[15]

The few labourers who gave evidence to the commissioners saw it differently, although ultimately the effect was the same. Even by 1837 the fear of the 'workus', which was to become a dominant part of English popular memory, was well established. John Wiscomb, a labourer from West Sussex, was asked if he thought he would be better or worse off in the workhouse and replied:

> I would not go in; I would not be parted from my wife and children for any man in England, unless God parted me; I would rather be shot first.

> You would rather die than be separated from your wife and children?
> Yes, I like them too well.[16]

The ballad 'Past', present and future' already quoted put the labourers' feelings precisely.

> They build up large workhouses now to part the man and wife,
> That they may no more children get, 'tis true upon my life.
> They take their children from their arms and send them different ways,
> And fifteen pence allowed to keep a man for seven days.[17]

There can be little doubt that an 'improvement' in the discipline of the poor was an intended part of the New Poor Law even if it was not its central aim. However, there was no such even slight ambiguity about the creation of the police. In the 'great' report of 1834 Chadwick pointed to the need for a police force in rural areas. C. H. MacLean, reporting on Sussex and Surrey in 1834, saw the police as an all-embracing agency of control who would deal with crime, the Poor Law, roads and paths and looked for the police to patrol the roads and communicate from district to district 'so that depredators could be traced, and the earliest intelligence of riot or robbery conveyed in every direction at the same time.'[18] In 1839 legislation was passed enabling counties and boroughs to raise police forces and this was added to in 1842 and 1850. Finally in 1856 the County and Borough Police Act introduced compulsion.[19]

Initially at least many of the forces set up under the voluntary legislation of 1839 acted very like the agencies envisaged by MacLean, especially in relation to the Poor Law and the control of vagrancy, categories of social identity which between them, as Carolyn Steedman points out, could cover all but the most respectable sections of the labouring classes.[20] But there were other areas especially in relation to poaching and other kinds of 'economic crime' where the police were brought into friction with the rural poor and we shall return to them in the next chapter. Again, as in the case of the repression following Swing and especially the Poor Law, it was not only the 'physical' reality of policing that mattered. All these changes represented a real break with the way things had been, or the way in which the labouring poor perceived them to have been in an ideological sense. The Old Poor Law to Cobbett, for example, was the sacred compact, the very embodiment of the reciprocity between rich and poor. He wrote in 1834, in one of his last pieces, on the New Poor Law,

> Obliterate the Act of Elizabeth, as this bill in fact does, and you dissolve the social compact, as far as it relates to working people; without protection on one side there can be no right to protection on the other.[21]

Keith Snell has argued a similar case, though without Cobbett's passionate certainty.[22]

The repression of the 1830s, the county police but above all the Poor Law marked the end of an era in the popular memory of the rural poor. Along with enclosure, changes in employment patterns, especially the decline of living-in in the south and east, and falling living standards, they isolated and demoralized the poor. By the 1850s, the real beginning of our period, this process was complete – indeed many were beginning to argue it had gone too far and that behind the sullenness and ignorance of the villager lay a peasant insurrection. The rick burners in Kingsley's *Alton Lock* are ignorant but they are much more dangerous and violent than the town radicals who come to address them.[23] The rural poor seemed to many to be completely alienated from their 'betters', a separate, secret people, impervious to change and influence. The old relationships had gone, swept away by the demands of agrarian capital, and nothing, apart from the harshness of the reform, had replaced them. As real prosperity and confidence returned to the agricultural sector in the 1850s the rural elites turned to put their own houses in order. There was also a very different impulse, often religious in origin, which sought, for its own reasons, to soften the harshness of the earlier period. While never totally successful these 'carrot' as opposed to 'stick' measures gained in popularity and effectiveness as the 1840s turned into the 1850s, and the 1850s into the 1860s.

A major element and agency in the new attitudes to the poor was the Church of England. The general history of the Church of England in the nineteenth century is far outside the scope of this book but some general points should be made. At the religious census of 1851 the strength of the Anglican Church lay in the rural areas. However, it was not an even strength. As Alan D. Gilbert has shown the real power of rural Anglicanism lay in the lowland arable zone of the south and east. Here 'parishes were smaller, more workable . . . [and] also better endowed.'[24] It was also in these areas that the 'ideal' parish existed, 'one in which a squire and parson presided jointly over a close-knit and deferential local community.'[25]

In the years before 1830 Anglicanism had gone through a period of what one historian has called 'disaster' and had been 'on the point of becoming a minority religious Establishment'.[26] This 'disaster' was a result of a number of problems but for the rural areas lack of provision of churches, especially in 'new' parishes, spiritual and pastoral neglect and the growth of nonconformity were of overwhelming importance. Worst of all the Church had always been closely linked to the landed elite. Not only were the landowners and farmers usually Anglicans but also it could be a clerical magistrate who sentenced a poacher or committed a rick burner for trial. Few, if any parsons had spoken for the poor in the desperate years of the 1820s and 1830s and the tithe remained a source of real grievance with many small farmers.

After 1830 this began to change, and indeed the period from that decade up to 1914 was marked by real growth in 'Anglican churches . . . Anglican clergy and . . . participation by laymen in the institutions of the Church.'[27] Gilbert has shown how between 1831 and 1871 nearly 4,000 new churches and chapels were built by the Established Church and the number of Easter day communicants doubled.[28] In the same period the old problem of non-resident clergy was tackled. In 1810 46.9 per cent of all clergy were non-residents not doing duty but by 1850 this had dropped to 15.5 per cent. However, many still remained non-resident even if they performed services in the parish. In the same period the number of clergymen rose from 10,261 to 11,728.[29]

Organizational change at the top was vital in both facilitating these changes and shaping the course they took, especially the establishment of the Church Commissioners on a permanent basis in 1836. However, more important for us were the broader religious/cultural changes within the Church itself and within our 'local world'. As James Obelkevich has written,

> It was . . . at the parish level that the battle was joined, and there strategy and tactics were determined not by politicians

> or theologians but by the parish clergy . . . The clergy were confident that their vigour and activity, contrasting with the neglect of their predecessors, would remove the grievances that had nourished Methodism and draw the discontented back to the parish church, where the entire village population would be united through participation in public ritual.[30]

Crucial to these changes was a new emphasis on the religious and pastoral aspects of the priest's role. From at the latest the 1830s, attacks from inside and outside the church on latitudinarian theology, moral laxity, worldliness and above all pluralism had assumed an all-pervasive character. Importantly both the Evangelical and High Church parties, whatever their doctrinal differences, were agreed that it was necessary to reform the priest's role. As the Evangelical who founded St Aidan's College, Joseph Baylee, said, a clergyman 'must be a man wholly given to his work or he must be content to be looked on in society as a careless shepherd of the Lord's Flock.'[31]

From the late 1840s both Evangelicals and High Churchmen began to acquire positions of power and influence within the Church of England and were increasingly able to push for reform of the parish clergy. A good example is Samuel Wilberforce who was Bishop of Oxford from 1846 to 1869. Wilberforce came to Oxford, as the editor of his letters notes, 'at a time when public clamour against clerical slackness was on his side . . . [and] he inaugurated an era of vigorous episcopal activity.'[32] He began by attacking pluralism. Within months of his appointment the stream of letters began. The Rev. A. B. Townsend, non-resident rector of Wheathampstead, was urged to 'appoint a resident curate', since 'I am informed that the present state of your health makes that continual attendance without which a Parish cannot spiritually thrive impossible to you . . . '[33] The Rev. James King, non-resident rector of Henley, was admonished more firmly.

> I am anxious to draw your most serious and earnest attention to the state of your important parish of Henley. It is over run with Dissent and Godlessness. Its population, now above 3000 souls most urgently needs the instant Care [*sic*] of another Curate . . . Souls committed to your charge and government are passing daily unprepared to their Eternal State.[34]

He also appointed active rural deans who were to keep him 'accurately informed of all spiritual details of [their] parishes', visit all churches in their charge annually and be 'a centre of spiritual influence to the clergy.'[35] He then turned to the quality of his priests. At any appointment over which he had control he sought to impose strict conditions of behaviour. He was especially opposed to hunting, and this remained a problem throughout his period as bishop although, like pluralism, the number of cases declined after the mid-1850s. His position is summed up in a letter in 1854 to the Rev. W. Bell who was applying to be licensed as a curate.

> I am convinced that a sporting clergyman is a great evil in a parish and I have uniformly refused to license as Curate anyone who intended to indulge in such amusements. Your assurance that you do not intend to be a sportsman would so far as shooting goes fully satisfy me without exacting any promise that you should never take a days shooting with a friend. But hunting stands upon a different footing. It is forbidden to clergymen by the Canon Law . . . and it is in all respects a far greater interruption to the studies habits and society to which a Parish Priest should be addicted . . .[36]

On the positive side Wilberforce pushed for, and usually got, a much more spiritually active clergy. A great part of the correspondence from the first years of his office is concerned with the frequency of services, catechism, communion and preaching. Those who are lax are instructed to do more, those who already perform are urged to greater things. Even the mundane, when it affects the priest's activity in the creation of the 'new community of prayer', is noted and acted upon. The Rev. W. I. Baker of Upper Heyford got short shrift when he complained his services were disrupted on Sunday afternoons. 'I have heard from your churchwardens . . . and they alledge [*sic*] that it is the great inconvenience of attending a service at 3 1/2 [*sic*] in a cattle country [*sic*] that prevents them being in their places on Sunday afternoons.' As a way of dealing with the problem Wilberforce suggests that service times are changed to 2.30 in winter and 3.00 in summer.[37]

Wilberforce's 'new' clergy then were to be resident, serious, spiritually and pastorally active in their parishes, and a force for moral improvement by action and example. There is an especially powerful letter, written in 1868 to one of his clergy who was filled with self doubt and clearly was having serious problems in his parish. In it Wilberforce puts forward his position on the new clergy.

> My advice then my dear Sir must go to the root of the matter. Shew the people you have a pastors heart & I do not think they will be long in giving you the natural return the support of the Parish . . . live in your parish; live for your parish; work in it as a man only can work who has come to his work from the intercession of his people. Do this and all 'improvements' will I have no doubt follow.[38]

'Live in your parish; live for your parish' increasingly became the maxim of rural Anglicanism as the 1850s and 1860s progressed, especially in the south and east of England. Elsewhere, there were still problems. As late as the 1880s the *Ormskirk Advertiser* could say of the parish of Croston, 'we have had no curate and our responsible minister has not been in our homes for more than nine or ten years.' Services when they were held were 'conducted in a very loose and heartless manner, and many of the regular attendants are obliged to go to the Methodist Chapel.'[39] It seems likely that this may well have been a result of continuing regional differences. The Anglican Church had always been weaker in the north, as we have already seen, and so by definition any real changes would have had much less impact there. Even by the 1900s a recent study of Lancashire notes that the Church of England was almost entirely identified with the gentry and that the farmers and labourers all attended the chapels.[40] In the north-east, in the mining/agricultural areas of the diocese of Durham, fifty new parishes were created between 1871 and 1881 and churches endowed. Nevertheless the miners and labourers of this quasi-rural district remained almost totally hostile to the Church of England. This was partly as a result of the identification between the coal owners and the Church and partly of the strength of Primitive Methodism.[41]

Elsewhere there were changes even within family-held livings, often the last bastion of the old, lax, clergy. William Turbitt who came to Powick in Worcestershire in 1833 was the first non-pluralist in that parish for over 40 years. He rebuilt the church and the vicarage house, built a school and ran a clothing club for the poor. He also introduced an evening sermon on Sundays. He was, 'representative of the clergy of his time who were much more diligent and conscientious priests than country gentlemen.'[42] At Souldrop in Bedfordshire the High Church Rev. G.-D. Newbolt also started a clothing club, an allotment scheme and rebuilt the church to accord with his High Church taste.[43]

Wilberforce's advice gave the village parson a new and different importance in village life. Where they stood in relation to the rest of rural society shifted slightly but decisively in many areas. From the 1850s, and earlier in some places, the parson became a key figure in the recreation of paternalism which at least broke gradually their simple identifications with the rural elite. Although this movement had far to go before it could become the open hostility that a minority of the Anglican clergy expressed towards the great landowners by the 1900s, it was a perceptible change and an extremely important one. A figure like Newbolt in Bedfordshire or the Rev. Edward Elton at Wheatley in Oxfordshire was very different from the aristocratic 'squarson' of the late eighteenth and early nineteenth centuries. This is not to argue that they were radicals in a political or social sense, rather that they sought to re-establish certain kinds of paternal relationships within their villages which involved not only control but also the creation of positive identification of the interests of the rural poor with the established social order while stressing the naturalness and inevitability of 'rank'. As the hymn had it,

> The rich man in his castle,
> The poor man at his gate,
> God made them high or lowly,
> And appointed their estate.[44]

Key elements in this were the expropriation and creation of communal rituals [always carefully monitored] and charity. Overlaying both was the argument that the priest had a special role to moralize, guide, and on occasions protect the poor who were literally their 'flocks' or, in a more striking metaphor, their 'children'. In this role they played a central part in the 'calm' that we mentioned at the beginning of this chapter.

An interesting example of the expropriation [or re-creation] of a communal ritual was harvest festival. The end of harvest had always been marked by celebration. As the ballad 'When this Old Hat was New' put it,

When the harvest time came round, or we went forth to shear,
How often were we merry made, with brandy, ale and beer,
When the corn it was brought in, and placed upon the mow,
The worker's bellies were well filled,
When this old hat was new.[45]

Such celebrations seem usually, at least since the sixteenth century, to have been secular, marked by drunkenness, sexual freedom and even violence. Often, as when 'largesse' was gathered, they involved the thinly veiled intimidation of tradesmen by gangs of harvest men and the celebration was then a single class one. Only those who had worked in the fields took part. Even farmers were excluded.

Celebrations like this were precisely the kind of 'folk' culture which was both actively suppressed from the early nineteenth century and, as we shall see later, positively attacked by the withdrawal of farmer and gentry support. Nor, more importantly for the moment, did the Church of England recognize any kind of harvest celebration although services of thanksgiving may have been used earlier. This changed in the 1850s. The originator of the present religious/secular 'Harvest Home' with its decorated church, thanksgiving service and secular tea and sports was, it is claimed, the Rev. George Anthony Denison, Archdeacon of Taunton and vicar of East Brent in Somerset. It was here in the early 1850s that the 'tradition' was revived [or invented]. By the late 1850s it had been taken up in several, usually High Church, parishes throughout England. In 1859 the Rev. Newbolt brought it to Souldrop in Bedfordshire and it was reported in the press that 'Harvest Home Celebrations on an improved plan having been successful in other parts of England, the first attempt was made at Souldrop on Wednesday Sept. 14th'.[46] By the early 1860s services at harvest appeared in Norfolk, although it is not clear if the decoration of the church, which was so much a feature of the ritual elsewhere, was widely used until the late 1860s.[47] In Lincolnshire the festival also appeared in the 1860s and 'it spread fast in the following decade and proved universally popular – with all varieties of churchmanship and with clergy and laity alike.'[48] By this date it had also reached rural Lancashire where the *Ormskirk Advertiser* called it 'a day of joy – not of drunken noisy joy, but sober and reasonable.'[49]

The basis of the festival's popularity among the clergy is not far to seek. In a theological sense it presented few difficulties although its origins usually lay with High Churchmen, as Obelkevich says 'it was part of a larger growth in moderate ritualism'.[50] Occasionally problems did arise, as at Souldrop when the festival was abandoned for several years after 1859 essentially because of attacks on the ritual by the Low Church party; however, even here it was resumed.[51] In 1862 Convocation in Canterbury issued an order of service giving it a religious seal of approval.

More importantly though was the social/cultural meaning. Harvest festival came to be one of the great ritual celebrations of the new paternalism – indeed it is from the original version of 'All things bright and beautiful', a harvest hymn, that the verse quoted above comes. In it the joint endeavour of the agricultural community was celebrated. In the gathering of the harvest master and man stood together, victorious, with God's aid, in the annual battle with the weather. The vicar of Morchard Bishop in Devon put this clearly to the 1894 *Royal Commission on Labour* when he said that the 'harvest service and festival' brought 'the farmers and men together in a most friendly way'.[52] At Souldrop in Bedfordshire in 1859 each farm's workforce appeared at the new harvest festival as a group led by their masters 'each farmer wearing on his breast a favour of distinctive colour, with an ear of corn projecting from it'.[53] This was reinforced by the myth of harvest. In this, all worked. Even the farmer stood with his men, his sleeves rolled back, working equally with them. The weather and the demands of speed knew no distinctions of status. Even if the seating plan of the church at Harvest Festival still divided men and women clearly by class, the equality of toil meant that a labourer could still carry the first sheaf into church at the service as at Rand in Lincolnshire in 1868.[54]

Harvest Festival in church was almost inevitably linked to a 'reformed' Harvest Supper often organized by the same person – the parson. This was the secular celebration of the same new paternalism. These seem to have appeared at the same point in time, the 1860s. In Norfolk, the Rev. Armstrong noted in 1868 that they 'are becoming quite a feature in Norfolk.'[55] At Souldrop the Rector combined with the farmers and gentry to integrate both festival and supper.

> . . . first publicly to offer tribute of thanksgiving to God for the abundant harvest . . . and next to check, so far as is practicable, those drinking excesses that have marked the peasantry for many years at the conclusion of harvest . . . [The] considerable expense was met by liberal donations from friends of the fete and subscriptions amongst the farmers.[56]

All the elements are here, control, religion, paternalist support and what Obelkevich calls the 'confident new-style clergy in association with the farmers.'[57]

Harvest Festival was only the most obvious of the liturgical reforms. To all the new clergy 'living for your parish' essentially meant the creation of what had been called 'a reconstituted community of worshippers, in which all villagers, labourers as well as squires, should take part.'[58] It was not that ritualism, except in the mildest form dominated, rather that the number of services was increased, as was the seriousness with which they were taken by both laity and clergy.

These changes did not of course come about overnight and there was opposition to them both from within the clergy and the laity. Even Wilberforce's rhetoric could not persuade the Rev. Burges to quit fox-hunting or the Rev. Paddon to return to High Wycombe, although ultimately his power as bishop did.[59] Older clergy sometimes simply refused change and often, being secure in private livings, were able to do so. The Rev. Benjamin Armstrong, a mild tractarian but certainly a new-style priest was deeply scornful about these figures 'whose churches are in a disgraceful state, services few and weekly ministrations *nil*' [emphasis in original].[60] Others within the clergy baulked at what they regarded as theologically incorrect instructions from their reforming bishops.

There was also opposition from within the villages themselves to such reform, usually specific and almost inevitably related to innovations in church practice or attempts at moral reformation. The Rev. Edward Elton of Wheatley in Oxfordshire, a Wilberforce appointee, battled for the best part of thirty years to reform his notorious parish. Edward King who was Elton's curate for a time and later Bishop of Lincoln wrote, 'Wheatley was at that time a peculiarly rough and lawless place and Mr Elton's attempts at moral reformation had roused the utmost hostility.'[61] Nor was

Hardy's account of the 'reformation' out of existence of a church band fanciful. As Vic Gammon has shown, from the 1840s onwards, there was a widespread attack on the old-style church orchestras which were seen as disruptive and theologically crude by reformers. Frederick Jones of Falmer in Sussex, a former church musician, saw the process clearly. 'Alas they were indeed happy meetings, notwithstanding the disdain, shall I say contempt with which a more educated public regarded our old compositions.'[62]

However, we should introduce a note of caution here. The gains made by the Established Church after 1850 were essentially relative to the disastrous problems of the early nineteenth century. In the north, parts of the West Country and the Welsh Borders Anglicanism never regained more than a third of all religious attenders even by the 1900s. Further, the continued close relationship between the Church of England and the rural ruling class meant that all but a tiny minority of clergymen continued to be at best ambivalent in terms of their relationship with their much poorer flocks. Both these aspects of the Church were to remain as real problems that were never overcome, and indeed worsened in the years after 1880.

The Church of England was only one part of the new paternalism. Equally important, were changes within the secular rural elites. The years between the 1800s and the 1840s saw the destruction of the old paternalist order and its replacement with a new order of the market. That is not to say every landlord or farmer suddenly began to behave like Adam Smith, rather that the general move was towards a more 'rational' system. From the mid-1840s with the repeal of the Corn Laws and the gradual but substantial growth in agricultural prosperity this began to change again. F. M. L. Thompson has argued that the twenty years after 1846 saw a period of 'renewed social stability and revived deference' in relationships between the aristocratic and industrial elites.[63] But it went much further than that. As David Roberts has written, after the 1840s there were distinct changes 'from the narrow and more formal paternalism of the eighteenth century village' as the duties expected of those in power increased as did the 'fervour and fullness' of the ideals of paternalism.[64]

The heart of this 'revived deference' was the construction of a 'natural social order' of ranks and obligations. In this order the aristocracy and the great landowners stood supreme. As Walter Bagehot wrote in 1872:

> I doubt if there has ever been any (country) in which all old families and all titled families received more ready observance from those who were their equals, perhaps their superiors, in wealth, their equals in culture, and their inferiors only in descent and rank.[65]

Beneath them, and bound together by reciprocities, were the descending orders of farmer and labourer. All added together, in the rural view at least, made the 'agricultural interest'; what the 1861 Census Report called 'the great central productive class of the country.'[66] This notion that agriculture was primary remained vital to the notion of the 'agricultural interest', and probably grew in importance, long after it had any basis in the economic structure of the nation.

The revived paternalism turned the clock back to the mid-eighteenth century by selecting key rituals, especially those around the gift, to revive carefully controlled idyllicist notions of rural social life and order. James Ewing Ritchie, who grew up in Suffolk in the 1830s, observed 'that charity had not become fashionable then' and that it was only later and selectively that 'coals and blankets' were distributed.[67] Yet there were clearly problems within this. Firstly, the demands of an agrarian capitalist economy frequently took control of the social order out of the hands even of those who had enormous personal social and economic power. This is clear in the years of depression after the mid-1870s, to which subject we shall return.

Secondly, the aristocracy were frequently remote from the lands on which their wealth was built. Alistair Mutch shows how Lord Derby, 'the premier landowner' in Lancashire, was seldom on his estate since, as he put it, 'no planting or building will make it other than a dull place.' Of the other major Lancashire landowners Lord Sefton 'owner of the second largest estate preferred life at Sefton House in London's Belgrave Square'; the two Scarisbrick brothers who held some 6,000 acres lived in Germany; Lord Lilford lived in Northamptonshire and the Marquis de Casteja spent much of his time in France.[68] In contrast, the Cholmondley's, one of Norfolk's greatest landowning families, spent more time in Lancashire, where they provided successive Lords Lieutenants, than they did in Norfolk.[69]

In such situations the only real representative of aristocratic power was a bailiff, estate steward or agent. As Mutch says, 'as local representative of the power of the landowner the agent was a figure whose influence and standing was rivalled only by the clergy.'[70] Elsewhere, the 'squire' at the hall was often not aristocracy but gentry. Again in Lancashire Mutch notes, 'it was left to the smaller gentry to govern the county.'[71] In many villages even this was not the case and here, as in Wheatley in Oxfordshire, the most powerful figure was the largest farmer in the parish, or the vicar. Yet the aristocracy and the great landed proprietors were vital even if distant for they provided the ultimate 'power base' for the paternalist system and the essential rituals which went with it.

Deference, the gift and paternalism were often in the hands of these lieutenant classes rather than the aristocracy itself. It was the 'middle' men and women who often distributed charity and received deference in return which they then 'passed on' to those above them through similar but separate rituals of gift and deference. To talk of a labourer or labourer's family 'deferring' to a 'paternalist' aristocracy usually made little sense then in real terms. Deference seldom worked directly but was mediated through a complex of ranks, unspoken but always 'understood', at least by those inside the system. At each point there were rituals to be observed and exchanges made.

The great rituals of paternalism, what Bagehot perceptively called 'the theatrical show of society',[72] like the new services of the Church of England, both represented and created deference and order. In March 1871 the birth of an heir to the Duke of Northumberland was celebrated with 'a good substantial dinner' at which 'no fewer than 400 of the principal farmers on his Grace's Land (*sic*) were invited to dine in the castle at Alnwick, while other large spreads were held at Tynemouth, Ovingham and Bellingham.'[73] In dinners like this the lieutenant class were acknowledged by being separated out and identified for particular treatment. In return they supported and deferred. In 1868 the tenants of John Eden Esq., of Beamish Park, Co. Durham, presented him with a 'magnificent piece of solid silver plate', accompanied by a letter coming from 'every tenant farmer'. This offered the piece as 'a token of our sincere esteem and respect for you as a landlord, and in recognition for your liberality to us in times of agricultural depression.' Mr Eden, well aware of the ritual replied,[74]

> I will ever value it as it deserves, and leave it as an heirloom to my successors; and I trust it will prove an incentive to them to cultivate the goodwill of their tenants. Where our interests are identical, this should not be a very difficult task.[74]

'Cultivating the good will of one's tenants' was a central part of paternalism from the landlord's viewpoint. In hard times this meant, as it did in the 1860s and especially the 1880s and 1890s, rent reductions. Even in the 1850s on the Courtenay estate in Devon we find the agent writing that a tenant's demand for a rent reduction should be met as 'there are many estates in that neighbourhood without tenants and reductions amounting to 30 or 40 per cent have been made in order to keep their Tenants (*sic*).'[75] In good times the more pleasant rituals of dining, socializing and perhaps most importantly hunting, shooting and fishing cemented this vital relationship.

The fox hunt or the 'right' to shoot occasionally on one's landlord's ground [even if you rented it the game rights usually remained with the landlord before 1880] were supreme rituals of the county order.

> Hunting was the activity *par excellence* which brought together local people and those involved in London Society. It had all the elements of aristocratic patronage and deference masked by male equality in sports . . . Hunting, too, allowed a limited amount of class mixing in the the field: that is local farmers, doctors and similar people could hunt along with the great . . .[76]

In the mythology of hunting all were 'equal' even, on occasions, women. Horsemanship, courage and knowledge of the countryside counted more than status or wealth. The farmer on his 'nag' who was a better huntsman than the London 'toff' was a well established piece of idyllicist folk lore before the nineteenth century began and was revived in countless anecdotal memoirs and stories. Nor was it only those who took part, essentially the lieutenant class, who were involved, but the whole of the county. John Simpson Calvertt, a hunting farmer if ever there was one, wrote in his diary of the first meet of the Heythrop's season in 1876, 'Supposed to be 1000, persons, witness the Opening, it has been an *annual custom* for *years* to give entertainment to *all comers*, on opening the season.'[77] Even those who could not ride were not excluded, for following on foot was common in hunting country, and there were frequently small perks of drink or even a few coppers to be had by a faithful 'follower' who opened the gates or pointed out the direction the fox had gone.

The big 'public' meets like the one described by Calvertt or the Boxing Day ones were rituals of crucial social importance, with the aristocracy and gentry 'on show' to the populace as a whole. Here paraded in hunting pink or clerical black were the rulers of rural England in a carefully worked out display. Here also was the young squire, dashing and 'devil may care' like the young Siegfried Sassoon, to whom nothing mattered but the chase and who produced, with his respect for a good horseman regardless of position, a notion of gentlemanly equality.[78]

What is represented by figures like the 'young squire' found constant expression at the social occasions of country life, especially dinners and celebrations associated with a range of county institutions. These ranged from the great gatherings of the county agricultural associations at the 'top' to the more mundane gatherings of village clubs at the bottom. These institutions, though often dating from the late eighteenth century, and, in the case of friendly societies (clubs) having origins which were often outside the deferential structure among working people themselves, seem again to increase in importance from the late 1840s.

Agricultural societies were, in origin, scientific, their aims being nearly always some version of those laid down by the earliest true agricultural society in England, the Bath Society. This was founded 'for the encouragement and improvement of agriculture, manufactures, commerce and the fine arts', in 1777.[79] Quickly, as in the case of Bath, these early societies became more and more agricultural in their purpose, publishing reports of improvements, encouraging experiment and organizing shows and dinners. These shows, and sometimes the dinners connected with them, developed into one of the great sites of paternalism. Individual aristocratic or gentry patronage under the umbrella of a society rewarded good tenants for fine crops or exceptional breeds of animal. The 3rd Earl of Egremont founded such societies in both

East and West Sussex before 1800.[80] Very quickly, and increasingly after the 1840s, these shows extended their patronage from the tenant farmers to the rural poor. For example, Kenneth Hudson notes that encouragement of improved cottage design by competitions 'multiplied during the second half of the century', while by the 1850s most of the county societies had established systems of one kind or another for rewarding labourers.[81] Rewards went for obvious things like skill at ploughing or stacking but correct social attitudes were also rewarded. Among those who received such 'encouragement' at Ormesby in Norfolk in the 1840s were Thomas Harbord 'now supporting five children under 14 years of age without parochial support', John Man who had served the same master for 14 years as team-man, Charles Plummer for having been '37 years with his present master and predecessors, without parochial aid' and William Warnes 'for neatness . . . of his garden.'[82] On the Acland Estates in Devon a ploughing match organized for servants stipulated that 'no Candidate will be eligible to compete . . . who has not been in the employment of his present Master or Mistress twelve months at least before the day of entry.'[83]

These rewards were given out at the shows or at dinners afterwards. Here again public display of paternalism was vital. At the dinner of the Petworth Agricultural Society held at the Swan Inn, Petworth, in 1844 His Grace the Duke of Richmond sat at the head of the table 'flanked by the bishop of Chichester and Archdeacon Manning and the leading esquires of western Sussex'. The labourers were 'at the other end of the room'. Two years later the prestigious West Sussex Agricultural Association admitted prize-winning labourers to dine with the members for the first time.[84]

From the late 1840s and 1850s onwards societies designed more directly for the poor themselves appear. Societies for rewarding labour had been a feature of the paternalist schema from the 1830s and even earlier but, as David Lane shows, in Sussex at least these societies grow in number rapidly in the 1850s.[85] Allotment societies and horticultural societies were widely supported by gentry and farmers because, as was said at Rye in 1850,

> . . . the tendency of such societies is to promote industry and morality to render the poor more careful, to keep the men

> from the public-house and employed, with their families, in that occupation which, of all others, tends to improve their tone of mind and provide nourishment for the body.[86]

After the Rye Society's meeting in 1860 the *Sussex Agricultural Express* noted with pleasure that 'all the gentry of the neighbourhood' had attended, showing ' . . . there was a universal kind and happy expression towards the cottagers' while the poor behaved suitably by showing 'that too rare expression of respectful confidence in and towards their rich neighbours.'[87]

The promotion of 'industry and morality' was also seen by the elite as the main purpose of friendly societies. These 'village clubs' were organizations of self help where for a few pence a week the labourer could insure himself against sickness and unemployment. Although friendly societies were never simply agencies of paternalism, most of them took on that aspect at different times.[88] Many village clubs were founded by the vicar. The Rev. Edward Elton at Wheatley in Oxfordshire founded a friendly society as did the Rev. G. D. Newbolt at Souldrop in Bedfordshire.[89] The one at Kidlington in Oxfordshire was founded in 1839 by the vicar, the Rev. Arrowsmith, and widely supported by the local gentry and farmers who made up the 'honorary members'. At Kidlington this group exercised total control of the officers of the society, its finances and the running of club day.[90] Even where the village society was 'in the hands of the members' as, in theory, branches of the great national societies like the Oddfellows and Foresters were, elements of paternalism remained through the system of drawing honorary members from among the local gentry. When an Oddfellows branch was formed at Burford in Oxfordshire in the 1840s 'many influential individuals declared their intention of becoming honorary members'.[91]

At club day dinners, harvest home suppers and society banquets the elite lost no chance to 'speechify' on the virtues of paternalism and the institutions it created. Central to all such accounts was the ideal and idyllic notion of the naturalness of the social order. This was clearly put in a club day sermon at Bampton in Oxfordshire in 1875.

> He [God] would have all people of one nature, from the Queen on her throne down to the labourer in the field, bound by one law of helping one another. Yes, we are all links of the same chain, whatever our lot or condition may be in this life . . . the strong

> helping to support the weak, the healthy waiting upon the sick, the rich administering to the wants of the poor.[92]

In 1860 the *Sussex Agricultural Express* used a fete given for the villagers of Wivelsfield Green by the vicar to comment that such meetings,

> . . . bind society together . . . and are doing an immensity of good in our part of Sussex, they are bringing round old times again and introducing the classes to each other, keeping up that spirit of unity and concord which at the present time is so much wanting in England.[93]

In this ideal notion of the social order duty reigned supreme – duty to 'your betters' and to your inferiors. The Earl of Chichester believed that as one whom 'providence has placed in a situation of greater wealth and influence' he had a duty to support the industry of his subordinates.[94] In return, deference, sobriety and industry were expected. Even club day dinners could not pass without warnings to be temperate.[95] At Barton in Oxfordshire in the 1870s it was suggested that lack of temperance had led to the withdrawal of 'more than one Honorary Member' from the local friendly society, and with such withdrawal the loss of vital support.[96]

If dinners and shows were the large-scale public manifestations of this ideal order, day-to-day charity, especially in winter, was its cement. Private charity literally held together social relations in many communities, a situation which the elites themselves recognized. The control of charity, of the gift, was vital to social stability.[97] Its granting could reward, its withholding could punish, its careful administration could, and did, shape all aspects of nineteenth century rural society. There was a generalized strategy which, for instance, opened soup kitchens in winter. The Rev. Elton's diary from Wheatley in Oxfordshire shows this kind of charity at work in the late 1860s.

> Dec 20th . . . Gave away coals & clothes tickets. Margaret nearly started her soup kitchen scheme. Dec 24th . . . Soup given out to a number of families . . . Dec 27th Soup given out with great success to a vast number . . . Dec 31 Gave out soup for 3 1/2 hours, engaged in giving out charity money to more than 100 families.[98]

This kind of relief was usually open to all and was designed, apart from genuine philanthropic notions, to give a general sense of caring and support. Few, if any, were refused such charity, at least by the 1860s. More specific charities though were refused. The Church often used its control of many village charities to increase its influence or to moralize those who it believed to be 'in danger'. The Rev. Thomas Hayton of Long Crendon in Buckinghamshire controlled a small charity in his village which was paid out in church and only to churchgoers. This deliberately excluded the large number of dissenters in the village from relief.[99] The letter books of Bishop Wilberforce show similar attitudes, as in 1849 when he wrote to the rector of Lillingstone Lovell in Oxfordshire,

> I should be no means advise you to exclude from alms which have been hitherto distributed to church people & dissenters indiscriminately any persons simply on ground of their religious opinions as such. But if the distribution of alms is left to you as *Clergyman of the Parish* (*sic*) to be made as you 'deem meet', I do not see how you can conscientiously deem those meet who for any reason systematically absent themselves from the public worship of the church.[100]

The account books of Howe's charity, Zeal Monachoram, Devon, show that after 1870 the new rector began recording not only if those applying for clothing had had relief before but also if they were churchgoers.[101] Elsewhere in the same decade this use of charities was to become a major issue in those areas where trades unions were strong.

Refusal of charity on political or social grounds was yet more common. The charities associated with the Petworth estate went only to those who could produce testimonials of good character and behaviour. Drunkenness, criminal conviction or reliance on the poor rates all led to refusal of relief.[102] Joseph Arch, the future agricultural trades unionist, found himself frequently refused charities by both parson and 'squire' – 'they would have dearly liked to drive me out of the parish neck and crop', he wrote in his autobiography.[103] Even when granted, charity was controlled. Money, for instance, was seldom given. The records of Howe's charity in the village of Buckerell in Devon show it was always given in cloth, clothes, blankets or coal. Occasionally a pauper objected as in 1862 when 'Sally Sparks – could not have blanket would not have anything else' but it did no good.[104]

These attitudes extended to the Poor Law, both formally and informally. As we saw above the 1834 Act marked a decisive break in treatment of the poor; however, after the mid-1850s this seems to change. It is as if the harshness has done its job and the old notions of the right to relief were broken. Once that had been accomplished the Poor Law became more flexible. As M. A. Crowther writes, 'at first the policy of deterrence was paramount, but the Board soon found that it needed to soften, if not obliterate, the workhouse's grim reputation.'[105] On occasions, for example in the lands of the Earl of Egremont in West Sussex, the Poor Law was effectively voided right from the start by the dominance in one area of a great family who simply refused to implement the new Act on paternalist grounds.[106] In other areas, factions within the Guardians, local problems, a real recognition of the seasonal nature of agricultural work, or simple arithmetic which showed that it was cheaper to pay out-relief than put a family into 'the house', led to widespread local modification of the law.[107]

Of these pressures on the Poor Law the seasonal nature of agricultural work was probably the most important, especially in arable or mixed farming areas. Although orders were issued to most rural areas in 1842 and then again in 1844 prohibiting the payment of out-relief, this was barely effective where seasonal labour requirements dominated the concerns of the Guardians. In these parishes the need for seasonal labour meant that the farmers who also acted as Guardians constantly resoorted to loopholes within the Poor Law, especially 'sickness', and use of the highway rate and private charity, to keep their workforce in the parish but out of the 'house'. As the Poor Law inspector for Buckinghamshire and Oxfordshire said in 1841 the discretionary powers were so great as to 'admit of the granting of outdoor relief under almost every contingency that can befall a man or his family.'[108]

As the century progressed, despite constant efforts by succeeding generations of Poor Law administrators, the situation became worse. Anne Digby's figures for Norfolk show that there were proportionally more 'able bodied paupers' receiving relief in that county in the 1880s and 1890s than in the 1840s.[109] By this later date Mr Lockwood, the Poor

Law inspector for the area, said 'during the last 20 years the rural workhouse has become almost exclusively an asylum for the sick the aged and children.'[110] This regional picture was reinforced by the reports of the Royal Commission on the Poor Laws between 1905–1909. Their examinations showed that in almost all rural districts the 'flight from the land' had reduced the seasonal workforce to such an extent that the typical country workhouse was 'an almshouse for the aged and infirm and the children'.[111]

However, the motives for such change were not entirely economic, although it does seem these were paramount, especially where farmers dominated the Board of Guardians. Norman McCord has pointed to the importance of private charity as an adjunct to the workhouse system and the Poor Law. Frequently the two went together and in this respect the same changes in ideology that we saw in relation to the Church and the rural elite certainly worked on the Poor Law. Treats for workhouse children and gifts to the aged poor become a central part of rural (and for that matter urban) philanthropy.[112]

Yet we must beware of too easily accepting this slightly rosy picture. 'Out relief', supplemented by private charity, was certainly not the equivalent of a living wage. In 1881 the Rev. Edward Elton wrote to the *Oxford Times* under the heading 'Destitution at Wheatley':

> I would be obliged for a small space in your paper to make known the extreme destitution and poverty existing here in the present severe crisis [winter] . . . The causes of such exceptional suffering are not far to seek, one of them is that much of the labour in adjoining parishes is done by the casual employment of people living in this, and in consequence, as soon as the work is over (no tie subsisting between employer and employed) the latter are left to their own resources, so that when any severe weather occurs they are reduced to exceeding misery.[113]

A coroner's court, also in Oxford, had heard thirteen years earlier of the extreme version of this when an inquest was held on the body of an elderly woman who had literally 'starved to death'. She was, the court was told, a casual farm worker, 'she used to work for Mr Higgins at Binsey'. But winter had set in and she, like others, was frozen out. This 'brought her to picking up (the) refuse of middens and dung hills.' When that failed she died, probably as much as a result of the cold as hunger.[114]

At a more mundane level the fascinating diary of George James Dew, a relieving officer in the Bicester Poor Law Union, records the day-to-day grimness of the Poor Law in action. 'It is rather a melancholy sight' he wrote in October 1870, 'to see so many poor creatures applying for relief, which, after all, is but just sufficient to keep body and soul together.'[115] Dew also had few illusions about the nature of the Poor Law.

> It will generally be seen that those persons who hold the most land are Guardians of the Poor; & when I consider the matter I can see plainly how it works. The Board of guardians have for the most part in their hands the power of giving or of withholding relief, &, taking human nature into account, it will not be surprising to find that those men who have to pay the greater amount of Poor Rates will naturally be *as careful as possible in the expenditure*, & hence the saving of their *own* money, & hence again, the scanty allowance to the poor. [emphasis etc as original][116]

On a day-to-day basis Dew's diary shows the petty tyranny and discrimination which was central to the Poor Law at local level. In 1871,

> . . . a woman of Kirtlington, Hanah Cato, 71 yrs of age, applied at the Bicester board of guardians for relief . . . The family of Cato's are bad & they have been before the magistrates some 20 times for poaching . . . The lands on which they have poached belong to Sir Henry Dashwood. & it was on this a/c that the woman was refused relief, other than an order for the Workhouse which she refused, & of which every poor person in the land hates the name. [as original][117]

To the elderly, even to my grandparent's generation who spent their old age under a welfare state, the workhouse remained, as it was to Hanah Cato, a terrible threat. The thought of dying in poverty and being buried in a pauper's grave dominated their last years. 'Rattle his bones, Over the stones./He's only a pauper, That nobody owns' was a great deal more than a children's rhyme. In 1878 a letter appeared in the *Oxford Times* concerning the death at Headington Workhouse of Richard Dover of Wheatley.

His children arrived at the workhouse to find 'that he had not been laid out, and had only a very ragged shirt on'. They asked for the body to be brought home and,

> accordingly on Tuesday about half an hour before the time fixed to bury him he was brought; it is true he was in a coffin, but Sir, would you believe it, he had nothing on but the afore said ragged shirt, in fact he had never been laid out at all, but simply placed in his coffin just as he had died, in fact, in every way just as one would bury a dog?[118]

But the old were not the only ones who still feared the 'house'. The majority of all adult recipients of the Poor Law after 1834 were women.[119] Much of the writing on the later Poor Law treats the problem of women and unmarried mothers and their children in the workhouse as if this was natural and inevitable, and suggests that it was probably not that bad. Those who lived through it saw otherwise. Fred Copemen, who was brought up in a Suffolk Workhouse just before the Great War, remembered the harshness and public humiliation attached to being a workhouse 'bastard'.[120] In 1851 the central board ordered that women who bore illegitimate children should pick oakum rather than do the more 'attractive' domestic work usually given to women in the workhouse.[121] In Norfolk a whole range of vile and petty discriminations worked against these women and their children which both publicly and privately damned them and reminded all of their sins. At Swaffam Union Workhouse they were excluded from the Coronation dinner in 1838, at Docking they were forced to wear distinctive clothing although the central board actually forbade this punishment. In most Norfolk workhouses these women were, as Anne Digby says, 'punished by being put to hard labour in the workhouse laundry a few days before confinement . . . ', a practice that was only stopped when women Guardians were elected at the end of the century.[122]

Years ago W. L. Burn, in an influential but now largely forgotten book, called the twenty years or so after 1850 'the age of equipoise'.[123] While we cannot have his total confidence, there are elements of truth in such a characterization. Certainly there was a feeling of social harmony and peace in the countryside after 1850 which was certainly not the case before. But it must be stressed, as we have seen in this chapter, that this was not some 'natural state' growing out of an organic social order; rather it was achieved balance. The reform of the Church of England, which moved it firmly back into the parishes, was probably the first step. Once in the villages, more regular services and a growing sense of clerical duty, summed up by Bishop Wilberforce's maxim 'live in your parish, live for your parish', gave the Anglican Church and its parson a new and important role in village life. Coupled with this new concern was a reappearance of paternalism in the secular sphere. Private charity, intervention in social institutions and the revival of *noblesse oblige* as a defining and structuring set of social axioms brought the rural elites into an active role in the community. Even where the appearance was greater than the reality such behaviour created a notion of a natural social order. Finally, the Poor Law, the main social institution for many areas of rural England, turned out not to be as harsh in practice, at least between the early 1850s and the 1870s, as many have supposed.

Yet we must treat this picture with caution. Behind Anglicanism's benevolent gaze could, and did, lie discrimination against those who did not fit. Behind the new paternalism stood the county police, the eviction order and the sack for any who stepped out of line. Behind the Poor Law lay the endless and crushing petty tyrannies and insults heaped on those least able to stand against it – especially the elderly and the single mother. Nor was the stability as firm and certain as it seemed on the surface. The contemporary or the historian does not need to scratch very deeply to find another side – the dark side of village life which threatened consensus and stability not perhaps with revolution but with constant problems and the ever present possibility of social disorder.

NOTES

1 David Jones, 'Thomas Campbell Foster and the Rural Labourer; incendiarism in East Anglia in the 1840s', *Social History* no. 1, January 1976.

2 ibid., p. 7.

3 See especially Barry Reay, 'The Last Rising of the Agricultural Labourers; the battle of Bossenden Wood, 1838' *History Workshop Journal* no. 26, Autumn 1988. Also P. G. Rogers, *The Battle in Bossenden Wood. The Strange Story of*

Sir William Courtney [London, 1961] and J. F. C. Harrison, *The Second Coming. Popular Millenarianism 1780–1850*, [London, 1979].

4 E. P. Thompson, 'The Moral Economy of the English Crowd in the Eighteenth Century', *P&P*, no. 50. There is now a huge literature around this concept.

5 See especially K. D. M. Snell, op. cit., especially Ch. 4 and Alun Howkins and C. Ian Dyck, op. cit..

6 *Political Register* 15th February 1834, p. 411.

7 For a discussion of this see Alun Howkins and Linda Merricks, '"Wee be blacke as hell", Ritual and Popular Protest 1500–1900', Peasant Studies Seminar Working Paper, SOAS, 1986.

8 James Obelkevich, *Religion and Rural Society: South Lindsey 1825–75*, [Oxford, 1976], p. 27.

9 'Past, Present and Future', Broadside by Hill of London, British Library L. R. 271a2. Vol. 1 f.48. It can be dated by a reference to 'new workhouses'.

10 Snell, op. cit., p. 105.

11 *PP 1837, XVII pt. 1*, 'First Report of the Select Committee on the Poor Law Amendment Act', p. 73.

12 ibid., Part II, 15th Report p. 21.

13 ibid., Part I, 1st Report p. 85.

14 ibid., p. 72.

15 ibid., Part II, 15th Report p. 21.

16 ibid., 10th Report p. 28.

17 Ballad, 'Past, Present and Future', op. cit..

18 *PP 1837, XVII Part 1*, 'Appendix to the First Report from the Commissioners on the Poor Law', p. 579.

19 See Carolyn Steedman, *Policing the Victorian Community. The formation of the English provincial police forces 1856–1880*, [London, 1984].

20 ibid., pp. 14–15.

21 *Political Register*, 12th July 1834, pp. 67–90.

22 Snell, op. cit., Ch. 4.

23 Charles Kingsley, *Alton Lock*, [Everyman ed., London, 1910], Ch. XXVIII, 'The Men who are Eaten'.

24 Alan D. Gilbert, 'The Land and the Church' in G. E. Mingay [ed] *The Victorian Countryside*, op. cit., Vol. I, p. 44.

25 ibid., p. 47.

26 A. D. Gilbert, *Religion and Society in Industrial England. Church, Chapel and Social Change, 1740–1914*, [London, 1976]. p. 27.

27 ibid., p. 29.

28 ibid., p. 28.

29 ibid., p. 131.

30 Obelkevich, op. cit., pp. 103–4. A great deal of the thought

behind the next few pages derives from a reading of Obelkevich's important book.

31 Quoted in B. Heeney, 'On being a Mid-Victorian Clergyman', *Journal of Religious History*, Vol. VII, no. 3, 1973, p. 217. A very important and interesting article.

32 *The Letter Books of Samuel Wilberforce, 1843–1868*, Transcribed and Edited by R. K. Pugh, Oxfordshire Record Society [Oxford, 1970] p. xv.

33 ibid., p. 58.

34 ibid., p. 56–7.

35 ibid., p. 60.

36 ibid., p. 295.

37 ibid., p. 140.

38 ibid., p. 406.

39 Quoted in Mutch, thesis, op. cit., p. 228.

40 ibid., p. 249.

41 Robert Moore, *Pitmen, Preachers and Politics. The effects of Methodism in a Durham mining community*, [Cambridge, 1974], p. 72.

42 J. S. Leatherbarrow, 'The Rise and fall of the Squarson', Unpublished PhD thesis, University of Birmingham, 1976, pp. 239–53.

43 *Some Bedfordshire Diaries*, The Publications of the Bedfordshire Historical Records Society, Vol. XL, [Streatley, 1959], pp. 207–21.

44 *Hymns Ancient and Modern*, no. 573.

45 Howkins and Dyck, op. cit., pp. 21–2.

46 *Bedfordshire Diaries*, op. cit., p. 206.

47 Herbert B. J. Armstrong [ed] *A Norfolk Diary. Passages from the Diary of the Rev. Benjamin John Armstrong*, [London, 1949], see pp. 100 and 129 for example.

48 Obelkevich, op. cit., p. 158.

49 Quoted in Mutch, thesis, op. cit., p. 265.

50 Obelkevich, op. cit., p. 159.

51 *Bedfordshire Diaries*, op. cit., pp. 206 *ff*.

52 *PP 1893–94, XXXV*, 'Royal Commission on Labour. The Agricultural Labourer. England. Report of Mr Cecil Chapman upon the Poor Law Union of Crediton, Devon', p. 265.

53 ibid., p. 221.

54 Obelkevich, op. cit., p. 159.

55 Armstrong, op. cit., p. 137.

56 *Bedfordshire Times*, 20th September 1859, quoted in *Bedfordshire Diaries*, op. cit., p. 221.

57 Obelkevich, op. cit., p. 160.

58 ibid., p. 127.

59 Wilberforce, op. cit., pp. 167 & 132.

60 Armstrong, op. cit., p. 125.

61 G. E. Russell, *Edward King, Sixtieth Bishop of Lincoln*, [London, 1912], p. 53.
62 Vic Gammon, '"Babylonian Performances"; the Rise and Suppression of Popular Church Music in England, 1660–1870' in E. and S. Yeo [eds], *Popular Culture and Class Conflict 1590–1914*, [Brighton, 1981], p. 80.
63 F. M. L. Thompson, *English Landed Society in the Nineteenth Century*, [London, pb. ed., 1971], p. 186.
64 David Roberts, *Paternalism in Early Victorian England*, [London, 1979], p. 130.
65 W. Bagehot, *The English Constitution*, [London, 1929], p. xxx.
66 *PP 1863, LIII*, op. cit., p. 35.
67 James Ewing Ritchie, *Christopher Crayon's Recollections*, [London, 1898], p. 37.
68 Alistair Mutch, *Rural Life in South West Lancashire, 1840–1914*, Centre for North-West Regional Studies, University of Lancaster, Occasional Papers, No. 16, [Lancaster, 1988], p. 22.
69 Ernest Gaskell, *Norfolk Leaders Social and Political*, [London, n.d. but *c.* 1910], unpaginated, under name.
70 Mutch, thesis, op. cit., p. 107.
71 ibid., p. 104.
72 Bagehot, op. cit., p. 269.
73 T. Fordyce, *Local Records or Historical Register of Remarkable Events which have occurred in Northumberland and Durham, Newcastle and Berwick-upon-Tweed . . . 1837–1866*, 4 Vols [Newcastle-upon-Tyne, 1867] Vol. IV, p. 131.
74 ibid., p. 13–14.
75 DRO 1508 M/Devon, Courteney Papers, Devon Estates, Letter Books, 12th December 1850.
76 Leonore Davidoff, *The Best Circles, Etiquette and the Season*, [London, 1973], pp. 28–9.
77 Calvertt, op. cit., p. 29.
78 Siegfried Sassoon, *The Complete Memoirs of George Sherston*, [pb. ed. London, 1980], p. 111 for example.
79 Quoted in Kenneth Hudson, *Patriotism with Profit: British Agricultural Societies in the Eighteenth and Nineteenth Centuries*, [London, 1972], p. 11.
80 See Rev. Arthur Young, *General View of the Agriculture of the County of Sussex*, [rep. Newton Abbot, 1970, original ed. London, 1813], pp. 445–7.
81 Hudson, op. cit., p. 110.
82 ibid., p. 51.
83 DRO 1148M add/28/32, Estate and Farming Correspondence, Acland paper, November 1850.
84 Quoted in Roberts, op. cit., p. 107.
85 D. J. Lane, 'Paternalism and Control in Mid-Nineteenth

Century Rural Sussex', Unpublished M. A. thesis, University of Sussex, 1985.

86 *SAE* 6th July 1850.

87 ibid., 1st September 1860.

88 For a brief discussion of rural Friendly Societies see Alun Howkins, 'The Taming of Whitsun' in E. and S. Yeo [eds] op. cit., pp. 187–209.

89 For Elton see W. O. Hassall, [ed] *Wheatley Records*, Oxfordshire Record Society. [Oxford, 1956]; for Newton see *Bedfordshire Diaries*, op. cit., pp. 213–14.

90 See Howkins 'Taming', op. cit., p. 197–8.

91 *JOJ* 9th April 1843.

92 ibid., 22nd May 1875.

93 *SAE* 15th June 1860.

94 Lane, op. cit., p. 24.

95 See Alun Howkins, *Whitsun in Nineteenth Century Oxfordshire*, [Oxford, 1973], pp. 25–8.

96 ibid., p. 49.

97 See Howard Newby, 'The Deferential Dialectic', *Comparative Studies in Society and History*, Vol. 17, no. 2.

98 Hassall, op. cit., p. 103.

99 Joyce Donald, [ed] *The Letters of Thomas Hayton, Vicar of Long Crendon, Bucks, 1821–1888*, Buckinghamshire Record Society, no. 20. 1979, pp. 79 *ff*.

100 Wilberforce, op. cit., p. 171.

101 DRO 1095/A/Ms 22, Account Book Holes Charity, Zeal Monachoram.

102 Young, op. cit., p. 446; Roberts, op. cit., p. 119; Ritchie, op. cit., p. 39 *ff*.

103 Joseph Arch, *From Ploughtail to Parliament. An Autobiography*, new edition, ed Alun Howkins [London, 1986], p. 53.

104 DRO 1091/PW 12. Buckerell Parish, Bequest of Mr. Howes to the poor of Buckerell.

105 M. A. Crowther, *The Workhouse System, 1834–1929. The History of an English Social Institution*, [London, 1981], p. 54.

106 *PP 1837, XVII, Part 1*, First Report, op. cit., pp. 85–6.

107 See especially Anne Digby, 'The Rural Poor Law', in D. Fraser [ed] *The New Poor Law in the Nineteenth Century*, [London, 1976].

108 Quoted in Digby, op. cit., p. 157.

109 ibid., p. 162.

110 ibid., p. 163.

111 ibid., p. 169.

112 See Norman McCord, 'The Poor Law and Philanthropy' in Fraser [ed] op. cit., pp. 100 *ff*.

113 *OT* 29th January 1881.

114 ibid., 4th January 1868.

115 Pamela Horn [ed] *Oxfordshire Village Life; The Diaries of George James Dew (1846–1928) Relieving Officer*, [Sutton Courtenay, 1983] p. 18.
116 ibid., p. 12.
117 ibid., p. 26.
118 *OT* 18th May 1878.
119 Pat Thane, 'Women and the Poor Law in Victorian and Edwardian England', *HWJ* no. 6 Autumn 1978, p. 29.
120 Fred Copeman, *Reason in Revolt*, [London, 1948], pp. 12–15.
121 Thane, op. cit., p. 32.
122 Anne Digby, *Pauper Palaces*, [London, 1978], p. 153 *ff*.
123 W. L. Burn, *The Age of Equipoise*, [London, 1964].

4

The Problems of Consensus: The Contradictions of the System

At the end of the last chapter we were left with a picture of order, of a society which had gradually achieved a new balance and harmony after a period of disruption and conflict. Yet, as we hinted, such a balance was achieved only with great difficulty and where it was achieved it seldom remained a permanent state. To begin with there were those problems which were internal to rural society and which presented a continuing threat to its stability, especially at local level. The most fundamental of these was the structural inequality of the nineteenth century rural areas. All the paternalist rhetoric, all the soup kitchens, all the *noblesse oblige* could do no more than mediate this inequality. The explanations of a paternalist code which told the poor or the middle ranks of society that this social and economic inequality was inevitable, desirable and permanent constantly came up against a much harsher and observable reality.

The most obvious inequalities were economic. The real distribution of wealth in mid-nineteenth century rural England is extremely difficult to establish. We saw in Chapter 1 that about 700 people (mainly men) held more than 5,000 acres of land in any one county in 1884. Between them they owned, 'more than a fourth of the soil of England and Wales, exclusive of lakes, roads, rivers, London, waste spaces and Crown property . . .'[1] Most of these great estates, though not all, produced substantial annual incomes which in turn created a culture and lifestyle of grand, opulent and occasionally beautiful conspicuous consumption. Even at the lower end of the scale the income derived from these estates was enormous compared with that of the rural poor. For example, John Bateman, who complied *The Great Landowners of Great Britain and Ireland*, fearing 'radical abuse' of his figures, created 'Squire' John Steadyman to show how landed wealth could be illusory wealth. Steadyman owns 3,500 acres producing an annual value of £5,000 but Bateman 'shows' how his outgoings on his estate reduce his annual income to £1,032. Even if we accept Bateman's deductions as real expenses our hard-done-by Squire is still 'earning' annually nearly 35 times what his labourers earned.[2]

In addition, this wealth was increasing in the years before 1875 at least, as rents rose for many, if not all landowners. Of course this is relative. F. M. L. Thompson argues eloquently that not only were returns on investment much lower in the years after 1835 than they had been in the years of enclosure, but that compared with even modest estimates of industrial profit they were very low indeed.[3] There were also regional variations. The profitability of an estate was crucially affected by its geographical position. Good land in the south and east produced higher rents and more regular rent increases, and the regional differences in elite wealth were very great. These differences were further stressed, although with a balance towards the north, by non-agricultural developments, especially railways and mineral rights, as well as urban development.[4] Yet even the poorest of Bateman's great families, or the most strained Irish peer, lived vastly more comfortably than most of the poor and even many of their tenants.

The middle rank are yet more of a problem. Centrally there were the enormous variations associated with region and farm size. As we saw in the last chapter the term 'farmer' covered a spectrum which ranged from the small family producers of Lancashire, the West Country or the Weald of Kent and Sussex who lived little better than labourers, to men like Calvertt in Oxfordshire or Clare Sewell Read in Norfolk whose annual income was probably equal to that of the owner of a small estate. To generalize from this presents insurmountable problems and the locality has to remain the unit of discussion. Nevertheless there was a substantial class of wealthy tenant farmers in all but a few English counties.

At the bottom were the poor. Again here there are differences associated with regional patterns. For all of the nineteenth century and much of the twentieth there was a divide between north and south. In the north of England, where agricultural workers were fewer, partly because of the settlement pattern and partly because of competition from industry, wages were higher and conditions better. A Northumberland hind who hired for a year, as Isaac Atkinson did in May 1865, was relatively well off. He got '16/6d per week in money, House and Garden rent free and coals led (ie brought to the house at cost price).'[5] At the other end of England, four years earlier, James Wallis, the senior carter on the Home Farm of the Courthope estate in Sussex, earned 15s per week with cottages and garden rent to find and no other 'perks'.[6] Fifteen years later, admittedly after the start of the depression in agriculture, Henry Middleton, a regularly-employed horseman on a large Norfolk farm, earned, including harvest money, 13/6d a week. He had no house but did get a 'Christmas Box' of meat and barley.[7] Equally typical though of eastern counties agriculture was a Mr Fields, working at Barnham Broom, also in Norfolk, who in the early 1870s, along with all other workers on the farm was paid by the day. In 1871 his daily earnings varied between 1/6d and 1/8d a day although he did some piece work. However, he did not work a full year and was laid off in bad weather and at slack times. As a result his real weekly wage was probably about 11s.[8]

There were also divisions within the workforce. All the wages above (with the probable exception of Field) are for the 'top' workers on arable farms, that is the men in charge of horses. Below this level wages dropped dramatically. In the same week that James Wallace earned 15s in East Sussex, the stockman George Tylor earned 13/6d; a labourer William French earned 11/3d hedging and planting; while a boy, Thomas Allen earned 8/6d helping with the milking and an old man, Henry Wilson, earned 6s breaking stones.[9] Below all these groups, and again regionally different, were the wages of women and girls. In Northumberland, as we saw in the last chapter, family hiring meant that women's wages, although relatively good, were usually paid to the husband or father. Isaac Atkinson's wife was 'to work when wanted and have 10d a day' (he was getting 2/2d). James Robinson who hired on the same farm in the same year agreed to 'find a good and sufficient woman worker during the Summer half years at 10d a day.' He was getting 1/11d a day but had a cow as well as house, garden and coals.[10]

In southern and eastern areas women were usually paid by the day and not hired for a long period. For example on the Courthope Estate in Sussex they appear simply as a 'cost' attached to a particular operation. In 1861 no women appear regularly or by name in the estate's outdoor wages book, but at haymaking in 1861 the ledger records 'Cash paid to women haymakers. £11. 3s. 6d.'. Although we don't know how many women were involved, this kind of entry recurs year after year – literally a case of 'hidden from history'. In Norfolk, as in most of the great arable areas, women's work was vital at weeding, hoeing, and stone picking, as well as at haymaking and harvest. A set of farm records from Barnham Broom shows women working at all these points in the year. The wages books show that in 1875 they were being paid 5d a day – exactly half what their northern sisters earned. There was also a good deal of piece work in these areas. In June 1875 Mrs Stone was paid 5s for hoeing 4 3/4 acres, while at a farm near Ditchingham Mrs Francis was paid 7s for hoeing and singling seven acres of beet. Interestingly a shilling an acre was also the male rate of singling and hoeing. On this kind of piece work, though nowhere else, a rough kind of equality appeared.

These great differences of wealth and the social and cultural practices which reflected them were concealed and structured by the institutions, formal and informal, repressive and paternalistic, which we looked at in the last chapter. By and large, on a national scale at least, these institutions were successful. However, from the 1850s onwards two separate forces outside the control of the rural world acted on this workforce to create the possibility of 'disharmony'. Firstly, under the pressure of urban demand, the acreage devoted to cereals continued to rise. This meant that the demand for workers also continued to increase. However, the demand was not mainly for permanent workers but for seasonal ones. The basis of this is straightforward. The farming year under arable production presents a series of peaks and troughs in labour demand. In the troughs, which make up the winter, much of the spring and part of the autumn, the demand for labour was small. At these times the horseman on the farm plus a few labourers were adequate. However, at hoeing, singling or the various harvests – hay, corn and roots – this workforce was totally inadequate. At these points the demand for workers rose dramatically.[13]

Secondly, especially after 1860, continued urban demand for labour meant that the part of the rural workforce willing to remain on the land was decreasing, as were the older village-based crafts and industries. As a result, as E. J. T. Collins says, 'The farm labour market entered its most critical phase of deterioration, the chief problem being no longer to absorb a labour surplus but to obtain sufficient labour for key summer operations.'[14] With a temporary respite in the depression years *c.* 1880–95, this problem continued to worsen as the century progressed – the labour market, so long the labourer's enemy, gradually became his friend. There was thus a period from the late 1850s through to the mid-1870s when demand for both food and labour from outside the rural areas put pressures on the rural elites which they could not easily control.

These pressures produced problems for the idyllicist world view of paternalism in two main ways. It perpetuated, even created, groups of workers who stood outside the paternal structures of regular employment, deference, and social order. In some cases this posed real problems of control – notably, for instance, with gangs of travelling workers. More often the problem was one of ideology; this is crucially the case of women and field work. Also, labour shortage at key points in the year produced endemic conflict between master and man, what I have called elsewhere structural conflict.

The model of paternalism and deference saw each person as having a 'place'. This was not only a matter of rank or status but physical situation – literally place in fact. The village was created as stable and unchanging with the church as a 'community' of worshippers. The ideal was the great estate where rank and place fitted together – your house and job precisely linked together with each one known exactly. In church, where you sat reflected the hierarchy with nicety and precision. The stress was on permanence and continuity; the good squire and the life-long honest servant being the ideal. In this, those who lived outside either physically or morally were an anathema yet the system of agriculture could not survive without them.

The travelling harvester, for example, was an essential part of Victorian farming – without him or her the increased demands for grain could not have been met. Yet they were the antithesis of the new paternalism's settled model of village life. Simply by moving around, especially when they came from Ireland or Scotland, they put themselves outside respectable society. They used their skill and their labour power to refuse the harness of regular employment and in so doing lived a rejection of the values of paternalism. This is not to suggest a kind of alternative ideal of the nomad; the work was hard and the conditions appalling, and many would probably have settled for paternalism if they had the option. Nevertheless their very existence was perceived as a material threat to harmony and order.

This was especially true of the Irish, and to a more limited extent the Scots, who appeared to the rural elite as a physical and moral threat on the one hand, while being accused of 'stealing the bread from the mouths' of native workers on the other. Simple racism had much to do with both these views. Anti-Irish feeling was common, and especially powerful in the 1850s and 1860s partly as a result of deliberate campaigns in the north-west but also because of the Fenian 'outrages'. However, the simple realities of travelling life meant 'normal decency', to use a Victorian phrase, was impossible or appeared so. Sleeping in barns meant little attention could be paid to hygiene but also that in what little leisure time there was the comfortless and draughty hovel was deserted for the comparative comfort of the public house. When the Irish travelled in gangs, as they often did, their very appearance was enough to produce moral panics, especially if women were among them. Even if, as was usually the case, such women were married and deeply respectable nothing could shake the English belief that they were 'loose and dissolute'. Another and different problem was raised by the fact that many were young and single – this was also true of English migrants – which produced different conflicts within local society.

These views are summed up in an editorial in the *Royal Leamington Spa Courier*.

> It is really too bad that fellows who take the bread from the mouth of our own surplus population should attempt . . . outrages at our very doors . . . the attention of the constables [should be drawn] to the doings of the emeralders who appear to be stragglers from the main hordes that have ravaged England like the eruption of the Huns of Attila . . . the vagrant labourers and beggars we meet with wandering through the country are about the worst specimens of barbarianism we could desire to meet.[15]

While such outbursts were common in the provincial press they have much more to do with the perceptions of a society seeking to create social order than with reality. The Irish, like most migrants, followed the same routes year after year, often visiting the same farms. Maggie Joe Chapman remembered one man who came to her father's farm every year for over twenty years.[16] Further north the account books of Northumberland farms show the same men returning again and again. At Castle Heaton Farm near Coldstream in the last years of the nineteenth century Barney O'Brien and Patrick McGee came for some years and then McGee was replaced by George O'Brien [probably a relative] to be replaced in turn by Teddy McFadden. As well as these two regular migrants others turn up, varying in number from year to year.[17]

In a similar way attitudes towards the Irish among labouring people and the farmers who employed them were much less extreme than the outrage of the rural elite would suggest. Mrs Brown, a labourer's daughter from near Wooler in Northumberland, spoke with positive admiration of them.

> . . . they made a lot of money when they came over, because the farm would give the milk and potatoes and that all they lived on . . . They would be in a different field to us, because when they were working everything was flying. They worked at full speed, because the harder they worked the more money they got. They would maybe take the field. Instead of just going in and working it, they would see how much they could take the field for.[18]

Maggie Joe Chapman, the Dales farmer's daughter, had real affection for those who came – 'they were a wonderful bunch, the Irish, very decent people.'[19]

Yet there were problems, usually a result of local resentment at competition for work. It seems likely that most problems of this kind were therefore southern where even in the 1850s and 1860s there continued to be a labour surplus in some areas.[20] Occasionally anti-Irish feeling of a different kind, political or racial, would break out and this knew no boundaries, as in Alnwick in 1851.[21]

> A serious affray took place at Ellingham, near Alnwick, between the inhabitants of the place and a party of reapers. During the disturbance an Irishman, named Bernard Dogherty, was wounded by a shot from a gun carried by Mr. James Adams, draper, from the effect of which he died. The gun was discharged by mere accident.[21]

Irish politics also broke into the supposed peace of rural England when, as in 1856 near Newcastle, a party of Orangemen 'quietly marching in procession in celebration of the victory of the Boyne' was set upon by a much larger force of 'Ribbonmen' armed with 'gun, bludgeon and scythe'.[22]

Irish migration peaked in the decade after the Great Famine. Thereafter, permanent emigration, by reducing the rural population in Ireland, reduced the number of temporary Irish migrants, although they continued to be of vital importance, especially in northern agriculture, well into the twentieth century.[23] However the demand for casual labourers continued high well into the 1870s and this supported and encouraged movement among English workers. As is the case of the Irish this caused problems to the social harmony as well as the ideology of rural society.

Most migrants were young and they frequently travelled in groups. Many were gypsy in origin which added further dimensions of moral panic. Earning decent money, often young and single, the travelling harvester became a classic 'folk devil' in the eyes of the settled Victorian community. There was also often an element of gaiety in these groups especially where the bonds of youth and friendship were reinforced by other ties like those that bound the harvesting Morris dancers of Finstock in Oxfordshire as remembered by Edwin Turner in the 1890s.

> He . . . used to go up to London every summer for haytime and would often go a month sooner than necessary in order to morris in the street, would go out day-by-day in different parts of London – Clerkenwell was the only name he could remember – often made 10 or 11 shilling a piece per diem.[24]

Youth and good earnings often put these young workers outside the law as well as outside settled morality, as at Bourton-on-the Hill in Oxfordshire in 1854.

> Jesse Thornett, Charles Thornett, Edwin Thornett and James Howse, calling themselves Wychwood Foresters were brought up in custody of the police, for being drunk and disorderly at Bourton-on-the-Hill, on the previous day. It appeared that they had been reaping, and having received their wages, were determined to have a spree; after they had been drinking some time, a quarrel arose, and then a fight.[25]

The seasonal demand for labour, especially labour for the cereal harvest, caused problems for the paternalist system. The demands of the market, which were outside the control of the rural elite, forced them to condone and even support social groups and behaviour which in 'normal' times were totally unacceptable. This contradiction between ideology and economic need exposed paternalism. At the end of the day all concerns for a settled and controlled community vanished before the demands of harvest and the god of profit.

Another area in which the demands of the economic system produced contradictions within the paternalist social order was in the employment of women. The paternal vision saw the rich man in his castle, the poor man at his gate and both their wives at home. The 'angel at the hearth', and the notion of separate spheres for men and women, created an ideal – the 'non-working' woman – which was reinforced by education as well as paternalism in the rural areas. Agrarian capital, like peasant production, demanded otherwise.

At the most simple level we see a situation where continued specialization of the economy, combined with changes in ideology as to the role of women, reduced the chances of permanent and skilled employment for them, while ideologically marginalizing and criticizing what work they did do. At the same time they were rendered increasingly 'invisible' by the insistence of an overwhelmingly male establishment that their work was marginal or temporary. The working woman, and especially the women who worked with her hands, was increasingly cast as unnatural and as such a threat to the normal order of things. However, in the rural areas, as elsewhere, the economy simply could not function without women's labour. Further, much women's work in the countryside was visible and public, as opposed to the acceptable and private work of the 'house'.

There was some work in rural areas which was considered 'fit' for women – essentially that which centred on the 'indoor' work of the dairy and the farmhouse. As this work was hidden, in the sense that it was to an extent out of public view, and because of the long-term links between the house and the dairy, it was accepted, or at least accepted while it was 'uncommercial'. For example, the household accounts of Anne Courthope of Whiligh in East Sussex show that she, the wife of George Courthope, who owned some 3,000 acres of good agricultural land, was still in the 1850s running a dairy. However, although she showed milk production in profit and loss terms in her accounts it was seen as part of the household rather than the farm and thus kept out of the commercial sphere.[26] As dairying and cheese making became commercial, as it did in many areas after the 1850s, women were replaced by men. In Derbyshire, for example, it was said in the 1880s that there ' . . . are fewer dairymaids and girls employed about the farmhouses than was the case formerly. In consequence of cheese making at home having about died out maid servants are no longer required.'[27] The keywords here are 'at home, for cheese making was actually going on on a larger scale than ever before – but in 'factories' run by men on the 'American system'.[28]

However, if the work of the dairymaid was acceptable to even refined Victorian opinion that of the field worker was usually not. The very difference in name is significant – the dairy*maid* and the field*woman*, the one with its stress on innocence and the rural idyll, the other with its connotations of experience and harshness. Hardy knew the distinction well when he made Tess a dairymaid at Talbothays in her period of innocence and love for Angel Clare, and a fieldwoman at Flintcombe Ash when she was deserted and truly 'a maiden no more'. Those men who reported on the employment of women in agriculture in 1843 and 1867–70 often felt the same. The Hon. E. B. Portman, for example, who reported on the three ridings of Yorkshire, Cambridgeshire, Hampshire, Devon and Cornwall made an absolute distinction between 'indoor' farm service and outdoor farm labour and concluded, 'girls should not . . . be employed in the fields at all.'[29]

Field work was, as the century progressed, regarded more and more as unsuitable and unnatural for women. Portman was only being more extreme than most of the other investigators when he wrote that as a result of field work 'such sense of decency' that girls have is 'entirely broken down' and that it made them 'entirely unfit . . . for their duties in the future as wives and mothers.'[30] By making these girls rough in manner and appearance, as it was stated field work did, it put them physically outside Victorian society and its model of womanhood which demanded delicacy of features, pale skin and elaborate dress. The Rev. James Fraser who investigated Norfolk, Suffolk, Essex, Sussex and Gloucestershire for the same report wrote of field work.

> Not only does it almost unsex a woman, in dress, gait, manners, character, making her rough, coarse, clumsy, masculine; but it

> generates a further very pregnant social mischief by unfitting or indisposing her for a women's proper duties at home. Some of the work on which women are frequently employed ... is work to which, on physical grounds, they never ought to be put at all. Exposure to wet or cold, from which no farm labour can claim exemption, is likely, owing to the greater susceptibility of the female constitution, to be specially injurious to them.[31]

Yet these opinions were not universal despite the Rev. Fraser's insistence that they were. In northern agriculture, and especially that of the border regions, women's work was stoutly defended not only by the women workers but by W. E. Henley who reported on that region. With an almost wry glance at those like Portman and Fraser who condemned women's work he wrote:

> There are many who hold the opinion that field work is degrading, but I should be glad if they would visit these women in their own homes after they become wives and mothers ... The visitor will leave that cottage with the conviction that field work has no degrading effect, but that he had been in the presence of a thoughtful, contented and unselfish woman.[32]

The difference between the attitudes of Fraser and Henley is not simply an individual one. Fraser was a deeply humane man whose report is a model of sympathy for the labourer be they man or woman, a sympathy he made real by his support, as Bishop of Manchester, for the agricultural workers unions in 1872–4. The basis of the difference lay in the disjuncture between the essentially urban and middle class ideals of 'unfitness' of work for women and the demands of both agrarian capital and simple poverty, for if capital demanded labour, labour desperately needed the wages. Both these needs were mediated through local custom and tradition.

Whatever working women thought, and there were many who accepted some versions of the 'unfit work' argument, there were many who clearly did not really see what the fuss was about and saw women's work not as unnatural or especially degrading but simply as necessary and inevitable. Fraser was told in Linton in Gloucestershire by a 'group of labouring women', 'that it would be a hardship if the law were to lay restrictions upon the employment of women in the fields,'[33] and field work for most working women was seen in these terms.

Time and again the evidence given to the commissioners on the employment of women and children point up its inevitability. Elizabeth Dickson, a widow from Norfolk, put the case eloquently and simply. 'My children were obliged to work very young, some before they were 7 years old. If you have nothing except what comes out of your fingers' end, as they say, its no use, you must let them; they want more victuals'.[34] The women of Linton who spoke to Fraser made the same point, 'their families would often have gone to bed hungry had they not earned their money in that way.'[35] The village elites, when they could overcome their moral fears about women working at all, saw the problem in the same way. The Rev. Thurtell of Oxburgh in Norfolk put it bluntly when he said 'The females of very large families *must* (sic) be permitted to work, in order that they may live.'[36]

It was not simply though a case of demand from labouring families but demand from farmers. As the number of casual workers from other sources began to decrease from the 1850s the labour of women and children became more and more important and it seems likely that women's employment in agriculture reached its peak. The Rev. W. G. S. Addison of Hartparry in Gloucestershire put this double demand clearly to Fraser: 'Female labour is absolutely required by the farmers, and the additional wages are as greatly needed by the labourers' families.'[37] James Freezer, who farmed 1,000 acres in Norfolk, required 'about 16 women all through the year to cultivate this quantity of land properly'. Crucially for him, as for so many others, 'the farm can be worked much cheaper with women than without them . . . For weeding a woman can do the work not only cheaper but better than a man.'[38]

As we have already suggested, although women's work was everywhere there were enormous differences in its regional nature. In the north and west women's employment was probably least casual. Here, shortage of labour because of the isolation of many farm settlements and, especially in the north and north-east, competition from industry meant that farmers had to employ relatively more workers all the year round as the 'residual army' of the southern villages simply did not exist. As we saw in Chapter 2, in Northumberland family hiring and the bondager system provided extra women workers for key agricultural operations. The farm accounts of Castle Heaton farm show women family members hired for the cereal harvest along with migrant Irish workers. For the harvest period in 1913 four Irish migrants were hired along with five women family members and two 'boy' family members.[39] This practice was however not only restricted to the north. In Dorset, family hiring performed the same function. The Rev. H. Moule of Fordington, a good friend to the poor of Dorset,[40] wrote to Hon. Edward Stanhope, commissioner for Dorset in 1867,

> . . . the smallness of the income of the agricultural labourer . . . (means) that advantage should be taken of any help which the wife, or which any of the children, may afford to add to that income. This facilitates the practice, so unfair to the agricultural labourer, *of hiring not the man alone, but his wife and family also*; (*sic*) so that whilst he continues in the employ of his master, his wife and any boys old enough must work when required.[41]

In Dorset, though, unlike Northumberland, family hiring was a result of weakness in the labourers' position since it was based not on labour shortage but labour surplus which meant that farmers were able to demand family labour as a condition of hiring.

In parts of the north and more so the west there were groups of women workers though who stood outside the family hiring system altogether. On the smaller farms of Northumberland where family hiring was not economically viable, or where there were off-farm sources of women workers as on the coastal plain, women were hired by the day for key harvest operations. The farm books of a 202-acre family farm near Dinnington in Northumberland show that most work was done by the two brothers who ran it plus three hinds. (Strictly hinds were married farm workers but the word was used frequently for a male worker.) At the hay, and especially potato harvest, casual workers, mainly women, were brought on to the farm. The small cereal harvest seems to have been taken entirely by regular workers. The numbers involved were relatively large. At potato harvest in 1908 sixteen 'girls' were employed over two weeks 'taking up potatoes'. Women workers were also brought on to the farm, to plant potatoes in the spring, to spread muck, also in the spring and for threshing on and off throughout the winter and spring.[42]

It is not clear from the records precisely who these women were since names seldom appear but there are no obvious family relationships between these women and the male workers, unlike the situation on the bigger farm at Castle Heaton. One assumes they were from the nearby mining settlements at Seaton. A few miles away Bob Thompson, a farmer, remembered

> there used to be a lot of women came out at harvest time ... lot of bottle makers wives, and they used to have a stretch same as they used to get stretches for potatoes, they had so many yards, where they had to make the band, tie the shef (*sic*) up and put it out of the way of the machine ... they all had their stint to do.[43]

Slightly further south in Co. Durham it was noted in the 1860s that there was no shortage of casual workers, 'extra women being easily procured from the numerous pit villages.'[44]

In the mainly arable areas of the south and east women tended to be more and more casual, brought into the production process at particular times from the wives and daughters, widows and spinsters of the village-based community, and paid by the piece for particular tasks. In the West Grinstead area of West Sussex, for example, women helped their husbands at hay harvest and young girls were employed in 'dropping peas after a dibbler'. A few miles north at Rusper they worked at hay harvest, corn harvest and weeding. At Hailsham in East Sussex women found seasonal work tying hops 'at so much an acre'.[45] In North Cerney in Gloucestershire women were employed throughout the farming year on a casual basis.

> They are useful for a variety of occupations: stone-picking, picking, drawing and cleaning turnips for sheep and cattle, weeding corn, hay-making, hoeing root crops, picking, raking and burning couch, harvesting, pulling, topping and tailing turnips, pulling straw for the thatcher, cutting chaff, untying the sheaves for threshing machine (*sic*) mending corn sacks &c. &c.[46]

It was in eastern England, in the great wheatlands, especially Norfolk, Cambridgeshire and Lincolnshire, that the casual employment of women seems to have been both most widespread and organized. It was in these areas that the infamous 'gang system' developed. This was basically a system of sub-contracting where a 'gangmaster' took a particular job for a price from a farmer and then employed women and children, boys and young men as well as girls, to do the work for day rates. For his 'trouble' the gangmaster took as much as a third of the wages of those he 'employed', making, according to one estimate in the mid-1860s, as much as 15s–£1 a week on a gang of 15–20 persons. The Rev. W. T. Beckett, the Diocesan Inspector of Schools for Norwich who made that estimate, summed up the system neatly. For the farmer, 'it enabled him to dispense with a certain number of labourers, as were it not for this system he would be obliged to keep a greater number of regular labourers . . . ' It also enabled him to do without a foreman or bailiff to supervise the work, this being done by the gangmaster. For the labourer though they 'are deprived of part of their fairly earned wages . . . [and] have often, to use a Norfolk phrase, "to play", that is remain unemployed on wet days, or when the weather is not altogether suitable for the kind of work required.' Most simply of all 'to the poor man it displaces labour and renders it less.'[47]

Agricultural gangs were usually based in the larger and 'open' villages, and went out day by day to work for the farms around. Occasionally they stayed away over night although this practice was uncommon. They undertook a range of agricultural tasks on a seasonal basis which added together covered much of the year. As a Norfolk gangmaster said in the mid-1860s

> There is work of some kind for my gang during most of the year, even in winter, except when there is frost or snow. Then the only work is perhaps for half a dozen or so of the bigger boys in topping and tailing turnips for food for sheep &c. From now, October, to March the work will be chiefly pulling and topping and tailing mangolds and turnips, forking twitch, and stone picking; then picking and burning twitch, puddling thistles and docks, weeding corn and other kinds of weeding, and this with singling mangolds and turnips, and so on, will last up to harvest . . . after harvest comes forking and clearing the land, and so work goes up to now again.[48]

Travelling from place to place, 'immodestly' dressed, young men and young women 'indiscriminately' mixed together, but above all public and visible, the agricultural gang embodied all that the Victorian elite attacked in women's field work. Unlike the 'dairymaids' of the pastoral regions hidden in the dairies and with their echoes, no matter how absurd, of Myssen figurines, the field woman could been seen everywhere in the huge fields and open places of the wheatlands. Bent double, clad in 'rags', heavy boots, short skirt and with a sack around her shoulders she was the antithesis of the ideal of the 'angel at the hearth' and a constant reproach to those who sought an ordered paternal idyll.

Yet their work, given the nature of farm organization, was vital. Like the gangs of travelling harvesters they stood 'outside' the system which projected a model of a settled, regular, deferential and male workforce. But without them the system, with its demands for periodic and massive labour inputs, would have collapsed. Yet the 'casual', especially the woman casual, could be and was marginalized. Physically they were seen as 'temporary' even if, as with many women workers, that was clearly nonsensical, they came into the village and went again, their threat to order was soon gone. But the system that produced demands for their labour produced tensions of a different kind within the regular workforce.

The long-term movement in the labour process within arable agriculture in the first three-quarters of the nineteenth century was, as we have already mentioned, towards the employment of fewer, but key, workers on a regular basis with a yearly hiring. This group was supplemented at key times by day-men and casuals. The core group of workers on an arable farm were the horsemen and a minimum number of labourers who could expect all-the-year-round employment, sometimes a cottage and, in the northern areas, a range of perks. However, for this group and, more importantly, those day-men who were in semi-regular work, there were several points in the year when the system of arable production increased the demand for labour and thus their chance of increasing earnings. In this situation conflicts arose which disrupted the 'harmony' of work relationships on the farm.[49]

The most important of these, although by no means the only ones, were the series of harvests beginning with the hay harvest in June and ending with the roots in October or even November. In addition there were other tasks, for instance hoeing or singling roots, which had to be done at a particular time even if they lacked the urgency of the harvests. The situation was put clearly by Henry Overman, a tenant farmer of 1,300 acres in north-west Norfolk, to the 1881 Royal Commission.

> There is this peculiarity in agriculture: that the work must be done at a particular moment?
>
> Yes and the men will wait and see how the harvest is coming on, or how the turnips are being got out. I grow a hundred acres of mangold every year, and my men have struck twice at the very time when they know that their labour is most needed for that crop.[50]

In a labour market which was usually overfilled, or at least where supply of labour was usually equal to demand, the sudden demands of a crop ripening, or the need for hoeing to be carried out, temporarily gave the labourer an advantage especially since much of this work, in the arable south and east, was done by the piece. Charlie Barber, of Great Fransham in Norfolk, who started work in the 1890s, led a 'strike' in this situation in the early 1900s.

> We struck for harvest wages . . . we was getting six pound, and of course we were supposed to be the first to start in the parish. We used to meet you know, see if we could make a proper bargain, like some of them used to give a shilling hire money. He was the first to start and we reckoned we wanted six-pound ten that year . . . so I asked him if he was going to give us the six pound ten. 'No', he said, he'd give the same as other people, he shouldn't give no more. And I said, 'That ain't an answer', but he wouldn't tell us no different. Anyway he wanted us to start next morning. I was team man then, and I had to go away and have a job done of the self binder . . . So I said to my brother, 'Don't you start unless he say he's going to give you that six pound ten, cos', I said, 'you know we're going to set the price for other people, 'cos we're the first to start'. When I got up there they were having their breakfast and I say 'Have you made a proper bargain?' 'No', they say, 'Well,' I said, 'don't lets start then . . . that ain't no good starting like that, 'I said', we set the price for other people, and they can give you what they like'[51]

Such strikes were very risky. Except briefly in the 1870s and after 1907 they could not have any union backing, and usually when unions existed they disliked this kind of spontaneous action. Even with labour shortage a farmer might be able to find travelling workers to replace striking labourers as at Mattishall in Norfolk in 1900 when a farmer 'set some tramps on in place of the men who left, but they had been threatened in the village and called blacklegs.'[52] There was also the problem of timing. If that was misjudged, especially at cereal harvest, the farmer had plenty of time to find replacement workers.

Failure also had long-term consequences. While the weather was in the labourers' favour and there were no alternative workers available he or she could win. Once it changed, or if the timing was wrong, the rural idyll was an unforgiving one. Henry Overman put it bluntly.

> About 11 out of 36 harvest men left me . . . (and) it ended in my having to come to London to get navvies . . . Before I commenced harvest the other men came back to me; but I would not have one of them, and never had one of them again, because I dislike dissatisfied men.[53]

In many cases it went further than just one master. Charlie Barber walked all round the district looking for alternative work.

> We heard of a man at Bradenham wanted some men, so we went to see him. Course he wanted to know where we come from. I told, 'Mr. Crane's at Fransham.' 'Oh well,' he said. 'I mustn't take you,' he say, 'you'll hat to go back to Mr. Crane'. Then we went from there to Newton, near Castleacre. There was a Mr. Smith there, he was advertising for harvest men . . . we went there and he was just the same. So of course we didn't get a harvest.[54]

If you were lucky though, or had gauged the season right, time and the weather would bring your master to your door.

> So we had orders to start the harvest, and we said 'What about the money?' We wanted seven pound . . . so he said 'Six pound ten', we said 'We want seven pound', and he said, 'No six-pound ten thats all I'll give.' So I said, 'All right,' I said, 'we shan't start.' So that was Saturday morning, so course we walked back down to the Hill (village 'green'), we leaned (*sic*) about the village, we met ourselves like. On the Tuesday night the farmer's son-in-law come round and said, 'You can start tomorrow, seven pound'.[55]

In the northern arable areas the situation was different. Here, a relatively much larger section of the workforce was regularly hired by the year and, in many areas, lived on the farms.

Thus little work was done by the piece and opportunities for bargaining were limited once a worker was hired. But the annual hiring took on some elements of the conflict around piece-work bargaining. Ian Carter has shown how on the arable farms of north-east Scotland a highly developed and quasi-formal organization existed among the young ploughmen which served, via the annual hiring, to control wages, warn against bad employers and even organize against them. 'The market (hiring) was the cockpit in which the social relations of farmers and servants stood out most sharply.'[56] A similar situation existed in Northumberland as Mr J. B. Pearrman, a hired man, remembered. He went to hire at Bellingham May Hirings but couldn't get a place except one offer for £6 which he turned down. In desperation at about 3 o'clock he went to find the farmer who had made the earlier offer.

> I was just about to speak to him when a fellow tugged me coat, and I turned round and this chap he says, 'Ah ye ganna hire with him', I says I was going to 'I've not gitten hired'. He says 'Diven gan there its a bad meat shop', he says 'I was there a week' . . . So I didn't get hired at Bellingham, so I came to Hexham, and I got £11 to go to Eachwick.[57]

The very 'threat' of hiring and the implied movement to another farm produced conflicts or at least bargaining, as this account from the East Riding of Yorkshire suggests. 'First hirings is generally a fortnight afore you leave the place you're at, 'Is ta stoppin'?', farmer'd say, and you'd say, 'Oh, I ain't bin asked yit!' And if you warn't, you'd tell him.'[58] Even if a labourer or hind intended to stay on in his or her place they often went to the hirings, partly to make the point that they could move and perhaps bring pressure to bear on a master, and partly simply to have a break. The hinds on the farm of the Rutherford brothers near Dinnington regularly went to the hirings even if they simply returned to the same farm. In 1910 the day book records, '2nd March 1910 Hiring day at Morpeth, Jack and Alec there.'[59] As Stephen Caunce says of the East Riding fairs, 'at the end of the first hirings it didn't matter that no hiring had been done. Both sides retired to consider their positions and in Martinmas week more realistic bargaining would begin.'[60] This flexing of muscles happened regularly at Dinnington as in 1910 when a week later Jack and Alec returned to the next hirings and were hired by the Rutherfords. As well as testing out the state of the market this going to the hirings gave what Mr Pearrman called 'our days . . . that was about three days at the hiring time. If you stayed on at a farm you got the term day [day your hiring finished] and about two or three days after that . . . '[61]

In the East Riding, where most of those who worked with horses were hired by the year and lived in, the hirings were a time to deal with other conflicts which had lain buried beneath the surface of order.

> Say you lived on a spot where you had a rough foreman-feller, always kicking the lad's backsides. We'll I've hear many a lad say, 'Oh well, waiyt while Driffield first hirings!' Theres many a bloomin' foreman-feller's getten his head broken at Martinmas at Driffield first hirings.[62]

But the fairs disrupted in other ways – simply by existing. They were proverbial for their 'licentiousness' and although they seem to have been harmless enough in a sexual sense the very gathering together of young men and women was seen as a threat to moral order and, especially in Yorkshire, there were moves from the 1860s to separate the sexes, with the women hiring in halls. In Northumberland mixed hirings remained and, according to the memories of those who attended them, were innocent enough.

> Hexham . . . oh, there would be anything from 40 to 60 or 70 lads all standing besides the shambles . . . then the girls always were at the east end . . . and the lads at the west end . . . It was a day out for most. And there was a place in Back Street, we used to call her Old Nonny Knight, she used to make pies and peas and we used to go there for a feed and it was really a good day . . . everybody was cheerful and sometimes there was a roundabout.[63]

Hardly the Sodom described by elite moralists. But the young men and women who lived for a year on the farms, isolated and remote from those of their own ages and often carefully watched by employers, did break out a little; and the position of relative power that they often found themselves in in an area of more or less permanent labour shortage certainly produced 'insolence' towards their betters. When men and women were separated at Bridlington hirings in the 1860s those organizing the women's indoor hiring remarked that 'the mistresses were greatly pleased, remarking with surprise satisfaction how much better behaved the girls were than when they hired in the street, where all was confusion and rude joking and jostling among the lads.'[64]

So, in the arable areas the very seasonal nature of the work and the increasingly large gap between demands for workers at harvest and requirements the rest of the year produced serious tensions in the rural areas of the south and east. Far from being calm and ordered, conflict was endemic in these areas, within the workplace at least, at key points in the year especially when harvesting operations were under way. In the arable areas of the north different tensions emerged. Here they were mediated through the yearly hiring. In all areas the employment of women and reliance on travelling workers disrupted both the physical model of a stable society in which all knew their place and the ideology which created 'fit work for women'.

In all these ways the surface of calm and order was constantly disrupted and threatened. A precarious balance was usually achieved but it was never permanent – the relentless demands of agricultural production could only be met by major changes which were in turn further disruptive. There were, however, other ways in which this calm was disturbed which were in a way outside production. Crime and 'pleasure', which to many Victorians were virtually identical when done by the poor, presented a different kind of threat to harmony and it is to them that we will now turn.

NOTES

1 Bateman, 'Introduction', op. cit., p. 12.
2 ibid., p. xxv.
3 Thompson, *Landed Society*, op. cit., p. 249–53.
4 ibid., pp. 256–68.
5 NRO, NRO ZBL/78, Hiring agreement from Hatton Hall Estate nr. Hexham.
6 ESRO, SAS Acc 126S Courthope Estate, wages/daybooks.
7 NNRO, R.154d. Labour Book. Ditchingham/Hemphall area.
8 NNRO, No Acc. no. Labour Books of a farm near Barnham Broom.
9 ESRO, Courthope, op. cit..
10 NRO, Hatton, op. cit..

11 ESRO, Courthope, op. cit..
12 NNRO, Ditchingham, Barnham Broom, op. cit..
13 For a more detailed account see Alun Howkins, 'Structural Conflict and the Farmworker', *Journal of Peasant Studies*, Vol. 4, no. 3, April 1977.
14 E. J. T. Collins, 'Harvest technology and Labour Supply in Britain 1780–1870', Unpublished PhD thesis University of Nottingham, 1970, p. 89.
15 Quoted in David Hoseason Morgan, *Harvesters and Harvesting, 1840–1900. A Study of the Rural Proletariat*, [London, 1982], p. 54. For this topic see ibid., Ch. 3, and Alun Howkins, 'The Great Momentous Time', op. cit., Ch. 1.
16 Maggie Joe Chapman interviewed in Charles Kightly, *Country Voices*, [London, 1984], p. 121.
17 NRO, NRO 302/172, Castle Heaton Farm, daybook.
18 NRO T/98 NRO 1208, Interview with Mrs J. Brown, b. Fenwick Steads nr. Wooler, 1876.
19 Kightly, op. cit., p. 121.
20 For anti-Irish feeling in the south in an earlier period see E. J. Hobsbawm and George Rude, *Captain Swing*, [London, 1969], p. 98.
21 Fordyce, op. cit., Vol. I, p. 270.
22 ibid., p. 317.
23 See Collins, op. cit., p. 133.
24 Cecil Sharpe MS, Folk Dance Notes II, ff 129–30 Clare College Cambridge.
25 *OC* 9 September 1854, p. 8.
26 ESRO SAS Acc 1276 GB, 'Anne Courthopes General Account Book, 1841–54'.
27 *PP 1881, XVII*, op. cit., Evidence of Hon. Edward Coke, Longford Derbyshire, p. 941.
28 ibid., p. 942.
29 *PP 1868–69, XIII*, 'Royal Commission on the Employment of Children, Young Persons and Women in Agriculture. Second Report by the Hon. E. B. Portman', p. 49.
30 *PP 1867–68, XVII*, op. cit., p. 95.
31 ibid.
32 *PP 1868–69, XIII*, op. cit., 'Report by Mr. Henley', p. 54.
33 *PP 1867–68, XVII*, op. cit., pp. 131–2.
34 *PP 1867, XVI*, op. cit., p. 89.
35 *PP 1867–8, XVII*, p. 132.
36 *PP 1867, XVI*, op. cit., p. 137.
37 ibid., p. 140.
38 *PP 1867–8, XVII*, p. 167.
39 NRO 302/172 Woods MS Castle Heaton daybook.
40 See Robert Gissing, *Young Thomas Hardy*, [London, 1975], pp. 36–7.

41 *PP 1868–69, XIII*, 'Report by Mr. Stanhope' op. cit., p. 20.
42 NRO 479, Farm Diaries of J. W. and J. E. Rutherford, North Masons Farm, Dinnington, Northumberland.
43 NRO T 34, Acc NRO 103, Interview Bob Thompson, farmer, Seaton Sluice, Northumberland.
44 *PP 1867, XVII*, op. cit., p. 181.
45 *PP 1867–8, XVII*, pp. 78–81.
46 ibid., p. 102.
47 *PP 1867, XVII*, op. cit., pp. 83–5.
48 ibid., p. 86.
49 See Howkins, *Structural Conflict*, op. cit..
50 *PP 1881, XVII*, op. cit., p. 741.
51 Interview AJH/Charlie Barber, Great Fransham, Norfolk, team man. Tape in author's possession.
52 *NN* 21st July 1900.
53 *PP 1881, XVII*, op. cit., p. 737.
54 Interview. Barber, op. cit..
55 Interview, AJH/'Billa' Dixon, Trunch Norfolk. Team man. Tape in author's possession.
56 Carter, op. cit., p. 144. See also Chs 4 and 5.
57 NRO T 151B, Interview Mr. M. J. B. Pearrman, labourer/farmer.
58 Quoted in Kightly, op. cit., p. 25.
59 NRO 479, Rutherford, op. cit..
60 Stephen Caunce, 'East Riding Hiring Fairs', *Oral History* Vol. 3, no. 2., p. 50.
61 NRO T151B Pearrman, op. cit..
62 Quoted in Caunce, op. cit., p. 48.
63 NRO T151B Pearrman, op. cit..
64 Quoted in Caunce, op. cit., p. 49.

5

The Problems of Consensus: Disorder and Crime

Although the endemic social violence of the first years of the century was by and large a thing of the past after the 1840s the maintenance of law continued to be a central problem. At the most public level, for example, the last 'serious' outbreaks of rick burning were in East Anglia in 1848–9, but this quintessential crime of social protest did not simply disappear. As late as the 1890s isolated attacks of this kind show the bitterness which lay behind the calm of paternalism. In 1899 for example, a labourer, William Mansell, told the jury at Norwich Assizes,

> I was upset when I left Gooch's having been turned out of my house, having nowhere to go. I went across Drakes Field to Mr. Murfet's wheat stack and set fire to that, and across the fields to the back of Kenny's and fired his stacks as I had a bit of a grudge against him as he owed me 15s to 17s and would not pay it.[1]

Even John Masefield, the 1900's poet, had a sense of this lurking anger when he made the poacher hero of his poem 'The Everlasting Mercy' cry out to a farmer,

> And one of these dark winter nights
> He'll learn I mean to have my rights;
> I'll bloody him a bloody fix,
> I'll bloody burn his bloody ricks.[2]

Nor did other violent conflict with the law vanish. John Archer has shown how cattle maiming, another crime of protest or revenge, continued in East Anglia until at least the 1870s. Indeed although there are 'high points' in this crime in the early 1830s and late 1840s as there are with rick burning, there is another highpoint in the mid-1860s, long after such 'primitive' methods are supposed to have vanished.[3]

More spectacularly, enclosure and enclosure riots are usually seen as a thing of the period between the 1790s and 1830s. Indeed the 'general enclosure' of 1845 is supposed to have put an end to such disturbances. This is simply not the case. The reports of the enclosure Commissioners of 1868–9 show that in the previous years there had been widespread opposition to enclosure which had often taken violent and 'traditional' forms. At Withypool on the edge of Exmoor the commoners fought a long battle to retain their rights to open pasture, cultivation of waste ground, cutting fuel and paring and burning areas of the moor for ashes which they sold. Even the population of the area seems to have stepped out of the eighteenth century. One of their critics, the Rev. Jekyll, who favoured enclosure, called them 'freebooters living entirely on plunder' and went on:

> For the last half century everyone has grazed the common and erected huts and enclosed small plots, without let or hindrance; predatory habits have been induced, which will take generations to eradicate.[4]

At Maltby in Yorkshire the enclosure was forcibly resisted and a petition sent to the commissioners after a noisy meeting. The main spokesman here was the 'hangman' of Rotherham who, mixing the deeds of the eighteenth century with words of the nineteenth, 'referred' the commissioners to 'the works of Mr Mill'.[5] At Headington Quarry in Oxfordshire, although it never reached the Select Committee, an enclosure dispute ran from the late 1850s to the 1890s involving all the trappings of an earlier and less ordered world. Fences were destroyed, animals turned loose on newly enclosed ground and the success of the rioters was celebrated with beer, 'which was handed out *ad libitum* to all comers', and with music from 'fiddles, tambourines etc.'[6]

Spectacular outbreaks like these were however rare, as they probably always had been, but they do represent, in an almost literal sense, the 'tip of the iceberg' the bulk of which was small-scale crimes against property.[7] Most of these were in turn crimes which while not necessarily acts of protest were often acts which seemed less than criminal to the poor themselves, and were often supported by local belief and custom. In Headington Quarry the most consistent acts against enclosure were not riots but the simple collection of wood or killing 'game', which the poor of the village believed they had a right to. In January 1861, for instance, William Webb, Robert Webb, George Webb, George Snow, Thomas Adams and Thomas Townsend were charged at Bullingdon Petty Sessions with 'cutting the Oak trees growing in the Open Magdelens and stealing and carrying the same away'. Mr Brunner, who defended them, told the court 'his clients admitted the act of cutting and carrying away, but they had done so on the supposition that they were entitled to the wood as well as the feed, as the right of common.'[8] Thirty years later the same George Webb defended himself against a charge of stealing wood in the same area by saying to the policeman who arrested him, 'he had cut wood there for the past fifty years . . . as the wood belonged to the poor of Headington.'[9]

Of all rural crime against property the most important were offences against the game laws, those laws which 'protected' hares, rabbits, deer, pheasant, partridge and other named fowl. To both rich and poor game had a special significance. To the elite it gave status, to the poor it was a 'right' but above all food. As a result, through the games laws, it is possible to assess the range of attitudes and behaviour present in the rural areas in relation to crime.

There is a very real sense in which what the law called poaching was simply the exercise of a particular version of other rights attached to land, especially common lands and woodland. Writing just after the Great War John Kibble, the working-man historian of north-west Oxfordshire, said of the Forest of Wychwood;

> When the forest was enclosed it was a sad blow to many who lived on its borders, for some of them got a great part of their living out of the Forest. Burdens [*sic*] of wood for firing, fallen branches, and furze were brought and sold to those who could buy. In spring wild birds eggs helped to make many a nice pudding. I knew an old man well when I was a lad who in earlier life used to go on Sunday morning around Topples and collect wild birds eggs for his wife to put into the pudding for dinner.[10]

The extent to which customary rights continued to be observed by both the gentry and the poor for at least some areas well into the nineteenth century is a matter of argument but on a day-to-day basis such obligations may well have been regular and all-pervasive. P. B. Munsche suggests that until the 1780s at least the application of the game laws was far from rigorous in most areas especially when cases did not involve deer and rabbits which could be tried as theft rather than game cases.[11] This fits well with that of Douglas Hay in *Albion's Fatal Tree* which sees the process of justice as a carefully manipulated ritual in which 'the benevolence of rich men to poor, and all the ramifications of patronage, were upheld by the sanction of the gallows and the rhetoric of the death sentence.'[12]

This balance, in relation to the game laws as in many other areas, came under increasing stress from the 1780s as conditions in the countryside changed. Although figures are difficult to come by it is absolutely clear from Munsche's work that prosecutions and probably offences under the game laws began to increase rapidly after the 1760s. Three reasons, or groups of reasons, lie behind this. Firstly there were changes in the nature of the ruling elite who, as in other areas, began to withdraw from the paternalist model of society which was important in the earlier eighteenth century. Part of this withdrawal seems to have been increasing game preservation and breeding which emphasized status and difference both between the rural elite and the growing urban bourgeois, and separation from their rural neighbours and inferiors. Game protection societies begin to appear in many areas in this period and the game laws seemed to have been enforced with increasing harshness.[13]

Secondly, and related to these changes, although in a kind of 'chicken and egg' way, growing urban demand for game, which could be bought but not sold under the old game laws, increased the rewards of poaching for an essentially urban criminal group. Finally, rural poverty, especially after the 1790s, drove more and more of the rural poor to casual poaching based upon economic needs.

As a result of these changes pressure for reform of the Game Laws began to mount. In 1796 John Christian Curwen brought a game Bill before the Commons which sought to make game a species of property. The Bill was defeated but it was the death knell of the old game code. In the next thirty years, and especially after 1820, pressure for reform grew.

That reform was accomplished with the 'Night Poaching' Act of 1828 and the 'Game Act' of 1831. The 1828 Act essentially brought together all previous statutes concerning the much more serious offence of poaching at night and provided sentences of up to transportation for life. The 1831 Act repealed twenty-eight statutes which had previously covered game offences, laid down closed seasons for winged game, gave the right to certified persons to kill game subject to the law of trespass, licensed game dealers and gave the right to sell game to those with certificates. Crucially, however, it reserved the right of shooting game to the landlord and his appointees. As Stephens, the nineteenth century writer on common law put it, 'the right to game becomes an incident to the ownership or right to possession of land'.[14]

The Acts of 1828 and 1831 were modified at various times during the next thirty years but remained the basis of legislation on game. In 1844 the 1828 Act was modified to cover public roads and highways, as well as enclosed ground. In 1862 both Acts were modified by the 'Poaching Prevention Act' which gave the new county police forces the power to stop and search in any public place 'any person whom (they) may have good cause to suspect of coming from any land where he shall have been unlawfully in search or pursuit of game.'[15]

The passing of these Acts, especially those of 1828 and 1831, was of fundamental importance. At the most basic level they completed the process which moved from custom to law by thoroughly criminalizing offences against a species of previously customary property. Connected to that they precisely located actual property in game – all game now had an owner who could dispose of it at will either to certified appointees to kill, or to kill and sell himself. [It should be noted though that it took the House of Lords until 1865 to finally settle this in case law.] The Acts also removed a whole area of negotiation from human relationships. Statute law now governed game and the last vestiges of the eighteenth century balance noted by Munsche were removed.

These aspects of reform were both clear to contemporaries. As Chester Kirby noted many years ago the bases of legal reform in relation to game were the demand to make it into real property and to 'open' the right to shoot to the game-eating middle classes.[16] The Marquis of Lansdowne put the case clearly in the House of Lords in July 1828.

> The great fault of the present system was that there were but very few persons interested in upholding it, while the great bulk of the community was interested in opposing it . . . Only by founding it [game] on the principle of property and not upon any ancient rights . . . upon the principle of property which was recognised by all, and which prompted a man to defend, not only that which was his own but that which belonged to others [could this be changed][17]

This position was shared by Stuart Wortley, later Lord Warncliffe, the most indefatigable of all the reformers. It was his efforts which eventually led to the changes of both 1828 and 1831. However, many opposed the changes, frequently basing their opposition on the defence of the old order. The Earl of Malmesbury firmly asserted the 'old country ways' which he said were under attack 'nowadays' with all 'classes running down country gentlemen'. He continued:

> Gentlemen now went out shooting, by sufferance, on the property of small farmers, and gave them a brace or two of partridges, and both parties were satisfied . . . [if qualifications were abolished] . . . the whole thing would be reduced to a question of pounds, and pence; every man would be anxious to make what he could by game . . . and there would be no more shooting on sufferance.[18]

The old Earl of Abingdon, who opposed enclosure on his estates around Otmoor, also opposed changing the game laws since they were 'institutions which had stood the test of time.'[19]

However it was not simply a matter for parliament. Game preservation, along with continued suppression of customary rights and the enclosure of wastes, brought custom into direct conflict with law. Mr Leycester saw this clearly in the Commons debates on the reform of the law in 1829.

> It had been said that the bill would clothe game with something of the character of property. What was that to the poacher? Would he trouble to read the book of Parliament? He read the book of nature. In that book he saw that the hand of

> nature made game wild, and 'unclaimed of any', and would act accordingly . . . [20]

Leycester could have added, like Cobbett, that the poacher could read in Blackstone's *Commentaries on the Laws of England*,

> All mankind had by the original grant of the Creator a right to pursue and take away any fowl or insect of the air, any fish or inhabitant of the waters, and beast or reptile of the field; and this natural right still continues in every individual, unless elsewhere it is restrained by the civil law of the country.[21]

The belief, among the poor, that 'the beasts of the field and the birds of the air were made free and alike for all men' derived not only from Blackstone, which they did not read, but from the King James Bible which they did. In the Book of Genesis the poor read of God's legacy to the children of Noah – to all men.

> And the fear of you and the dread of you shall be upon every beast of the earth, and upon every fowl of the air, upon all that moveth *upon* the earth and all the fishes of the sea; into your hands are they delivered. Everything moving thing that liveth shall be meat for you; even as the green herb have I given you all things.[22]

This idea finds constant expression in more or less sophisticated terms throughout the late eighteenth and nineteenth centuries. In Thomas Berwick's *Memoirs* we find Anthony Liddell, 'a village Hampden'.[23]

> Acts of Parliament which appeared to him to clash with the laws laid down [in the Bible] as the word of God, he treated with contempt. He maintained that the fowls of the air and the fish of the sea were free for all men; consequently game laws or laws to protect fisheries, had no weight with him.[23]

Less sophisticated was the evidence given to the 1828 Select Committee on Game Laws by a Yorkshire general dealer who said, 'God made Game, and I consider it every mans right, that it was for every body to judge for himself; but when God made man he did not say what he was to eat'.[24] Frequently during the nineteenth century country benches issued warnings about this belief, as at Bullingdon in Oxfordshire when the magistrates said that there 'appeared to be a notion among the peasantry' that 'all the wild things under heaven were free for all'.[25]

Although any right to kill game had long vanished by the nineteenth century the pattern of agrarian life and society and the customary structure kept aspects of it alive. As a late nineteenth century author wrote of the forest areas of Buckinghamshire,[26]

> Here was a race of people, who for generations had roamed the forest at will, *sans* serious let or hindrance, till they honestly believed their 'privileges' to be immutable rights, suddenly, and, to their minds, unjustly bereft of their heritage, in many cases their livelihood, and . . . of their supply of fresh food.[26]

Custom, both as a belief in 'lost' rights or as a system of activity, provided a legitimating structure which was given a sure and powerful underpinning of material reality. This was put by both Joseph Arch in his autobiography, and by a later agricultural trades unionist in an interview almost a hundred years later.

> Years ago you still had to live. I've heard my father say hundreds of times, 'If I hadn't stolen my children would have went hungry' . . . I don't think there was anything wrong with that . . . People had to poach to live.[27]

At the most basic level, killing animals provided food and the killing of wild birds and the gathering of their eggs was widely recognized as essential and subject only to prosecution for trespass. In the same way wood gathering provided fuel, sells were used to make baskets, flowers were gathered to sell, cattle, sheep or donkeys turned to fatten or graze, and nuts were gathered for sale or pig food. Custom taught, by repetition, not only the right time to do these things but also legitimized them by constant usage. The law might distinguish between 'wild' ducks and blackbirds, between 'vermin', like otters and the pheasant that ate an allotment holder's small crop of barley, but custom and agrarian practice did not, and could not. Joseph Arch put this point eloquently in his autobiography and to the Select Committee on Game Laws in 1872. 'The plain truth is, we labourers do not believe hares and rabbits belong to any individual, not any more than thrushes and blackbirds do.'[28]

This combination of agrarian customary practice, a belief in rights, and harsh economic reality was supported by the village community and celebrated in its popular culture. Even John Bennet, MP for Wiltshire and no friend of the labouring poor, told the 1828 Select Committee on the Game Laws that 'not the slightest disgrace attached to poaching among the lower classes', while Henry Hunt, perhaps a less reliable witness, said 'I have no hesitation in stating that the poacher did not consider himself guilty of any moral crime, nor did his fellow parishioners'.[29] Nearly a hundred years later, J. A. Wilson, a respectable trade unionist, wrote of his father's poaching, 'the law of the land could lay no charge against him except . . . poaching [which pure ethics cannot condemn]'.[30] Even Arch's stern Primitive Methodist puritanism defended poaching, marking it off as totally different from all other crimes.

> I have worked, and would work, with a man who has been convicted of knocking over a hare or a rabbit, but I should not go to work with a man who had taken a hen off a roost. If the poacher was a good workman, it would be all right in my eyes and the eyes of the other labourers; but let a man who had stolen a hen off a roost be ever such a good workman, I should have nothing to do with him . . . because he would be a felon. What is more; if I saw any man steal six-pennyworth from an employer of mine, I should at once report that man.[31]

'Billa' Dixon, formerly landlord of the Trunch 'Crown' in Norfolk, talked about the conspiracy of silence which defended poachers.

> They wouldn't give nobody away. People wouldn't, oh no. They wouldn't give nobody away. *You* didn't give nobody away not if you knew. We knew one time a bloke come up into the pub . . . and he had a little sack tied up under his arm . . . Well Sunday a chap went to feed his bullocks, he see feathers lay every where. Well he told his boss, so the police come down on Monday morning . . . they wanted to know if we see anybody but nobody wouldn't give nobody away. I knew and one or two more knew, they say "That was old Wacky Hardman got them right enough" . . . but you wouldn't give nobody away, not in

> them sort of little things, he hadn't murdered anybody, and you kept quiet and let them get away with it.[32]

'The book of nature' that Mr Leycester's poacher read was a powerful force in popular belief. Hares and especially rabbits were obviously, in some sense, wild. Nobody bred them any more for food or for sport, indeed by the 1830s they were already on the way to becoming a major pest to all members of the agricultural community except the landlord. In that case the double notion that they were somehow 'different' from the other 'gifts' of nature and that a man or woman could be sent to prison for killing them was especially galling as well as irrational to the poor. There was also a harsh economic reality. With a countryside in some areas teeming with game it was a foolish man who saw his family starve. As James Hawker, whose memoirs are a remarkable account of a Victorian poacher, says 'Poverty is the mother of invention; poverty made me poach.'[33] Added to custom and the confusion of the law these feelings created a notion of rights which, especially in the hard years of the 1820s–1850s, seems increasingly to have defined game as one of the lost birth rights of Englishmen and the poor in particular. Even after the Law Lords had decided the question once and for all in legal terms in 1865 these ideas persisted in and out of court. In the diary of an Oxfordshire relieving officer we find his comments on the game laws in the 1870s.

> Hares and rabbitts [*sic*] are wild animals and know no bounds in their settlement. This young man is gone to prison for three weeks with hard labour because he exercised a right which every man undoubtedly has . . . that of killing wild animals in his native land.[34]

What figures we have for convictions under the game laws bear out this view. Far from the Acts of 1838 and 1831 stopping poaching it increased. As a direct result of this failure the Poaching Prevention Act of 1862 extended to the police the role of gamekeeper. The debates on the Bill in both the Commons and the Lords make it clear the august members of both Houses realized that 'the poor' simply did not accept their definitions of law. As Lord Henley said, 'In the minds of the common people there was a great distinction between game and other kinds of property.'[35] Mr Hunt said that 'if another winter were allowed to pass by without any steps being taken to guard against the(se) evils' then murder and further increases in poaching would inevitably result.[36]

The 1862 Act was probably one of the least popular pieces of legislation of the mid-nineteenth century. In it we see clearly the other side of the policy of paternalism. By giving powers to the police to stop and search anyone they thought had been on enclosed ground in search of game it extended the hatred and contempt in which gamekeepers were held by the local community, to the local police forces. This feeling continued even into the early years of the twentieth century as 'Billa' Dixon said

> Course the police were so much against the population then. In them days . . . the police was sort of a bit of an enemy, you put him down. Them days he used what he could against you whether that was a fair deal or not.[37]

Ten years after the passing of the Act at least two Chief Constables, those of Norfolk and Derbyshire, who gave evidence to the 1872 Select Committee, felt that it was setting the poor against the police and hampering their real work.[38] These kinds of feelings led, in 1876, to rioting in the village of Blockley in Worcestershire. Richard Boswell Belcher, a respectable Baptist tradesman who was involved in the case, left an account of the riots and the problems which lead to them.

> A Police-sergeant 'Drury' began to distinguish himself by extraordinary activity in summonsing and arresting by warrant an unusual number of men. At the same time a very busy Gamekeeper, under Lord Redesdale, prosecuted various innocent men for poaching, traps being laid for them . . . With these tyrannical doings of policeman and Keeper our men were driven to exasperation and they vowed vengeance. The keeper kept out of the way but the policeman's doings became more unbearable than ever and an awful riot ensured.(*sic*)[39]

In the 'riot' Drury was chased to his house by a group of ten men who broke all the windows, dragged him into the street, beat him up and threw him into the stream. Only the intervention of other villagers prevented, according to an eyewitness who gave an account in the 1930s, the murder of the policeman. Five men were arrested and four got eighteen months in gaol. On their return they were, according to the same account, welcomed home as heroes. 'They closed the mill . . . and all the women wi' tin cans and pots and pans and trays went down the station to meet 'em and drummed 'em into the village.'[40]

Events like the 'Blockley Riot' and the battles between poachers and keepers were presented, represented and legitimized in the popular songs of the poor. In 'William Taylor' the hero is a young man who turns and fights a group of keepers and kills one of them. When challenged to save his own life by betraying his friends he replies, like all 'real' heroes in his situation,

> 'Oh no says young Taylor that won't do at all,
> For now that you've got me I'll die for them all.'[41]

The last verse of the song ends with the praise of the Taylor and defiance of the keepers,

> There's none like young Taylor nor never was yet
> Theres' none like young Taylor, you keepers all know,
> That fought in yon coveys some winters ago.

In 'Rufford Park', a Lincolnshire ballad, not only are the poachers, who are also murderers like Taylor, justified by the old appeal to Biblical law but they are also urged to 'keep you gallant lark'. In 'Thorneymore Woods', a song from the East Midlands, a poacher having been betrayed but 'got off' vows revenge on the keeper who betrayed him and shot his 'mate'. He ends his song,

> Now the bucks and hares shall never go free,
> A poaching life is the life for me,
> A poacher I will always be, until the day I die.[42]

Outside the ballads, the poacher also becomes a hero in popular culture. In John Walker's famous melodrama *The Factory Lad*, Will Ruston, 'an outcast', is the instrument of just and final revenge on the tyrannous factory owner. At one point Rushton delivers, with suitable melodramatic flourish, the classic defence of the poacher.[43]

> The Game Laws, eh? As if a poor man hadn't as much right to the bird that flies and the hare that runs as the rich tyrants

> who want all, and gripe and grapple all too? I care not for their laws. While I have my liberty, or power, or strength, I will live as well as the best of 'em.[43]

However, after the 1862 Act subtle changes took place in the attitude of both the poor and the elite. Whilst the main legitimation of poaching continued to take the form of appeal to rights derived from custom a new strand entered the argument, that of political radicalism. This was apparent in the debates on the 1862 Act when Cunningham, the radical member for Brighton, told the Commons to a mounting barrage of interruption,

> . . . they would not succeed in silencing him. They represented the monopolists of the country, they were representatives of the [dusty?] acres . . . The supporters of this game preserving bill would have to answer to the people . . . At a time when the people of this country were famishing for want of bread he thought that a parliament which reverted to the feudal and antiquated notions about the game laws had better return as soon as possible to the constituencies.[44]

Cunningham's arguments had been present since the foundation of the Anti-Game Law League in the 1840s[45] but were given new impetus after the Act of 1862 by growing radical and popular feeling against the police, who it was argued were public servants, enforcing what many saw as a class monopoly of an illegitimate kind. It was this that lay behind the inclusion of the abolition of the game laws in the 'objects' of Arch's National Agricultural Labourers' Union, a widespread campaign which embraced organizations like the National Secular Society as well as local radical associations and clubs.[46]

Gradually, this essentially 'modern' and political argument seems to have found more and more support among the poor themselves. The reasons are fairly straightforward. In all but marginal areas the customal framework was finally crumbling. Although elements remained, especially in labour practices, the foundations had gone with the general enclosure and with the rationalization of agriculture and the associated changes which we have already discussed. However the *ideas* of the old customary framework did not vanish totally, indeed in some areas they continued to be strong. More usually they co-existed with newer radical ideas often running into them. We see this in two remarkable late nineteenth century autobiographies, those of 'The King of the Norfolk Poachers' and James Hawker. Both these writers, especially Hawker, legitimized their poaching by appeal to 'lost rights' and criticism of class monopoly, bringing together both the 'old' arguments and the new. Both also firmly linked poaching to a wider range of customary activities, especially those associated with commons. Hawker makes the links clearly.

> We had no voice in making the Game Laws. If we Had I would Submit to the majority for I am a constitutionalist. But I am not going to be a serf. They not only stole the land from the People but they stocked it with Game for Sport, Employed Policemen to look after it, neglected their Duty in Looking after Private Property . . . And we the Toilers have to Pay the Piper . . . I have poached more for revenge than gain. Because the Class poached upon my liberty when I was not able to defend myself. [As original][47]

'The King of the Norfolk Poachers' was less politically sophisticated than Hawker, although he supported Arch, and right at the end of his book returns to the 'old' justification of 'right'.

> There is one thing I should like to say and that is that I never raided a hen Roost with all the bad deeds that I have done, I have always had the Idea that game was as much mine as any one elses. Did not God say that he gave all the Beasts and Birds for the use of Man, not the rich alone, and the Green herbs for the Healing of the Nation. [As original][48]

In some ways the Ground Game Act of 1880 confirmed the new view. This gave the ownership of hares and rabbits not to the landlord but to the tenant and did away with one of the reformers' main grievances as well as an area of real conflict between landlord and tenant, although this remained a problem, as we shall see later.[49] It also made it a lot more difficult to prosecute anybody for poaching ground game since 'ownership' was more diffuse and shooting rights, even over a very small area of land, was usually adequate defence. In the end the gradually rising standard of living among the rural poor combined with an increasing respectability probably did more to change attitudes than all the acts of parliament. By 1889 the Chief Constable of Lincolnshire could write: 'There is a considerable decrease under the Game Acts, and poaching appears this winter to have been little practised, not only in Lindsey, but throughout the County.'[50] Significantly the autobiographies of Arch, written in 1898, of Hawker, written 1904–5, and 'The King of the Norfolk Poachers', written in the late 1920s, all talk about poaching as either declining or finished and their impressions are borne out by what figures there are.

Through looking at the Game Laws and the different positions taken in relation to them we have seen how 'crime' could take on different meanings to different groups. However, this was not true of all crime, nor were the game laws the only areas where the law was broken. In the first case clearly many acts of anti-social or criminal behaviour were condemned by all in rural society. 'Billa' Dixon's remark that 'he hadn't killed nobody' points to areas where usually consensus was achieved. The line was difficult to draw though and class often had a lot to do with it. Both Arch and the 'King of the Norfolk Poachers' said they would condemn those who robbed hen roosts, classically the cottagers' 'beast shed', but it is very clear that many, if not most small-scale thefts were by the poor from the poor.

Probably the most common crimes in the rural areas, along with offences against the game laws, were drunkenness and casual violence, in fact the two frequently went together and presented a constant threat to order. Those involved were usually young, though some were 'rough' elements who rejected any attempt at integration within the framework of village society. George Swinford writes with unconscious irony of this world.

> Of course there was plenty going on in Filkins besides work. For one thing there was fighting. Every village had what was called a best man at fighting, and some times the best man in one village was expected to take on the best man in another village . . . When we met boys from other villages there was often a fight . . . There is not much fighting these days or quarrelling between the villages as there was years ago.[51]

This sentiment was echoed precisely by 'Billa'Dixon.

> I didn't take no notice of fighting years ago, you never took no notice. Yet later years . . . [if] two of them got wrong you'd nearly be frightened out of your life about it. But in them days, if two of

> them got wrong, the pub would go out, nearly the whole of the pub would go out, and stand round in a ring, and see them fight it out, but latter years that faded out.[52]

'Billa' Dixon's memories point to another important area, the close association believed by contemporaries to exist between any kind of uncontrolled popular recreation and public disorder. We saw in Chapter 3 how the new paternalism of Church and elite sought to mould aspects of popular behaviour. However, this was not always as straightforward as these groups hoped. Even something so closely linked both to controlled recreation and representations of paternal harmony as fox hunting had to be carefully watched, as a letter written by his agent to Lord Spencer concerning a Hunt Kennel Supper in 1862 shows.

> I have ordered roast beef and plum pudding, 3 pints of ale per man and a bowl of punch after supper to drink your Lordships health. I have desired Mrs. Gage to mix the ale with bitter beer, and not to make the punch too strong and to take care that the quantity I have ordered is not exceeded.[53]

Outside these rituals of paternalism, disorder seems to have been endemic in popular recreations. This was especially so where a 'traditional' feast or celebration survived. The Forest Fair held in Wychwood Forest in Oxfordshire every September until the late 1850s was invariably marked by widespread drunkenness and violence. In 1852 excursion trains of the Oxford, Worcester and Wolverhampton Railways (the Old Worse and Worse as it was known locally) alone brought 2,000 people to Charlbury from where they walked to Newhill Plain in the middle of the forest.[54] Here, well outside the control of law, squire and parson, old scores were settled, and illegal prize fighting continued, as the memories of Ambrose Preston testify.

> A lot of fighting went on here too. Preston remembers Will'm Busby, a bakers son of Minster Lovell, quarrelled with Crow Lockett (in fact Luckett, a well known prize fighter) . . . at skittles over a matter of twopence . . . So Crow put up 5L for the fight. Will'ms friends tried to stop him from fighting . . . When they started Crow tried to 'stand off from him and pick him about' but Busby 'went straight for him every time' and being a 'cruel powerful man cut Crow all to pieces.' [As original][55]

Hiring fairs in the north of England, as we saw in Chapter 2, were the special arena of youth, and therefore particularly prone to disorder, even if then, as now, the elite were inclined to exaggerate the scale of the problem. Nevertheless it was real enough on occasion. On successive years in the 1860s and 1870s hirings in the East Riding were seriously disturbed when rioting broke out after fighting started between plough-boys and the police. At Bridlington in 1875,

> a great disturbance took place . . . between police and the farm servants. During the afternoon a young man who was drunk made a disturbance. He was taken to the police-station, when several of his 'mates' set on the policemen and kicked and knocked them about . . . There were only a few policemen in the town, and they were quite unable to repress the rioters, who for a long time had it their own way.[56]

Even the innocuous 'club day', the annual dinner and parade of the village friendly societies, which we looked at in Chapter 3, could present problems. At Leafield in Oxfordshire at Whitsun 1875, 'the morning passed off very well, but long before evening set in the extra policeman's services were much needed.'[57] Nor were those sports organized by the gentry free from threat. At Abingdon in Berkshire in 1882 a sports meeting, even though it was a temperance affair, erupted into violence when 'soon after the commencement of the proceedings several disgraceful fights occurred which at one time threatened to seriously prejudice the success of the sports.'[58]

However, even in the 1850s, many of these 'traditional' feast days and holidays were under attack from reformers both within the elite and within the poor themselves. As far as the elite were concerned their reforms were often a part of the battle to establish a new paternalist order. In this they began to take their support away from 'rough' amusements and transfer it to more 'rational' forms, especially fete and sports days where no alcohol was served. This was crucial since most traditional customs relied on gentry support for money and often the site of a fair or feast. In Oxfordshire the support of the Dukes of Marlborough had been vital to the Whitsun/spring festivities. The Dukes allowed their land to be used, gave the tree for the Maypole, the material for the 'Bower' (a construction of tarpaulin and wood which served as a dance hall and bar), as well as generous contributions to the common fund. By the end of the 1850s this support, like their support for the traditional, violent and drunken, 'Whit-Hunt', had been transferred to the local friendly societies club-day, a much more decorous, though still 'boozy', celebration. By the 1880s even this had become too much and Whitsun was marked, within the Marlborough domains, by an athletic sports day and temperance fete.[59]

Among the poor and 'middling sort' there was a growing tide of opinion which saw traditional sports and their associated drunkenness as insulting. Thomas Wright, who wrote under the name 'A Journeyman Engineer', divided the working class into the mass of about 90 per cent who drank and were therefore subservient to their masters and unable to think for themselves and the top 10 per cent who were sober trades unionists and political radicals.[60] To Lloyd Jones, an ex-Chartist, looking at the country districts from London in the early 1870s the farm labourer was also a victim of this and worse, 'the squire is his King, the parson his deity and the tap-room his highest conception of earthly bliss',[61] However, even within the country districts things were changing. The generation of labourers who led 'the Revolt of the Field' were, as we shall see in Chapter 7, often temperance reformers who like Lloyd Jones and Thomas Wright made the connection between drink, festivity and control, especially when these were in the hands of the elite. Finally, the 'nationalization' of British culture after the 1890s–1900s brought new sports and interests to the rural poor, as we shall see below, which rendered the 'traditional' simply 'old-fashioned'. Morris dancing, rush bearing and any number of traditional ceremonies and celebrations may have been beaten down by the elite's wish to control and structure the recreations of the poor; however, their ultimate demise usually came as a result of the neglect of those who, in earlier generations, had loved and nurtured them.

Nevertheless, much popular culture remained impervious to such assaults, adaptable enough to survive, or simply out of sight. The public house, for example, remained probably the most important site of plebeian leisure and culture throughout the nineteenth century. Further, the public house was increasingly a class institution outside the gaze of the respectable. As Peter Clarke has shown, from the early years of the nineteenth century, the elite gradually abandoned the public houses, leaving them, as Sir Nicholas Conant wrote, 'to the poor more than the rich and laborious persons more than any other description'.[62]

Even so, despite fifty years of attack, there were still more 'on-licences' in England in 1900 than in 1800 and the vast majority of these were beer shops or former beer shops which were exclusively the domain of the poor. Here, virtually unseen to the elite, flourished a dense and occasionally subversive culture, 'where folk might carouse and dance, gossip and enjoy themselves as best they could'.[63] Here also the village friendly society, pig club, or, later on, trade union branch could meet in self-activity kept from the elite by their own ideal of respectability. Nor was it an exclusively male culture. Tess seeks her mother out in a beer shop in *Tess of the d'Urbervilles*[64], and especially on Friday and Saturday nights respectable women of all ages went into rural public houses and beer shops.

Beneath the surface of order, and in many areas not far beneath the surface, there was always real or potential disruption. However, the social order of the complex and differentiated society that we have looked at in the last five chapters was remarkably resilient. There were problems, and the historians' aggregation of endless local disturbances can make them appear large. Certainly the effects of one of these breakdowns of the veneer of order, like the Blockley Riots, on a village must have seemed profound. Yet we should beware. These disorders never 'came together' and in some very fundamental way could not be generalized any more than the local harvest strike, reliant on local wages, hours and conditions could be turned 'national'.

Against the forces of disruption were ranged a formidable army. The New Poor Law, the County Police, and the Game Laws were the visible tips of icebergs made up of endless petty tyrannies which every village experienced in the forms of blacklisting, eviction or refusal of support or charity. Yet they were not all, nor were they enough – alongside the stick was the carrot. Changes in the attitudes of the rural elites and especially the growing social conscience of the Church made the manipulation of charity a key element in the re-creation of a deferential social order. And that order was maintained, indeed seemed to be growing more stable as the years of agricultural prosperity continued. By the 1860s even the labourer was beginning to feel some benefits with a real, if slight, increase in wages. But a chill wind was blowing from the west which was to cause a crisis within this social system which all its deference could not control. Harvest 1875 was wet and stormy. Five more were to follow which were, if anything, worse. More serious, though unremarked initially, were the first major arrivals of American wheat on the English market. The golden age was over.

NOTES

1 *EWP*, 9th December 1899.
2 John Masefield, *The Everlasting Mercy*, [London, 1912], p. 28.
3 John Archer, '"A Fiendish Outrage?": A Study of Animal Maiming in East Anglia: 1830–1870', *AHR* Vol. 33, Pt. II, p. 151.
4 *PP 1868–69, X*, 'Report from the Select Committee on Inclosure Act', p. 46.
5 *PP 1878–79, VII*, '2nd. Report from the Select Committee on Commons', p. 68.
6 For all this see Alun Howkins and Raphael Samuel, 'The Fight for the Headington Magdelens', unpublished paper, 1971. The quotations are from *OT*, 12th August 1871 and *JOJ*, 2nd September 1871.
7 Clive Emsley, *Crime and Society in England, 1750–1900*, [London, 1987], p. 27.
8 *JOJ*, 26th January 1861.
9 ibid., 11th March 1895.
10 John Kibble, *Historical and Other Notes on Wychwood Forest and Many of its Border Places*, [Charlbury, 1928], p. 52.
11 P. B. Munsche, *Gentlemen and Poachers. The English Game Laws 1671–1831*, [Cambridge, 1981], Ch. 4.
12 Douglas Hay, 'Property, Authority and the Criminal Law' in D. Hay, *et al.* (eds) *Albion's Fatal Tree. Crime and Society in Eighteenth Century England*, [London, 1975], p. 63.
13 Munsche, op. cit., Chs 4 & 6.
14 ibid., Ch. 6; see also Alun Howkins, 'Economic Crime and Class Law: Poaching and the Game Laws 1830–1880', in S. Burman and B. Harrell Bond (eds) *The Imposition of Law*, [New York, 1979], p. 276.
15 25 & 26 Vic. c.114.
16 Chester Kirby, 'English Game Law Reform' in *Essays in Modern English History in Honour of William Cortez Abbot*, [Cambridge, Mass., 1941].
17 *Hansard*, 6th May 1828.
18 ibid., 11th May 1827.
19 ibid..
20 ibid., 6th April 1829.

21 William Blackstone, *Commentaries on the Laws of England. A Facsimile of the First Edition of 1765–69 . . .* , 4 Vols. [Chicago, 1979] Vol. 2, p. 411.
22 Genesis 9 v.II.
23 Thomas Bewick, *A Memoir of Thomas Bewick*, [Oxford, 1975 ed.] p. 25.
24 *PP 1828, VIII*, 'Select Committee of the House of Lords on the Game Laws', p. 423.
25 *OC*, 3rd March 1852.
26 Communicated to the author by Raphael Samuel, from *Old Oak*, p. 21.
27 Interview AJH/Jack Leeder, op. cit.
28 *PP 1872, X*, 'Select Committee of the House of Commons on the Amendment of the Game Laws', p. 274.
29 *PP 1828, VIII*, op. cit., p. 372 and p. 382.
30 J. A. Wilson, *Memoirs of a Labour Leader*, [London, 1910], p. 25.
31 Joseph Arch, *From Ploughtail to Parliament. An Autobiography*, ed. Alun Howkins [London, 1986], p. 163.
32 Interview AJH/Dixon, op. cit..
33 James Hawker, *A Victorian Poacher*, ed. G. Christian [Oxford, 1961], p. 77.
34 Dew, op. cit., p. 54.
35 *Hansard*, 23rd July 1862.
36 ibid., 16th July 1862.
37 Interview AJH/Dixon, op. cit..
38 *PP 1872, X*, op. cit..
39 A. W. Exell and N. M. Marshall [eds] *Autobiography of Richard Boswell Belcher of Banbury and Blockley (1898)*, [Blockley, 1976], p. 15.
40 ibid., p. 23.
41 From the singing of George 'Pop' Maynard, Copthorne, Sussex.
42 'Thorneymore Woods' from an undated Nottingham Broadside *c.* 1860.
43 John Walker, 'The Factory Lad', *Dick's Standard Plays No. 930*, [London, 1885]. Play first performed July 1834.
44 *Hansard*, 23rd July 1862.
45 Chester Kirby, 'The Attack on the Games Laws in the 'Forties'', *Journal of Modern History*, IV [1932].
46 See Arch, op. cit., Ch. VII. On support see *National Reformer* 8th & 22nd August 1880.
47 Hawker, op. cit., p. 95.
48 'The King of the Norfolk Poachers', *I Walked by Night*, ed L. Rider Haggard [Ipswich, 1974], p. 180.
49 J. H. Porter. 'Tenant Right: Devonshire and the 1880 Ground Game Act', *AHR*, Vol. 34 pt. II [1986].
50 Quoted in Ian Beckwith, 'The Pattern of Rural Crime,

1856–1876', unpublished research paper, 1975.

51 George Swinford, *The Jubilee Boy: The Life and Recollections of George Swinford of Filkins*, ed. Judith Fay and Richard Martin [Filkins, 1987], pp. 71–2.

52 Interview AJH/Dixon, op. cit..

53 Peter Gordon (ed.), *The Red Earl. The Papers of the Fifth Earl of Spencer, 1835–1910*, 2 vols, Northampton Record Society [Northampton, 1981], Vol. I, p. 48.

54 *OC*, 22nd September 1852.

55 Bod L, MS Top Oxon d.191a, ff 174–5.

56 *ENRC*, 13th November 1875.

57 *JOJ*, 29th May 1875.

58 ibid., 3rd June 1882.

59 For this process see Alun Howkins, *Whitsun in Nineteenth Century Oxfordshire*, [Oxford, 1973].

60 Thomas Wright, *The Great Unwashed by the Journeyman Engineer*, [London, 1868].

61 *The Bee-hive. The People's Paper*, 13th January 1872.

62 Peter Clarke, *The English Alehouse. A Social History 1200–1830*, [London, 1983], p. 309.

63 ibid., p. 323.

64 Hardy, *Tess* op. cit., p. 50; see also dancing in the pub in the same book, pp. 94–7.

6

The Crisis of Rural Society: 'The Wealthy and Great'

The social system of rural England in its 'golden age' after 1850 appeared to have an unshakable character resting on forces over which those in power had total control. 'The rich man in his castle'; the large tenant farmer with his hunters and the parson in his church appeared unchangable and all powerful. Yet ultimately, power lay outside their control. The golden age rested on high wheat prices arising from urban working class demands for bread. If this was shaken then the prosperity which lay at the core of the perceived harmony of rural society was threatened. In the mid-1870s that began to happen.

In 1870 Britain imported 28,827,000 hundredweight of wheat. By 1875 this had climbed to 42,763,000 hundredweight and by 1880 to more than 44 million.[1] More significantly, in 1870 52 per cent of this wheat came from the USA and Canada whereas by 1880 this proportion had increased to about 90 per cent. This pointed in the direction of a long-term change from which British arable agriculture was not to recover until the post-Second World War era.

Initially at least, these monumental changes were concealed (if exacerbated) by a series of bad harvests. As early as 1873 the papers of John Oxley Parker, an Essex land agent, show that farms were not being let and some tenants, even reliable ones, were beginning to fail.[2] Two years later things were worse, as Oxley Parker wrote to one of his clients, 'I am very apprehensive that difficult times are in prospect' and went on that he had several farms in hand and was loath to let any good tenant go.[3]

In the five disastrous years after 1874 the depression spread from the vulnerable Essex clays to most of the arable areas of the south and east. By 1877 John Simpson Calvertt, the substantial Oxfordshire tenant farmer, wrote in his diary,

> 1877 was wet and cold, in the Spring – a short hot, Summer – very wet later Harvest – wet all through November, and rain, snow and wind last 8 or 9 days of December ... very few Apples, scarcely any Stone fruits, no acorns – but abundance of Nuts, only!!![4]

Rowland Prothero, later Lord Ernle, looked back on these years in his famous account *English Farming Past and Present*, first published in 1912.

> During the sunless uncongenial summer of 1879, with its icy rains, the series of adverse seasons culminated in one of the worst harvests of the century, in an outbreak of pleuro-pneumonia and foot and mouth disease among cattle, and among sheep a disastrous attack of liver rot ... In similar circumstances, farmers might have been compensated for the shortness of the yield by an advance in price. This was no longer the case in 1879. America, ... poured such quantities of wheat into the country as to bring down prices below the level of the favourable season of the proceeding year.[5]

Even where a harvest had been gathered the wet continued to make trouble for the farmer, as George Rope of Grove Farm in Blaxhall in Suffolk wrote in his diary at the end of 1879.

> The wettest season since 1860 and similar but not so cold ... A great deal of corn has been carted in bad condition – many stacks have been taken down because of heating – and many wheat stacks will not be fit to thresh till well up in the summer.[6]

In Oxfordshire Farmer Calvertt saw the harvest dragging on and on.

> Sept. 13th. Only cut Harvest *one* (*sic*) day this week!!! – today worse than ever – ruin to all Farmers – such a rainy Spring and Summer, has never occurred in my time ... Sales of farms all over the District ... Sept. 16th ... the worse Harvest I ever gathered – neither quality, or yield, & acres of wet heavy veins, *worthless* (*sic*)[7]

He ended his diary for 1879 with the sentence, 'So ends the most *ruinously* ugly *seasoned* year, of *this century*',[8] a sentiment echoed 200 miles east in Stowupland, Suffolk, where Thomas

Carter of Green Farm wrote in his diary, 'the year 1879 is called the black year . . . '[9]

However, the very harshness of the weather served to conceal from all but a very few the fundamental shift in wheat prices. Even the Royal Commission of 1882 was misled in this respect. As its 'final report' said, 'all the witnesses we have examined have agreed in ascribing it (the depression) mainly to a succession of unfavourable seasons.' It went on, having barely noted 'unprecedentedly larger importations, chiefly from America',[10] to conclusions which were at best ironic in view of the years to come.

> On the immediate causes of the agricultural depression it cannot be said that any one of them is necessarily of a 'permanent character'. Bad and good seasons appear to come in cycles, and with the alterations of agricultural prosperity and depression. This, the main cause of depression, no legislation can control.[11]

Within the next ten years just how 'permanent' the changes which were occurring were to be become clear.

The depression, like English agricultural society itself, was regionally specific and its effects varied. It affected most areas by the early 1890s but not with equal harshness nor at the same time. Most vulnerable to both the short-term effects of weather and the longer term effects of imported wheat were the arable areas of the south and south-east. As P. J. Perry writes these were,

> high cost systems in which high levels of investment were the basis for high returns. Such systems are particularly vulnerable to any downward turn in prices; economies in the use of fertilizers, in cultivation, in labour, tend to be quickly reflected in diminished output.[12]

The claylands of Essex came almost to symbolize the problems of the farmer on vulnerable wheat lands. When Aubrey Spencer visited the Denegie Hundred of north-east Essex for the Royal Commission on Labour in 1893 he wrote a powerful description of the area in decay.

> The heavy clay land . . . is essentially a wheat producing district . . . This part (of England) has suffered terribly by the agricultural depression – probably as much or more so than any other part of England . . . A considerable amount of land

> is altogether out of cultivation . . . A more melancholy sight from an agricultural point of view can scarcely be imagined than this part of the district presents.[13]

John Oxley Parker handled a good deal of land in this area and charted its decline in his accounts and letters. At the end of 1879 he, like Calvertt, looked back over the worst year in his memory and wrote, 'No such trying time for farmers for the last fifty years. Many farms in the hands of the owners; other paying no rent . . . '[14]

Already in 1879 Parker had recommended to many he acted for that rents should be reduced. In 1877 he wrote the kind of letter to a landlord which was to become more and more common in the next few years.

> You have an honest tenant, working the farm fairly and rightly, but unable . . . to continue to do so and to find the rent . . . He could do so by selling off, lessening stock, but an impoverished tenant would be no use to you on such a farm. I have considered that forbearance and delay were the better course and have trusted to the future to bring up the arrears.[15]

It was a dismal hope. The seasons improved a little in the early 1880s but a recurrence of bad weather in 1884–5 finally exposed the weakness of arable agriculture in many marginal areas. J. Todhunter, tenant on Manor Farm Parndon in Essex, put the worsened situation bitterly in a letter to Parker in 1886, 'the prospects of agriculture grow more hopeless day by day, and I can really see nothing for it except the poor clay lands be abandoned.'[16] By the mid-1890s that had begun to be a reality as Aubrey Spencer observed, 'I . . . saw fields once arable but which now have ceased to grow any crop but thistles . . . '[17]

Elsewhere, even in the 1880s the situation appeared much less serious. Many years ago T. W. Fletcher pointed to the continuing relative prosperity of parts of Lancashire throughout the depression, and although his optimistic views have been modified the area still remains a stark contrast to Essex.[18] The central reason for these different experiences was the urban market. Until the 1840s Lancashire agriculture was backward and inefficient. This was, according to Alistair Mutch, 'dramatically changed' by 'the spectacular growth of the urban areas of South Lancashire, and the development of communities which brought new markets within the reach of farmers'.[19] These were the 'new' and successful peasant farmers mentioned in Chapter 2. From 1840s urban growth and the spread of railways supported, even created, a system of relatively small farms based on liquid milk production. Milk was first sent to Manchester by rail in 1844; by 1893 76 per cent of its daily needs came in this way.[20]

But it was not only milk. Urban growth in Lancashire, as elsewhere, especially around London, encouraged market gardening and small-scale poultry farming whose produce was moved swiftly to town centre wholesale markets by train or simply brought in by cart and sold by the producer.[21] In south-west Lancashire in particular the production of potatoes for the urban market was vitally important. By the 1870s nearly 20 per cent of land in the Ormskirk district was under potatoes. The smallest farms specialized in 'earlies', new potatoes at high prices, while the larger units produced maincrop varieties which were often clamped and sold.[22]

This very direct relationship with the urban market which protected much of Lancashire agriculture from the worst effects of the depression at least until the 1890s could also be found elsewhere. Urban demand for milk and other diary products remained bouyant throughout the period after 1875 and in relation to liquid milk at least there was no other source but local farmers. This is reflected in the national statistics. David Taylor has written that increasingly in the period after 1860, 'milk production was the largest single sector of English agriculture and the fastest growing of the major sectors.'[23] Between 1860 and 1900 total milk consumption rose from some 600 million gallons annually to 830 million gallons, and consumption per head increased from roughly nine gallons a year to 15 in the same period with the greatest increase in the 1870s.[24] These figures found precise reflection in the growth of an urban oriented, liquid milk industry encouraged by the railways. Along the Great Western's line in Wiltshire, Dorset and Gloucester farmers turned to milk production for the London market while the Midland Railway's line to Derbyshire provided a route in that direction. As Druce's report on Derbyshire in 1881 says, milk was sent to 'London, Manchester, Sheffield, Birmingham, and other large towns. Some milk from Derbyshire I was told, went even to Newcastle-on-Tyne, and some to Hull.'[25] Just as Lancashire produced for the cotton towns, regional economies of milk supply developed elsewhere, for example in Wensleydale, the economy of which was transformed by the opening of the railway.[26]

If the production of milk for urban centres provided protection against the worst of the depression in some rural areas, different regional variations protected others. Kent, for instance, along with parts of East Sussex and Herefordshire and the Vale of Evesham, relied on fruit and hops which, like liquid milk, were both areas of real growth throughout the depression. 'A large, and in some parts rapidly increasing quantity of land in the Southern Counties is devoted to the growth of fruit' it was written in 1881, which led the author to think Kent had a 'hopeful future'. In West Kent, he continued, 'large quantities of Strawberries and Raspberries are grown on land which a few years ago was poor woodland.'[27] Hops were equally successful. Although beer consumption *per capita* began to decline in the 1870s it was many years before this was seriously to be felt in the hop fields of Kent, Sussex, Surrey and Hampshire which produced 86 per cent of the nations crop in the late 1870s.[28]

However, it was not only crops which could make a difference. Urban life which operated to support fruit, dairy and vegetable production on a large scale in some places, supported much smaller production almost everywhere where there was a concentration of non-rural workers on some variety of industrial trade. In Co. Durham for instance small farmers were able to resist the problems of the depression,

> because they have freedom to sell their hay to the collieries, they have good markets for their dairy products, and they have the opportunity of getting manure very reasonably, almost for the expense of moving it from those colliery villages.[29]

The farm books of North Masons Farm, Dinnington, Northumberland, show similar strategies at work on a small farm in the early 1890s. Pit ashes provided them with manure and every year the farm's two hinds went back and forward to Dinnington Pit carting ashes. In 'return' the colliery company bought turnips for feed and hay for the pit ponies, while the colliers bought potatoes.[30] A similar situation developed in parts of East Sussex where use of common land and waste coupled with demand from London enabled the smallholders of the area to survive and even expand by chicken cramming.

Cramming was at its most basic simply forced feeding of fowl to bring then up to 'dinner' size more quickly.[31] The depression acted in two main ways on the cramming industry. Firstly, as elsewhere, it stimulated innovation. As Henry Rew put it in 1895, many were 'bound to find something beyond corn and stock to make . . . farming pay in these times'.[32] Secondly, by reducing the cost of corn, the major food input, it made the whole business financially more viable. Again the railways were vitally important. New stations at Ticehurst (mid-1850s), Uckfield (1868) and especially Heathfield (1880) enabled birds to be moved quickly to London. By the mid-1880s the London Brighton and South Coast Railway added a special van to passenger trains three time a week from Heathfield and between 1885 and 1900 the value of poultry sent from this station increased from about £60,000 a year to over £150,000.[33]

At the other end of the farming scale very large enterprises were often protected from the worst effects of the depression simply because their overall profit margins could bear the losses caused by imports and bad seasons. Evidence here is more difficult to come by since the two great reports on agriculture of the early 1880s and early 1890s sought, at one level, to prove to government that there was a depression. What there is tends to be negative. John Simpson Calvertt for example cried 'rain and ruin' through his dairy and did cut the scale of his farming operations but in many respects, particularly his own lifestyle, seems to have been remarkably untouched by this agricultural disaster. For instance in 1894, when he moved to a slightly smaller farm to allow his son on to his previous tenancy, he ended his yearly account with the words, 'a further ruinous year, for Agriculture' yet he had continued to hunt, to visit London, Coventry, Oxford (frequently) and Ascot as well as shooting and entertaining.[34]

On the good wheatlands of Norfolk the impact of the depression was also not as serious as many believed. In many parts of the county, especially in the north-west, the large size of the farms protected the county as did the good lands in the east. As Mr Druce said in 1881, 'the external indications of agricultural depression in those parts of this county that I visited were not so apparent as in other parts of my district.'[35] At about the same time the Rev. Benjamin Armstrong commented from his Norfolk vicarage on the continuing prosperity of the 'Prince Farmers', 'surrounded by every luxury and the beau ideal . . . such as Norfolk produces'.[36] R. H.. Mottram, looking back in the 1940s at the Norfolk town of North Walsham in the 1890s, wrote, 'whatever farmers may say they can go on living on their farms, not only when they are not making their fortunes, as their great grandfathers did, but when they are sustaining losses that would bring any other kind of business to a standstill.'[37] Other areas were protected by similar economies of scale, Mr Coleman wrote of the large farms of north Northumberland, 'I do not consider the depression so serious or deep seated as that which prevails in the midland or southern district . . . '[38]

Yet we should beware going too far down this road especially if we look at the whole period from the late 1870s through to the 1900s. Initially many areas did weather the depression so that when the Richmond Commission inspected them in the 1880s things were not that bad. By the 1890s a further ten years had wreaked havoc. What Wilson Fox said in 1895 of Lincolnshire could without much alteration have been applied over and over again.

> Generally speaking, it may be said, that owing in the first place to bad seasons, commencing in 1874, and then to the rapid and continuous fall in prices commencing in 1882 and 1883 coming at a time when there had been great losses, through decreased yields and sheep rot, and also when the land was much deteriorated, the farming industry has suffered blow after blow, until the present time when the situation is extremely critical, and the future outlook of the gloomiest character.[39]

This was at the other extreme to Calvertt and the great 'wheat barons' where many thousands of less well-to-do farmers clearly did go to the wall. Essex has already been noted as an area of extreme depression and in terms of unlet farms and land 'going back' this was certainly true. As E. J. T. Collins has written of southern Essex,

> Thomas Whitmore (the local landowner) is once said to have stood on the tower of Rettenden Church and looked southward over 22,000 acres of vacant land returning to its wild state. A few years later his son rode from Orsett Hall to Chelmsford and saw not a single field of wheat.[40]

The local effects of bankruptcy could be, and often were traumatic, but actual failure was only one of a number of results which were possible – what is of concern here is other changes which could be made.

There were changes which could be made within (loosely at least) the existing methods of farming. The most common of these was simply to let standards drop – farm dirty. This was probably most obvious in those areas which weathered the depression reasonably well since elsewhere more dramatic measures were needed, although it was a frequent resort in all areas in the years up to 1881–2. In Norfolk in 1881 after seven bad years Mr Druce said the land 'remains fouler that it was prior to 1874'. Where farms were unlet and in the owners' hands they 'are for the most part cultivated, though not well cultivated.'[41] Twelve years later things had become worse even in this good wheat area. As Henry Rew observed, 'I think the balance of testimony indicates that as regards cleanliness certainly and as regards condition probably, there has been some deterioration in the past few years.'[42]

Elsewhere conditions were no better. Tidy hedgerows, weed-free cereals and straight, even planted lines of turnips or mangolds vanished as costs, primarily of labour, were cut. From the Yorkshire Wolds even in 1881 it was reported that 'those well acquainted with the district (said) that farming had gone back very much of late years.'[43] In 1892 when Wilson Fox visited Northumberland he was told by Mr George Rea of Middleton, 'There is a lot of dirty land all over the country. At present prices farmers have to economise in every way . . . '[44] Even in the pastoral areas there were signs of change. From Bromyard in Herefordshire it was reported in 1892, 'land is being put down to grass or allowed to run down',[45] while in prosperous Lancashire a land agent from Preston said, 'the land is not so tidy or well farmed.'[46]

When the corners had been cut, another, and much more important change occurred in the move away from the production of cereals. The total area under cereals on the eve of the depression was 9,431,000 acres. By 1898, when the worst of the depression began to lift, this had fallen to 7,401,000, a decrease of about 22 per cent. Of course this did not mean that all this land went out of cultivation or that it was simply laid down to grass although permanent pasture did increase by about 19 per cent in the same period.[47] What it did mean was that the system of agriculture which had been based on the production of cereals, and in which cereals produced high profits was changing and was going to have to change still further.

Less obvious, although locally at least as significant, were the almost endless changes to a more complex alternative husbandry. Many of these built on existing demand or agricultural structure. This would be true for example of the Lancashire vegetable and dairying industries where the depression gave an impetus to expand already existing agricultural practice. Growing urban demand for a diversified diet and the marginally increased spending power to go with it led also to new departures. Most significant here, in crop terms at least, was fruit and vegetable production. Nationally the figures are difficult to obtain since the categories conceal vegetable production and figures for small fruit were not collected before 1888; however, we can see some increases. The area under orchards increased from 155,000 acres in 1875 to 226,000 in 1898 and continued to rise until the Great War. The area under small fruit shows a still more dramatic change, increasing from 37,000 acres in 1888 to 72,000 acres ten years later.[48]

Mapping these figures locally is an endless task but they were regionally very significant and in the long term substantially altered the farming map. Lincolnshire, for instance, now a major vegetable growing area, emerged as such during the depression. In 1895 Wilson Fox reported on the Spalding area which was clearly very prosperous.

> In the neighbourhood of Spalding I made a somewhat exhaustive enquiry among some of the market gardeners. A great variety of vegetables, fruit and flowers are grown for the northern and London markets. The following produce is raised in this district: early potatoes, early cabbages, horse radish, carrots, celery, rhubarb, asparagus, turnips, mangold and mustard seed, beans, peas, black and red currants, gooseberries, apples, pears, plums, greengages, cherries, bulbs, chiefly narcissus, daffodils, lilies, crocuses and snowdrops, also violets. Strawberries are also grown at Long Sutton, this industry having been started by some Kent growers.[49]

Similar if less dramatic changes were happening elsewhere all over East Anglia where 'marginal' wheat lands were turned over to fruit and vegetable production. In the Maldon and Tiptree districts of Essex fruit production was stimulated both by urban demand and more directly by the opening of jam factories at Tiptree and Tolleshunt Knights.[50] Similarly in Cambridgeshire the opening in 1873 of Chivers jam factory at Histon did a great deal to enable and encourage the switch from cereal to soft fruit production in that area. In addition Chivers owned and farmed about 3,000 acres mostly under fruit by 1900. In the nearby Wisbech district fruit growing appeared in the mid-1880s and was followed by flower growing in the early 1890s. Rider Haggard argued in 1902, this had saved the area as had Chivers in Histon.

> So far . . . trade in fruit and flowers has added greatly to the prosperity of the district. Orchards with dwellings on them had sprung up all round the town, between 100 and 200 houses having been built in Wisbech itself during the previous three or four years. Also the population had increased considerably.[51]

As well as changes within the arable sector there was, as we have already seen, an overall shift to dairying and changes within the pastoral sector. Within this move there was a long-term shift away from cheese and butter production and into liquid milk. By 1900 it has been estimated that English farmhouse cheese production had fallen by as much as two-thirds in less than forty years as imported cheeses, especially North American and Danish, undercut the native product in price.[52] More important was the shift to liquid milk production across the agricultural sector as a whole. Firstly there was continued development within established dairying areas, secondly a shift within mixed farming units to more emphasis on livestock, and finally a move within traditional arable areas towards dairy, and especially liquid milk, production. By the end of the century liquid milk production had appeared in Norfolk, Cambridgeshire, Lincolnshire and especially Essex, all previously overwhelmingly arable areas.[53]

The effects of these essentially economic changes on the social history of rural England were enormous and complex, direct and indirect. For the farmers, for instance, falling profits were the most obvious and immediate result of the fall in wheat prices yet that fall has to be seen within a social and cultural context. As Lord Ernle wrote in 1912 of the years after 1879: 'to a generation familiar with years of prosperity which had enabled English farmers to extract more from the soil than any of their foreign rivals, the changed conditions were unintelligible.'[54] Farming prosperity had created a rural middle strata of wealth and power in the great tenant farmers. Benjamin Armstrong's 'farmer princes' or men like John Simpson Calvertt or the 'sheep barons' of Sussex dressing for dinner every night created and supported but in turn were created and supported by a whole culture. Separated from this culture to some extent, though intersecting with it, was the 'country house' culture of the landowning gentry and aristocracy. This, based on high rents, in the end rested on the same farming prosperity.

In the first instance it was this culture that the depression attacked. In A. G. Street's novel, *The Gentlemen of the Party*, based on family memories of the years after 1872, we see a wealthy sheep/corn farmer confronting depression and unable to comprehend that his day was gone. 'Sell his hunters? Not he! Why, that would mean that every damn fool in the neighbourhood would know that he was in queer street.'[55] As we have seen, Calvertt kept hunting right through the depression and in many ways his lifestyle was very little affected. However, many did have to alter their standards for the simple reason that farming, especially in the arable areas, could no longer support luxury. In 1881 John Coleman already saw signs of the change when he commented that the lifestyle of the Yorkshire Wold farmers was already changing, adding 'it must be admitted that during the years of plenty Wold farmers became more expensive in their habits and did not save money as much as they might . . . '[56] Similar reports came from Lincolnshire ten years later.

> Those who lived too extravagantly, who did not pay sufficient attention to business, or who were not sufficiently masters of their calling, have since 1874 disappeared, the harder times proving too much for men who were not prepared to put forward all their skill and energy and exercise rigorous economy.[57]

Although we must beware of exaggeration it seems that, in many areas of England at least, the need for 'rigorous economy' severely damaged the 'gentleman farmer'. In Street's novel of Wiltshire the gentleman farmer Martin, whose status and power was based on wheat, is replaced by a West Country 'cow-keeper' who puts the land to grass, negotiates reduced rents and gets the outraged, but helpless landlord to build him cow-sheds.[58] These changes were duplicated spectacularly in the 'real' world of Essex, although the pattern seen there, albeit on a smaller scale, was repeated over many parts of midland and eastern England in the next few years.[59] In Essex the disruption, especially in the north-east of the county, took on a peculiarly acute form. On the heavy clay lands, which as we saw were particularly badly hit, landlord and agents were by 1880–81 finding it impossible to keep or get tenants. The central reason was of course the fall in wheat prices but, and this is crucial as it was to Street, it was how the fall in prices was dealt with. In Street's novel Martin dies rather than sell his hunters, and the response of some Essex farmers seems to have been the same. It was a cultural response which conditioned men to think that they could live like gentry on 200 acres of wheat and, when prices fell, they seem to have abandoned farming rather than drop their standard of living significantly.

Those who replaced them, or who survived by adaptation, were a different breed. E. Lorraine Smith's study of Essex carried out in the 1930s points to these differences even if a little politely.

> The difference which the immigrant farmers noticed between themselves and the native farmers was in the manual labour which they expended on their farms. They were 'working farmers', while the natives were 'collar-and-tie farmers' . . . The native farmers in the period of depression . . . made a sharp distinction between the duties and responsibility of management and the manual work . . . and the time which was not necessary for managerial duties was occupied by leisurely and gentlemanly pursuits.[60]

A Devon migrant to Oxfordshire put it slightly more bluntly when he described the 'native' farmers as 'driving about in carriages and pairs, hunting three times a week, card parties and top hats, and cigars'.[61] Nearly 80 years on, the son of a Scots migrant to Essex was able to talk of the differences between his father and most native farmers.

> My father was a Scotsman and he came down in 1896 and took over this farm. At that time of day he was the only farmer round here for several miles . . . All this land here, all the way round, these woods and all was all dormant and brambles, and thousands and thousands of rabbits . . . Nothing, no farming whatever . . .

> How do you think you father managed to make it pay where other people couldn't then?
>
> Worked like hell mate. He went into all sorts of things . . . growing seed for Maples Seeds . . . milk . . . when these Scots people came down here to farm they worked . . . previous to that the farmers never worked. That was – that was – oh no you mustn't work.[62]

We need some caution here, as Lorraine Smith says, 'very likely the style of the native farmers has been exaggerated . . . but all the same, it contains an element of truth.'[63]

The numbers involved in these changes are difficult to work out. Smith calculated that 22 per cent of farmers in Essex in 1930 were immigrants, and he also calculated that about 20 per cent of farmers in the grazing area around Rugby were of Welsh origin.[64] Today over half the farmers of Essex are of Scots origin. At local level the change could be more startling still. As E. J. T. Collins says in his study of the Orsett estate in southern Essex,

> On the heavy lands between Orsett and Horndon, and in the Hundreds further east, the old order disappeared. On the Thurrock portion of the entire Orsett Estate, on more than thirty farms, only one of the original, pre-1860, tenant families, the Wordleys, survived the depression.[65]

The Wordleys were though precisely those who survived by rejecting the old order.

> The George Wordleys, father and son, were in every sense 'working farmers'. They were parsimonious in all things and strictly avoided the sort of expenditures – on for example sport and entertainment – that had consumed the best energies and most of the profits of the old Essex farmers.[66]

Like the Scots and A. G. Street's mythical Ebenezer Crumpler, the Wordleys abandoned wheat and barley and switched to livestock and reliance on family labour. Another Orsett family who survived, the Coles, did so with a mixture of sheep, provisioning ships at Tilbury and steam plough contracting.[67] In 1902 in Norfolk Henry Rider Haggard was told that in the North Walsham district 'In the old days corn paid the wages and the root crop the landlord . . . now there were only three people in the district whom he called legitimate farmers. Nearly all the landholders there had a trade which they combined with their farming.'[68] Edward Faulkner of East Bergholt in Essex grew up on such a unit. His father 'started up at the Carriers Arms' but as he said 'all my family have been in the dealing world.' His grandfather was a horse dealer and his father, as well as keeping the pub, was a scrap merchant and sold goods from door to door. The scrap 'was all collected up at the – what we call Michaelmas sales . . . there used to be twenty or thirty sales a year, farmers giving up, they couldn't make a go of it . . . ' Finally his father had 50 acres which he worked with his son's help and occasional casual labour.[69]

It was men like these, whether migrant or 'native', who often survived and prospered in the harsh climate of the depression but the cost, in the short term at least, was a subtle but profound change in social relationships. Of course many gentlemen farmers survived especially in areas like north Norfolk, and parts of Lincolnshire, Yorkshire, and Northumberland where economies of scale protected the cereal farmer. But elsewhere there were changes. This was especially so where the landowners were, for whatever reason, vulnerable. Most usually this was in the same areas as the farmers, for low wheat prices translated almost directly into rent reductions which in turn produced a crisis of varying intensity among the landowning gentry and aristocracy similar to that experienced by the farmers.

In 1895 Oscar Wilde wrote of these problems in one of the funniest (and most accurate) accounts of the agricultural depression's effect on the English elite.

> LADY BRACKNELL . . . what is your income?
> JACK. Between seven and eight thousand a year.
> LADY BRACKNELL [makes a note in her book]. In land, or in investments?
> JACK. In investments chiefly.
> LADY BRACKNELL. That is satisfactory. What between the duties expected during one's lifetime, and the duties exacted from one after one's death, land has ceased to be either a profit or a pleasure. It gives one position and prevents one from keeping it up. That's all that can be said about land.[70]

In this famous scene Wilde was simply repeating what many believed, that the depression was the death blow to a long and established rural elite. Although this view was certainly exaggerated – the death blow, if it has ever come came in the early and mid-1920s – there is no doubt that in reality, and possibly more importantly in perception, the power of the landed class was undermined by the economic events of the years after 1875. As J. V. Beckett writes,

> As the key for unlocking the door to social and political status and power, land retained its significance down to the 1880s . . . At that point a combination of agricultural depression, the partially successful conclusion to the long campaign to reform estate settlement legislation, and the shifting balance of political power in the state finally began to deflate the mystique of land . . .[71]

But it was not only mystique, for that was to remain vital, even to be revived in the first years of the twentieth century, it was real economic decline for some.

The most immediate effect on landowners were demands for rent reduction and/or the handing in of notice. Throughout the middle years of the nineteenth century rents had continued to rise, albeit slowly, and this had meant that land seemed a certain and secure basis of elite wealth. What R. A. C. Parker says of the wealth of Lord Leicester at his death in 1842, that he 'passed on to his son a secure prosperity, solidly based on a rich and flourishing Norfolk estate', was true for a whole generation of aristocratic landlords.[72] Such solid bases were built on in the 1840s, 1850s, and 1860s although few great estates had an unproblematically cheerful economic history.[73] Equally importantly, the development of urban property, railways and mineral rights added to aristocratic incomes although this was often concealed behind the ideology of landownership.

The depression challenged this position. By forcing down rents it ruined a few, and pauperized some, usually at the bottom end of the gentry. Crucially, by exposing the weakness of those families who were entirely reliant on agricultural rents for their income, it delivered a body blow to the ideology of landownership by showing that only those who had invested elsewhere could survive. As Beckett says, 'the estates which survived most successfully tended to be those where land alone was not necessarily the principal source of income.'[74]

The fall in rents were dramatic but again regionally variable. In Lancashire Lord Derby's Fylde estate actually increased its rental between 1870 and 1896 but this was exceptional.[75] Generally speaking the pattern we have seen in farming fortune was, as one would expect, reproduced. The pastoral areas by-and-large saw much less serious decline in rents than the arable. In Norfolk the rents on Leicester's Estates were reduced by an average of 45 per cent between 1878 and 1894. Even so he had farms in hand and believed that eight farms coming up for renewal in 1895–96 would not be renewed despite reductions or remissions of between 40 per cent and 60 per cent.[76] In Lincolnshire, where the land was less firmly arable rents fell by between 20 per cent and 60 per cent; however, as elsewhere, as Olney points out, 'net income fell even more sharply because landlords were not able to cut back their expenditure in proportion.'[77] Farms in hand had to be kept up if new tenants were going to be attracted, and repairs and other improvements carried out if good tenants were to be kept. The dairies of John Oxley Parker, the Essex land agent, reveal the day-to-day problems.

> Sept. 28th 1884. [Wrote] to Mr Todhunter in reply to letter giving notice to quit Manor farm if rent is not reduced to 10 shillings an acre. Oct. 18th. After wards at Mr Inglis' office to meet Mr May . . . Long discussion as to reduction of rent. Mr May said he could not give more than 10 shillings an acre. Saw Mr Royce and agreed that his rent should be £150 instead of the nominal amount at which it had been – £200.[78]

In Oxfordshire John Simpson Calvertt contemplated the disastrous effects of the depression on the Crown Estates, which was his landlord, and then put in for a rent reduction, backing it up with a threat to 'quit'. As a result the Crown's original offer of £600 a year was reduced to £450 for 660 acres 'including 7 cottages and tithe free', a reduction of 25 per cent.[79]

Rent reductions 'exaggerated differences that had always been significant in landed society'[80] between those who relied solely on rents and those who had other sources of income. The former group, generally the less wealthy, often suffered badly or even went to the wall. In Lincolnshire, 'F. W. Alix let West Willoughby Hall to a Captain Rennie and retired to Brussels, where he died in 1894.'[81] In Norfolk the papers of the Rolfe family, middle range 'squarsons' show a similar decline. Hampered by a disastrous Chancery suit the depression was the final blow. Living abroad Eustace Rolfe received from the mid-1880s demands from renewing tenants for rent reductions. As the 1890s came and the depression saw no signs of easing, the small family estate at Heacham made loss after loss and even good tenants fell behind with the reduced rents. The final blow was the realization that the new 'Death Duty', introduced in 1894, would make the position of any heir untenable and in 1899 the estate was sold.[82] Theirs was an example of the position pointed to by David Cannadine some years ago, 'on an estate which was heavily mortgaged . . . death duties might well come as the last straw'.[83]

Those who survived tended to be the larger landowners who were perhaps already slightly more separated from the rest of rural society. As Olney says of Lincolnshire,

> The great owners survived in most cases, but their contribution to the day-to-day running of the county had always been limited. It was the impoverishment of the small gentry class and the lack of recruitment into it that in the long run had the most important effect on the society and administration of the county.[84]

As a result some of the realities of paternalism began to crumble although the ideology remained strong, as Henry Rew remarked of Norfolk in the 1890s:

> Apart from the trouble and difficulty from which the owners themselves suffer, through the operation of economic causes over which they have no control, it will not be contended in any quarter that such a state of affairs is favourable to the interests of the community. The owner of an estate is the centre of a wide circle of interests and individuals, all of whom are more or less affected by his actions. When his position is disturbed the disturbance of necessity spreads itself in concentric rings, so to speak, over a considerable area.[85]

If we add to the gentry the tenant farmers, as it seems we may have to in some areas, Rew's account was more worrying still. The paternalist model in reality as well as in its representation relied on face-to-face contact and personal interaction for both its 'good' and its repressive side. Charity or justice had to be seen to be done by a particular group and experienced directly by those receiving it. By removing or altering the nature of the vital middle group in the paternalist hierarchy the whole structure and nature of rural society was opened up and potentially destabilized.

An additional element appeared in the depression period which further acted to undermine aspects of paternalism – the growth of a professional and/or elective local state machine. Although this had nothing directly to do with the depression, coming at the same time as a weakening in the power and local influence of the rural elite, it contributed to the major changes taking place. The creation of elected school boards in some areas in 1870–71, of elected County Councils in 1889 and Parish Councils in 1894 represented a move away from the informal and paternalist social organization of the years from 1850–1880.

Although the change was not immediate – it was remarked in Norfolk that the new County Council was little different in composition from the old county bench[86] – the potential for change was there. In the medium term, as more and more power passed to these bodies and their importance became more clear, so their composition changed further. By the early 1900s for example 'working-mens' candidates (some of them women!) frequently contested Parish, County, and District Council elections as well as standing for school boards (up to 1902 when they were abolished) and Boards of Guardians. We shall return to this below, but it was the growth in power of the institutions themselves, especially after 1900 which did most to attack paternalism.

Potentially much more serious was the strain imposed on the relationships between landlord and tenant. The whole question of 'tenant right', especially compensation for unexhausted improvements and fixity of tenure, had long been a bone of contention in English rural society although how contentious is a matter of debate.[87] What seems certain is that the depression raised the issue in new and more serious ways as it did the question of rents and cropping agreements which were part of most leases. In the end the relationship between landlord and tenant held, in England if not in Scotland and Wales, although it was changed. Crucially the balance of power within the 'contract' altered. This is again put neatly in A. G. Street's *The Gentleman of the Party*. Confronted with unlet farms the landlord (or rather his agent) sees the changed situation clearly.

> He hated this business. Never before during his stewardship had a farm on the Ashton Estate been hawked around. Generally he had a waiting list of would-be tenants, most of whom courted favour in a suitably humble fashion. It was one thing for a tenant to apply for a farm, but very definitely another for an agent of a large estate to have to apply to a possible tenant.[88]

In this situation a new tenant was not only able to insist on rent reductions or a sitting tenant able to negotiate them but other more subtle changes took place in the relationship between landlord and tenant. Cropping agreements, one of the most potent symbols of landlord power, often went out of the window. As Henry Overman told the 1881 Commission: 'I farm pretty well as I like, but I am in the middle of a 16 years' lease. There I have got a slight per-centage off too'.[89]

The abandonment of such agreements was a mixed blessing. In the case of Overman it probably encouraged sensible change – he was a progressive and responsible farmer who introduced a new flexibility into aspects of Norfolk agriculture. Elsewhere it led to the 'sucking' of land by taking straw crop after straw crop and real deterioration in both long- and short-term soil productivity. But it was the shift in the balance of power that mattered most. No longer was the landlord a demi-god whose power was absolute. Good tenants were held on to, and their demands for improvements listened to and often granted. A new tenant coming on to a farm, like Street's mythical grass farmer Crumpler, could make demands on taking a tenancy which would have been unthinkable in the 'golden age'. One example will give a sense of these changes. The Hastings family had farmed as tenants on the Earl of Leicester's Holkham estate in Norfolk since 1757. In 1882 the elderly John Hastings who had farmed since 1869 became ill and his son faced the task of taking over. There were already rent arrears and he gave notice to quit while also asking Lord Leicester for a loan to continue until his notice expired. The loan was granted and the son (also John Hastings) persuaded to stay. In 1884 when the older John died the estate loaned his son £500 for two years at 5 per cent and provided a mortgage on family property. In 1885 the rent was reduced by 30 per cent and by a further 30 per cent on the new rent in 1888. Despite this Hastings still continued to have problems and in 1891 he gave his notice to quit for the third time. Again the estate intervened, keeping the rent at the same level but carrying out repairs and building a new field house for cattle and a turnip house. In 1895 his rent was reduced again to £477 per annum compared to the £1,013 which was the rent when his father died. He himself died in 1907.[90]

At Holkham the problems of the Hastings family were dealt with amicably even if the cost to the estate was great. Elsewhere problems arose. A certain sense of independence began to appear in the tenant farmers once they were freed from the total subservience that the constant demands for farms had placed them under in the twenty years after 1850. One source of disquiet was the example of Ireland where the Land League had successfully turned tenant farmers' grievances into a mass anti-landlordism. In the early 1880s some aspects of this were beginning to spread into Scotland and Wales. In the autumn of 1881 the Scottish Farmers Alliance was formed in Aberdeen to press for revaluation of farms, reform of the land laws, security of tenure and tenant rights – demands with a very Irish feel to them.[91] Even before this date though the Richmond Commission had set as one of its tasks the investigation of the relationship between landlord and tenant and often the questions to witnesses were put in the context of the land agitation in Ireland.[92]

Although anti-landlord and tenant right agitation never reached Scottish let alone Irish dimensions in England, in some areas it was a real issue and one which was directly raised by the depression. In Lancashire, as Alistair Mutch's work shows, tenant farmers' organizations became a major force in the 1890s. The most 'militant' of these, the Lancashire Tenant Farmers' Association, led directly to the founding in January 1893 of the National Federation of Tenant Farmers Clubs at Chester. The whole tone of these organizations was totally different from the gentlemanly ethic of the old agricultural societies and even the chambers of agriculture where landlord and tenant sat down together to celebrate the virtues of a united agriculture. The stress, as in Ireland and Scotland, was firmly on the distinctive position of the tenant. As one delegate put it at the founding conference, it would be 'an insane thing to admit landlords to their counsels. They might as well ask colliery proprietors and agents to come to the ranks of their men.'[93]

The demands of the NFTFC were essentially, like those in Scotland, the notorious 'Three F's' of the Irish Land League

– fixity of tenure, fair rents and free sale of improvements. However, even within Lancashire, the movement's heartland, support was a problem. Firstly, as Mutch points out, 'it may be doubted as to how far the membership shared the exact opinions of their leaders, or held an intellectually cohesive view of their problems. What they wanted were reductions in rent and improved security of tenure . . .'[94] This inevitably weakened them in the face of the second problem of farmers' organizations – landlords' hostility. In Lancashire the landlords dealt with these organizations in the way the farmers themselves had dealt with the labourers' unions – by refusing to recognize them and meeting members only as individuals. Thus on the Earl of Sefton's estate the agent refused to meet a delegation from the farmers' club but saw each tenant individually and offered rent reductions. In this way the traditional 'vertical' relations between landlord and tenant were apparently preserved even if it was in fact the farmers' pressure which brought about such reductions.[95] Finally, and probably most centrally, it was the lack of a national element which weakened English tenant farmers' organizations of this openly political kind. In Scotland and Wales as in Ireland there was a close connection between the landlords as a class and cultural grouping and their English nationality which clarified the nature of their exploitation as well as separating them off as a group. In England this clearly was not the case and the vertical integration which characterized relationships between landlord and tenant survived the storm.

Nevertheless, relationships were changed. New farmers, like the Scots in Essex, the Devonians in Oxfordshire or the Welsh in Northants were a different breed and knew their worth. They also came from a harder tradition often mixed with religious nonconformity and even political Liberalism, a tradition which in some ways put them closer to the labourers and certainly did not endear them to the Toryism and Anglicanism of landlord culture. Similarly, the older family farmers who survived did so, like Calvertt in Oxfordshire or the Wordleys in Essex, by adopting a more instrumental approach to their landlords, even when, as in Calvertt's case, his landlord was also his sovereign. Economic circumstances ruined many farmers but those who survived the depression were in a much stronger position to bargain than their fathers and were much more aware of their power. As a Norfolk farmer put it to assistant commissioner Henry

Rew in 1895, 'Land courts were necessary 25 years ago, but now the tenant has the whip-hand of the landlord.'[96]

Beyond tenant right, other problems connected with landlord control became more and more important as points of conflict between landlord and tenant during the depression period. We have already mentioned cropping agreements and in most places these were abandoned, albeit reluctantly, without too much bother. However, in some places there were difficulties. The NFTFC talked on occasion of the fourth 'F' – freedom of cultivation, although this was not a problem in Lancashire.[97] In Northumberland, on the other hand, Bob Thompson from Seaton Sluice remembered the agent coming round to farms in the early 1900s to make sure farmers adhered to the four course system, 'we adhered to the system – we were wedded to the system . . . '[98] Similarly, in the Marshland districts of Cambridgeshire and Norfolk, cropping seems to have continued to be enforced at least to the early 1890s.[99]

Another area of contention which arose directly out of leases was game. Under the legislation passed between 1828 and 1862 all game including rabbits and hares was reserved to the landlord. As rabbits in particular increased in the century and as shooting became a source of landlords' income as well as prestige some many farmers resented the destruction caused by game. The depression again affected this in terms of cropping practice. Returning again to Street's Wiltshire we find the major worry of the Earl when the grass is taking over is his game.

> 'What?', spluttered the Earl, 'turn Sutton into a dairy farm . . . Damn it! The two best drives on the whole estate would be ruined. You find a man that'll keep a ewe to the acre on the arable, and then he'll be bound to grow some cover for the partridges'.[100]

Smallholdings were, in the Earl's view, worse for the same reason. 'Bloody little buildings all over the place, the shootin' spoilt, and the countryside lookin' like a lot o' blasted allotments.'[101]

The drop in cereal prices after 1875 precisely affected those crops most vulnerable to game, and to hares and rabbits in particular. In addition the Liberal Party, seeking farmers' support, made game, especially hares and rabbit, a major political issue.[102] As a result conflict began to appear in local agricultural societies and in the columns of the local press. In 1880 the Liberal government passed the Ground Game Act giving the occupier concurrently with others the right to kill game. However, in practice it was often not that way. As a Lancashire farmer told Wilson Fox in 1894, 'there is a written law to give us the hares and rabbits and an unwritten law that says we may not take them.'[103] J. H. Porter's work on Devon suggests that this was often the case, and certainly where game provided an impoverished estate within some revenue farmers got short shrift from their landlords and game continued to be a source of friction between landlord and tenant. Mr Gray, the agent for the Marquis of Waterford in Northumberland, put it clearly when he said 'whenever the man lets the game to a shooting tenant there is discontent . . . Farmers cannot endure a shooting tenant.'[104]

The depression hit the wealthy and great hard although the blow varied in power from region to region. The marginal wheat growing lands fared worst. Here tenant farmers suffered catastrophic drops in profits and landlords' rents fell dramatically. Elsewhere things were not so bad especially where regional farming systems were able to adapt to new demands. Apart from the personal tragedies of bankruptcy though there were other more subtle changes. A gap opened between tenant farmer and landlord which was not so much one of hostility (although that element was present) as of independence. The 1890s saw the emergence of tenant farmers' organizations, like the East Anglia-based Farmers' Federation, which went on to be the basis of the National Farmers Union. Significantly an attempt by a landowner, Lord Winchelsea, to heal the growing rifts between all three agricultural classes in the 1890s, the National Agricultural Union, failed to attract any widespread support. Other changes were harder still to trace. A drop in landlord income especially among the vulnerable minor gentry seems to have presented problems for the paternalist system, problems which were exacerbated by the quite separate growth of the local state.

Yet we must be cautious: it was reshaping that was taking place rather than revolution. Nor were the losses that great if you stood at the other end of the scale. It is invariably asserted by historians that it was the landlords who suffered most from the depression yet even the most serious drop in rent or even near bankruptcy like that suffered by the Norfolk Rolfes was nothing compared to the situation of labour. Flora Thompson writing in the 1930s about the depression years put it neatly when she said 'everybody seemed to do well out of agriculture in those days except the labourer'.[105]

NOTES

1 B. R. Mitchell and Phyllis Deane, *Abstract of British Historical Statistics*, [Cambridge, 1971], p. 101.
2 J. Oxley Parker, *The Oxley Parker Papers*, [Colchester, 1964], p. 128.
3 ibid., p. 148.
4 Calvertt, op. cit., p. 45.
5 Rowland Prothero (later Lord Ernle), *English Farming Past and Present*, [1917 ed. Rep. New York, 1971], p. 376.
6 Joan Thirsk and Jean Imray, *Suffolk Farming in the Nineteenth Century*, [Ipswich, 1958], pp. 53–4.
7 Calvertt, op. cit., p. 64.
8 ibid., p. 67.
9 Thirsk and Imray, op. cit., p. 101.
10 *PP 1882, XIV*, op. cit., p. 13.
11 ibid., p. 32.
12 P. J. Perry, *British Agriculture 1875–1914*, [London, 1973], p. xxxviii.
13 *PP 1893–94, XXXV*, 'Royal Commission on Labour. The Agricultural Labourer. England. The Report of Mr Aubrey Spencer on the Poor Law Union of Maldon (Essex)', p. 699.
14 Oxley Parker, op. cit., p. 150.
15 ibid., p. 151.
16 ibid., p. 153.
17 *PP 1893–94, XXXV*, op. cit., p. 76.
18 T. W. Fletcher, 'The Great Depression in Engllish Agriculture, 1873–96', *EcHR* [second series] XIII; also 'Lancashire Livestock Farming During the Great Depression', *AHR* IX 1961. For a more critical account see Alistair Mutch, 'Farmers Organisations and Agricultural Depression in Lancashire, 1890–1900', *AHR* Vol. 31 pt; also Alistair Mutch, *Rural Society*, op. cit..
19 Mutch, *Rural Society*, op. cit., p. 30.
20 ibid., p. 35.
21 *PP 1894, XVI pt. 1*, 'Royal Commission on Agricultural Depression Reports by Mr. A. Wilson Fox on the Garstang District of Lancashire and the Glendale District of Northumberland', p. 7.

22 Mutch, *Rural Society*, op. cit., pp. 59–63.
23 David Taylor 'The English Dairy Industry, 1860–1930', *EcHR* [second series] Vol. XXIX no. 4, p. 589.
24 ibid., p. 592.
25 *PP 1881, XVII*, op. cit., p. 35.
26 Christina Hallas, 'The Social and Economic Impact of a Rural Railway: the Wensleydale Line', *AHR* Vol. 32, no. 1, 1986.
27 *PP 1882, XV*, op. cit., p. 41.
28 ibid., p. 39.
29 *PP 1881, XVII*, op. cit., p. 129.
30 NRO 479, op. cit..
31 For much of what follows see Brian Short, '"The Art and Craft of Chicken Cramming". Poultry in the Weald of Sussex, 1850–1950', *AHR* Vol. 30, pt. 1.
32 Quoted in Short, ibid., p. 22.
33 ibid., p. 21.
34 Calvertt, op. cit., pp. 199–213.
35 *PP 1881, XVI*, op. cit., p. 375.
36 Herbert B. J. Armstrong, [ed] *Armstrong's Norfolk Diary. Further Passages from the Diary of the Revd. Benjamin John Armstrong* [London, 1963], p. 147.
37 R. H. Mottram, *Bowler Hat. A Glance at the Old Country Banking* [London, 1940], p. 152.
38 *PP 1882, XV*, op. cit., p. 6.
39 *PP 1895, XVI*, 'Royal Commission on Agricultural Depression by Mr. A. Wilson Fox on the County of Lincolnshire', p. 35.
40 E. J. T. Collins, *The Orsett Estate, 1743–1914*, [Thurrock, 1978], p. 65.
41 *PP 1881, XI*, op. cit., p. 370.
42 *PP 1895, XVII*, Norfolk, op. cit., p. 359.
43 *PP 1881, XI*, op. cit., p. 134.
44 *PP 1893–4, XXXV*, Northumberland, op. cit., p. 125.
45 *PP 1893–94, XXXV*, 'Report of the Royal Commission on Labour. The Agricultural Labourer. England. Report by Mr. Roger C. Richards . . . upon the Poor Law Union of Bromyard', p. 163.
46 *PP XXXV*, Garstang, op. cit., p. 163.
47 Mitchell and Deane, op. cit., p. 78.
48 Mitchell and Deane, op. cit., p. 78.
49 *PP 1893–4, XXXV*, Lincs, op. cit., p. 105.
50 *PP 1893–4, XXXV*, Maldon, op. cit., p. 75.
51 H. Rider Haggard, *Rural England*, [London, 1902], 2 Vols, Vol II, p. 53.
52 ibid., p. 56.
53 Taylor, *EcHR*, op. cit., p. 590.
54 Ernle, op. cit., p. 377.

55 A. G. Street, *The Gentlemen of the Party*, [London, 1936], p. 46.
56 *PP 1881, XVI*, op. cit., p. 134.
57 *PP 1895, XVI*, Lincs. op. cit., p. 63.
58 Street, op. cit., Ch. IV. Significantly this chapter is called by Street 'The Coming of the Grass'.
59 E. Lorraine Smith, *Go East for a Farm*, [Oxford, 1932], pp. 15–18.
60 ibid., pp. 38–9.
61 ibid., p. 39.
62 Interview with Mr Hugh Smith, Kelvedon, Essex. b. 1898. EOHC.
63 Lorraine Smith, op. cit., p. 39.
64 ibid., pp. 19–21.
65 Collins, *Orsett Estate*, op. cit., p. 71.
66 ibid., pp. 71–2.
67 ibid., pp. 72-3.
68 Haggard, *Rural England*, Vol. 2, op. cit., p. 457.
69 Interview with Mr. Edward Faulkner, East Bergholt, Essex b. 1893. EOHC.
70 Oscar Wilde, *The Importance of Being Ernest*, Act 1, in Richard Ellman, [ed] *Oscar Wilde: Selected Writings* [Oxford, 1961], pp. 303–4.
71 J. V. Beckett, *The Aristocracy in England 1660–1914*, [Oxford, 1986], p. 85.
72 R. A. C. Parker, *Coke of Norfolk. A Financial and Agricultural Study 1707–1842*, [Oxford, 1975], p. 198.
73 For much of what follows see Thompson, *English Landed Society*, op. cit..
74 Beckett, op. cit., p. 85; see also Thompson, op. cit., Chapter X *passim*.
75 Thompson, op. cit., p. 310.
76 *PP 1895, XVII*, 'Royal Commission on Agriculture. England. Report by Mr. Henry Rew . . . on the County of Norfolk', p. 342.
77 Olney, op. cit., p. 179.
78 Oxley-Parker, op. cit., p. 152.
79 Calvertt, op. cit., p. 180.
80 Olney, op. cit., p. 179.
81 ibid..
82 Berry, *The Rolfe Papers*, op. cit., Chapter 7 *passim*.
83 David Cannadine, 'Aristocratic Indebtedness in the Nineteenth Century: The Case Reopened', *EcHR* [second series] LXXX no, 4, p. 64.
84 Olney, op. cit., p. 182.
85 *PP 1895, XVII*, Norfolk, op. cit., p. 329.
86 *EWP*, 9th February 1889, p. 5.

87 J. R. McQuiston, 'Tenant Right: farmer against landlord in Victorian England 1847–1883', *Agricultural History* 47 1973, argues for its importance. J. R. Fisher, 'Landlords and English Tenant Right 1845–1852', *AHR* 31 pt. I [1983] argues against this view.
88 Street, *Gentleman*, op. cit., p. 52.
89 *PP 1881, XVII*, op. cit., p. 737.
90 Susanna Wade Martins, *A Great Estate at Work. The Holkham estate and its inhabitants in the nineteenth century*, [Cambridge, 1980], pp. 119–25.
91 Ian Carter, op. cit., p. 169.
92 See for example the evidence of George Turnbull, tenant farmer of 2,100 acres at Belfort, Northumberland, *PP 1881 XXVII*, op. cit., p. 548.
93 Quoted in Mutch, 'Farmers' Organizations', op. cit., p. 31.
94 ibid., p. 31.
95 ibid., pp. 33–4.
96 *PP 1895, XVII*, Norfolk report, op. cit., p. 380.
97 ibid., p. 31.
98 NRO T.34, op. cit.
99 *PP 1895, XVII*, Norfolk Report, op. cit., p. 415.
100 Street, *Gentleman*, op. cit., p. 48.
101 ibid..
102 For much of what follows see J. H. Porter, 'Tenant Right: Devonshire and the 1880 Ground Game Act', *AHR* Vol. 34 ii 1986. For the campaign against the game laws earlier see Kirby, 'The Attack on the English Game Law System', op. cit..
103 *PP 1894, XVI i*, op. cit., p. 7.
104 ibid., p. 188.
105 Thompson, *Lark Rise*, op. cit., p. 41.

7

The Crisis of Rural Society: 'The Labouring Poor'

As with the elite the effects of the depression upon the labourer were complex and both direct and indirect. In the most direct sense dropping the 'standard' of farming, making changes within the basic agricultural structure, and changes in cropping to alternative husbandry in particular had important effects on labour. At the first level dropping standards or laying down to grass, which were the most obvious resorts of the farmer in the depression, needed fewer and, in some cases, different kinds of workers than arable farming, especially the high arable farming of the mid-nineteenth century. This drop was frequently noted by the commissioners in the 1880s and 1890s. At Maldon in Essex it was said in 1894 'there is not so much labour employed here as there used to be'[1]; while from Driffield in Yorkshire in the same year came the report that 'no doubt there has often been a reduction (in labourers)'.[2] It was however in the great corn areas of the east where putting down to grass reduced labour demand most obviously, Wilson Fox, reporting from Swaffam in Norfolk in 1892, wrote of, ' . . . the conversion of arable land into grass by farmers, who, driven by the lowness of prices, are dispensing with labour by giving up growing corn, which they say cannot possibly pay at its present price and with wages at their present rate'.[3] In the Glendale area of Northumberland the same commissioners noted a change in the rotation from a five course to a six or seven course shift 'since the fall in the price of corn' which 'means a considerable saving of men and horses'.[4]

Initially, at least, it was the casual workers who suffered. The reasons for this are straightforward. We saw in Chapter 4 how arable agriculture relied on a core of regular workers plus a large number of casuals who came in at busy seasons. Many of these busy times were in fact created by high farming. Weeding, stone picking, hedging and ditching, even certain harvest operations like raking round were all, in part at least, the product of a belief in farming neatness. They were also the great areas of casual employment. Reduction in weeding, dock pulling and stone picking all hit directly at the labour of casuals, especially women. By 1900 this was seen in terms of rural depopulation and low wages but it began, to some extent at least, in the farmers' lowering of farming standards during the depression.

In the great corn areas of the south and east in particular the reports of the Royal Commission on Labour in 1894 and the more general reports on the farm labourer in 1900 and 1905 return time and again to this reduction in the casual workforce, whether men, women or children. In 1900 Wilson Fox wrote,

> The employment of women and children in agriculture . . . has nearly ceased to exist . . . thus depriving the farmers of cheap labour at busy seasons, and in the last few years the resident casual labourer who could be secured for hoeing and weeding, hay and corn harvest, and potato lifting, &c. has almost entirely disappeared in many districts.[5]

We can see this change in the papers of the Courthope estate farms from Sussex, both in terms of the reduction in the number of casuals employed and in terms of increasingly intensive use of regular workers. In 1851 the farm employed twenty-nine workers. In the week beginning 28 August, near the end of harvest five of them worked every day (including Sunday). These were key horsemen and stockmen. A further sixteen worked six days and eight worked between one and five days. In addition there are entries for unknown numbers of men and women (money only is entered) for weeding, mowing and threshing. For the same week in 1894, although the number of regularly employed was roughly the same (twenty-seven), ten worked on Sunday, including four who were mowing as well as those on essential duties. All the rest worked a six-day week and there were no casuals employed at all. In 1894 even the gardener was employed during harvest.[6]

Casual workers remained an important part of the workforce in many areas, especially in the north, as we shall see later, but in the south and east they were rapidly becoming a thing of the past by the 1900s. However, and it is an important qualification, numbers of women employed did not drop as swiftly as the number of casuals. Women remained, despite the insistence of many observers like Wilson Fox, quoted earlier, a resident reserve army of labour. Their 'disappearance' was much more to do with ideological blindness and throughout the depression women remained a central part of the workforce.

Reduction in labour demand of this kind was probably worse of all when a farmer, either out of necessity or because a new and different tenant arrived, switched more to the use of family labour. We have already discussed this in terms of the farmers' culture but here we should see it as another effect of falling prices on labour supply. The *Royal Commission on Labour* put it neatly in relation to the migrant Scots and northern farmers who moved into Essex. 'These north-country farmers and their families, including frequently the female members do a considerable amount of manual work themselves and they employ comparatively little labour'.[7] Nationally the figures involved here were small but significant in village or farm terms since the lowering of farming standards usually affected a whole parish or area. In this case movement was the only answer. As Rider Haggard put it in 1902.

> But what became of the poor labourers? Perhaps they know in Whitechapel – for two of the causes of rural depopulation are the shrinkage of the demand for labour in these bad times, and the perpetual laying away of arable land to grass.[8]

Simply laying down to grass as a short-term expedient was one option; a switch to dairying was another. As the depression wore on into the 1880s this option, as we have already seen, was taken more and more, especially in the counties with access to an urban market. This also reduced labour demands and caused other workers to change their jobs, learning new skills. Street's *The Gentleman of the Party* described such a change when Ebenezer Crumpler, the Dorset 'cow-keeper', takes over the sheep/corn farm of farmer Martin and switches it to dairy.

> This increase in the dairy herd, and consequent reduction of the flock . . . brought about many changes at Sutton Manor. The

> head shepherd refused to take less wages for handling a smaller flock, thinking the new tenant could not do without him . . . 'Let the fool go', ordered Ebenezer, 'an' gi'e the under shep the job . . . Now then, what about all they carters? Some on them'll ha' to go . . . (and) we wants another chap in the dairy'.[9]

So Sutton Manor was transformed with a reduction in men and fields to grass. In 1906 Mathew Hunt of Sherborne in Dorset sung a slightly fragmentary song giving the shepherd's version of these changes to the folk song collector H. E. D. Hammond.

> Now the fields they are let out and the ditches tossed about,
> It will break the heart of every man
> With the posts and rails we'll make them rakes and pails
> . . .
> And a-milking we must go, or follow the plough-tail
> to reap and plough and sow, aye, and to harrow we must go.
> For we must all away, we can no longer stay,
> And there's nothing for poor shepherds to do.
>
> A poor man's pay is but eighteen pence a day;
> You have need to double the price.
> And what is that [d'ye think] to find them bread and drink
> Six children, the man and his wife?
> Whilst the rich do play their cards, aye, the poor will all be
> starved,
> And we must all away, we can no longer stay,
> for there's nothing for poor shepherds to do.[10]

It was not only shepherds. Pastoral farming, whether growing beef or mutton, as well as dairying, needed a much smaller workforce. As at Sutton Manor many a Wiltshire carter or Essex horseman found himself without a job as a result of his master's recognition, along with Ebenezer Crumpler, that the 'Cows be the only thing what pays nowadays'.[11] Near Thame in Oxfordshire this reduction in labour demand was given a mathematical certainty. 'Mr Thomas Franklin says that the average on his farm is (1) arable, 50 acres, three men and one boy; one woman to 150 acres; (2) pasture, 50 acres, one man; extra required at times', a reduction in labour force of over 60 per cent.[12]

The effects of changing to fruit and vegetable production are much more difficult to chart. Market gardening did encourage small units worked intensively with family labour which increased employment but it also meant little regular demand for hired workers. For example, it was said of the switch to vegetable farming on the Isle of Axholme that although it meant increased demand for labour 'this should be no drawback to the small farmer whose family labour is at home'.[13] On the other hand there were periods of intense labour activity, especially associated with harvesting and picking, when the local labour force had to be supplemented from nearby towns, as well as the employment of women and children. In the Thurrock area of Essex, where there was a rapid expansion of vegetable growing after 1880, local labour was insufficient even when local schools closed for a fortnight for pea-picking. This was dealt with by selling the crop standing to vegetable dealers from London 'who put in their own workmen – East Enders, gypsies, even travelling Irish, as well as locals – to harvest and cart off the crop.'[14]

This pattern of a small regular workforce plus a very large seasonal labour input, which was in a sense only a continuation of nineteenth century arable patterns, was also dominant in fruit and hop areas. Kent and Sussex hopping and Evesham fruit picking both relied on urban workers, mostly women and children. George Meek went hopping from the slums of Eastbourne up to Mayfield in north-east Sussex in the early 1880s and found his fellow workers, 'a rough lot from the perlieus of Edward Street, Brighton'.[15] The migration to Kent was the most spectacular and most famous of the nineteenth century movement of seasonal labour. The total seasonal labour force travelling into Kent for the hopping is difficult, if not impossible, to estimate – even contemporary figures range between 80,000 and 150,000 – but it was certainly a massive influx.[16] However, like much of the Essex work, it did little for country dwellers, since, while it provided both seasonal and regular work for locals it was declining. Although hop cultivation was certainly intensive the acreage under hops was decreasing in the last years of the century despite being essentially unaffected by mechanization until the 1950s.

Commercial fruit production was different. Wilkins at Tiptree and especially Chivers at Histon in Cambridgeshire seemed, to contemporaries at least, to have transformed and saved the agriculture of their areas. The commercial production of jam by Chivers meant that by 1902 they employed a regular workforce of over 1,000 pickers in season. Chivers' argued that fruit production employed many more 'hands' than cereal production as it needed 20 men to cultivate 150 acres of fruit against about 5 for an ordinary farm.[17] Haggard waxed lyrical, as did the government a few years later, on the benefits of fruit growing, ending his account, 'How powerfully such an establishment works for the well-being of a district will be readily understood by the reader. I only wish there were many more of them scattered through the length and breadth of England.'[18]

Changes such as these in employment and farming practice which were a more or less direct result of the agricultural depression have to be seen in context with two other areas of change – continuing rural depopulation and gradual mechanization. Neither of these was caused by the depression but both were significantly affected by it although the relationship is a complex one and way outside the scope of detailed exploration here. However, both areas need to be looked at, albeit cursorily.

As the figures below show all the ranks of agricultural society were decreasing in numbers throughout the period 1871–1901. These figures are at best a guide but they do indicate the extent of the problem as contemporaries saw it. The decline in the agricultural population which had been going on from the 1850s and 1860s continued and indeed got worse. In the three decades which included the

Table 7.1 Numbers (male and female) engaged in agriculture 1871–1901 in England and Wales

Year	Landowners	Farmers	Labourers	Total
1871	25,431[a]	605,589	980,166	1,611,096
1881		575,434[b]	870,798	1,500,555[c]
1891		497,171	780,707	1,305,878
1901		475,633	621,068	1,124,701

[a] After 1871 there is no figure for landed proprietors in the census. I have simply assumed this figure would remain constant over the period and added it on. Bateman gives a figure of 38,000 owners of more than 100 acres. But this is a very small holding for a 'landowner'. See Chapter 1.

[b] In 1881 the census stopped counting the wives and daughters of farmers as employed. I believe this seriously misrepresents the position on the majority of English farms. This figure therefore includes farmers' relatives, male and female, as did the census before 1881. The figures after 1881 are adjusted assuming that proportions remain roughly the same. Clearly this isn't so but it does give a more accurate picture.

[c] A constant number of landed proprietors is added.

depression the number of labourers, male and female, in England and Wales dropped by almost exactly a third. In the same period the numbers of farmers fell by nearly a quarter.

How the depression relates to this ongoing problem also seems fairly clear. In the 1870s the number of labourers fell by about 10 per cent, in the 1880s by about 11 per cent, and in the 1890s by nearer 20 per cent. As in other aspects, such as changing cropping and rent reductions, it seems it took 10–15 years of depression for the fact that the pattern of English agriculture was permanently altered, to sink in. Further, it seems likely that the various strategies adopted by farmers to reduce costs took time to work their way down. A similar pattern can be seen in relation to farmers, although given the nature of my figures this is much less accurate. Here the real drop in numbers comes in the 1880s, which fits in with Perry's study of farming bankruptcy. He suggests that the 1880s, especially the early 1880s, were the worse decade overall for farmers.[19] The 1891 census also noted this drop especially in relation to 'close male relatives of farmers . . . This is a decline of over 10%, and appears to indicate unmistakably that the younger generation are not so nearly disposed to adopt agricultural life . . . '[20]

The other factor which affected the labourers was mechanization. At the most basic level English agriculture was essentially non-mechanical before the 1870s. Only the threshing machine, and then only regionally, was widely used.[21] It was not that the machines were not available, rather it was that hand labour was much cheaper. However once labour supply began to fall, as it did noticeably in some areas from the 1860s, and the sources of migrant labour described in Chapter 4 began to dry up, machinery became a more attractive proposition to many farmers. As E. J. T. Collins writes, 'machines were introduced as a reaction to shortages of labour at high points in the trade cycle'.[22] The gradual switch away from hand technology, especially at harvest, is documented in relation to Oxfordshire by John Walton. Walton shows that it 'was only when it became evident that there was a harvest labour crisis . . . that the reaping machine was adopted in any great numbers'.[23] The spread of such harvest machinery was swift. No Oxfordshire farm in Walton's sample had mowing or reaping machines in 1850; by 1880 30 per cent did; about 35 per cent had hay rakes at the earlier date; 40 per cent by the latter.[24] Mutch's work on Lancashire shows a similar pattern, but with higher wages and possibly more acute labour shortages machinery arrived slightly earlier and had a greater impact. In this area 19.3 per cent of farmers had some form of mechanical reaper as early as 1871, a figure which had increased to over 60 per cent by 1881.[25] There were however many problems. Labour remained cheap even in the 1890s. For example Henry Rider Haggard did not buy a self binder until 1898, mainly because it had not been worthwhile before that date given low labour costs. Even so there were still problems as Haggard found in that the machines would not cut 'laid' crops.[26] On very small farms where the quantities of cereals grown were tiny, machinery was not viable until after the Great War. On top of that there was the conservatism of those who believed that things could not be changed. A Northumberland pitman whose father was a labourer remembered the first self binders in the Alnwick area,

> When Mr Blakey come in here with the self binder . . . some of them would say 'Ha-wey, what good's that, its going to be nae good round here.' Well he got set in and went round . . . but they wouldn't have it till he got under way.[27]

At Seaton, also in Northumberland, a small farmer said 'we didn't mechanise 'til the 1930s . . . at that time (1914) there was only one drill in the neighbourhood . . . the self binder only came out in this area about 1900, there were very few . . . '[28]

If we look then at the economic effects of the depression on the working population of the rural areas – the farmers and the labourers – they are fairly clear. For the arable farmer the drop in wheat prices accompanied by bad seasons led to a fall in profits. To a lesser extent in pastoral areas frozen meat imports and cheese imports had a similar effect. As profits fell farmers adapted or went out of farming. This adaptation frequently had the overall effect of reducing labour demand. However, seen in the context of already existing rural depopulation, this became doubly serious. The important thing here is that for a time quite how serious this was was concealed by a desire on the farmers' part to reduce their labour bill.

In some senses, as far as labour was concerned, the depression acted as a catalyst, speeding up a process which had already begun. This was also the case as regards machinery, although the argument here takes on a 'chicken and egg' form. Machinery was often available from the 1850s. But it was not widely adopted until increasing labour bills, caused partly by labour shortage and partly by trades unionism which is looked at below, made it economically viable. Then and only then were machines adopted but once they had come into an area they seem to have spread quickly. In this sense they did force men off the land by replacing human labour by that of machine, but only very slowly and with a muted effect. As Collins says, 'technological unemployment appears not to have been a major social problem in English agriculture in the nineteenth century.'[29]

If we move away from these very direct effects of the depression we see in relation to the labourers, as we did with the 'wealthy and great', a set of further changes, in essence the social consequences of depression. Sometimes one thing leads clearly to another. For example, falling profits could begin a process involving farm sale, a new tenant, a new cropping system, new labour requirements, and new social relations. In these cases, as we have already seen to some extent, links and determination are straightforward. Other changes in the years after 1875 are less easy to structure. Trades unionism, for instance, or growing conflict between Church and chapel, were not created in any direct way by the depression but were indirectly influenced by the physical and ideological disruption the depression caused. Similarly, changes in the infrastructure had ambiguous results. Reform of education or local government, although designed to reinforce the established order, could also challenge it.

As we saw in the last chapter the depression had an indirect effect on the paternalist model of social organization. By reducing rents and profits, by altering the personnel of the village elite and, crucially, the elite's view of its role within the village community, subtle but important changes took place within the social relationships of that community. These had both direct and indirect effects on the labourers.

At the core of the paternalist set up was the relationship, at work and in the village, between master and man. The ideal, as we saw in Chapters 3 and 4, was of a settled 'family' unit headed by a male wage earner living in the same village and owing allegiance and deference to parson and squire. Even before the depression this model was challenged by the realities of casualization, especially in the arable areas. The increased rate of emigration during the depression opened those cracks still further. It was the young who left, men and women, driven by the conditions of country life but also attracted by the towns. As the Rev. Augustus Jessopp, Rector of Scarning in Norfolk, put it:

> The noise and conflict, the glare and fire, the gas and the shop windows, the circus, and the crowds, the savoury tit-bits, so toothsome and so succulent, that are to be had for a groat, whose like comes rarely from the parson's lady in the village . . . the cheap trains and the loud talk . . . these are the things that attract far more than the mere consideration of another shilling a week.[30]

With the depression reducing employment the town grew in attraction. As young men and women went to the towns so those 'left behind' had more contact, through letters and visits, with those who went. A Norfolk horseman interviewed in the early 1970s saw five males of his family move to London where they were found work in Truman's Brewery by an uncle who was employed there as a drayman.[31] Young women often followed a route set by an older sister or other relation. If none such existed another link with the urban world, frequently the vicar's wife, would be asked.[32]

The possibility of movement and its increasing frequency meant those left behind were less and less integrated into the rural world. Through the last years of the century there are constant complaints of the increasing unwillingness of young men and women to accept their lot as inevitable or unchanging. In North Devon for example it was said of the labourer, 'he well knows that the great Welsh coal field lies only a few hours sail from any of the little harbours that dot the coast . . . '[33] Most farmers and landowners who gave evidence before the Royal Commissions of the 1880s and 1890s used the much more general notion of 'independence'. From Glendale in Northumberland Mr James Fox, a farm steward, said in 1892, 'There has been a great change in the demeanour of the men in the last 10 years. They are more independent'.[34] In the same year, but from the other end of England, Credition in Devon, these sentiments were echoed by a farmer, Mr Charles Mortimer. His men were 'more independent and careless of their masters' interest'.[35] Nor was it only the rural elite who noticed this change. Even the labourer and the labourers' champions saw it and its difficulties. As F. E. Green wrote in 1912,

> That the younger country labourers are becoming more independent one does not doubt, but the process of exfoliation is, I admit, not a beautiful one . . . They have in some way to show what they consider their 'independence', to regain their self respect which they lose in their parasitic service – hence their surliness to those who in no way govern their lives.[36]

Within this process education had, as we suggested earlier, an ambiguous role. There is no doubt that educational reformers in the mid century saw education as a method of civilizing and thus controlling the rural as they did the urban poor. Until the 1870 Education Act this task fell to two main bodies – the Church of England National Society, founded in 1811, the schools of which were known as 'National Schools', and the British and Foreign School Society founded between 1808–11, which was essentially a nonconformist body. Its schools were known as 'British Schools'. The schools of these bodies were 'inspected' from 1839 and thus received government grants. In return they taught agreed subjects and from 1862 all students at these schools went through a graded series of standard examinations. This was the infamous 'payment by results' system where the teacher was paid only if pupils reached the expected standard.[37] To many a country rector like Augustus Jessopp in Norfolk or Edward Elton in Oxfordshire, education was to be the salvation of the rural poor. Teaching them, or rather their children, to read and write, to speak properly and to dress cleanly was to civilise them. One of the first things Elton did in his troubled and violent parish was to raise money to open a National School.[38]

Such hopes were often quickly dashed. Resentment on the part of the poor against 'interference' by their betters and, more importantly, simple economic pressure meant that schooling in any real sense reached only a small proportion of the rural poor. In 1847, National Schools in Suffolk, for example, reached about 10 per cent of the rural population while nationally it was stated that the figure was nearer 8 per cent.[39] Even if the British Schools were added the figures are little better. As the *Morning Chronicle* investigator in East Anglia in 1849 put it, 'the education of the children of the agricultural labourers is . . . remarkably deficient.' As an example he quoted the following 'dialogue' between a vicar and pupils at Wrotham in Suffolk.

> 'Why was Lazarus seen afar off in Abraham's bosom?'
> 'Because he was Abraham's father'.
> 'What is a publican?'
> 'A Pharisee'
> 'How many Houses of Parliament are there?'
> 'Three – two'
> 'What is the upper one called?'
> 'The house of dukes'
> 'What is the lower one called?'
> 'The house of gentlemen'
> 'Who puts on the taxes?'
> 'The Queen'[40]

Things were a little better by the time commissioners went out to look at the employment of women and children in agriculture in the late 1860s. There were still widespread and serious problems, including a sense from some sections of the rural elite that education might civilize but it might also teach the poor to question their station in life. However, the central problem remained the need for child labour. This need was felt both by families needing the money and the farmers to whom children were an essential part of the labour force. Benjamin Etheridge, aged 12, told Mr J. E. White who collected evidence in Norfolk, 'I never was at school in the weektimes since I went to work in the gang. Cannot say how long that is; its a long time.'[41] Smith Lusher, a man in his 40s, told the same commissioner, 'My children (aged 8 and 9) go to school on Sundays and I teach them a little at night. I do not know if they would take them at school if they were off work a few days now and then'.[42] In Gloucestershire, the Rev. James Fraser met James Brown of Swanley who, although he has been to Totworth school, had left at 10 unable to read or write and had not been back since.[43] The problem was put clearly by Rev. W. T. Beckett who was Diocesan Inspector of Schools in Norwich. 'The great reason for (leaving school early) is the importance to farmers of boy labour from an economical point of view.'[44]

Yet things were improving. Those who actually went to school often did learn and stayed on as late as possible. On the same day the Rev. Fraser met James Brown at Swanley he also met another boy called William Stephens working in a field with a pair of horses. He had left school at 11 1/2 but 'could write very well, and I tried his reading powers on a somewhat difficult and perfectly strange passage which he made out very intelligently.'[45] Elsewhere it is clear that parents were changing their minds about education, especially where good wages lessened the need for child labour except occasionally, or local custom placed a high value on education as a means of social advancement. Both these came together in Northumberland where an almost Scottish stress on the merits of democratic education seems to have been common. Although there were problems of access because of the remote nature of many Northumberland farms the reports of both 1868 and 1894 remark on the enthusiasm for education among the working people in this area. As W. E. Henley said in 1867, 'I cannot too often repeat, that in this district the pressure for education comes from the people themselves.'[46]

This very improvement exposed the ambiguities of education. As Rev. Beckett, the Norfolk schools inspector, put it,

> One great objection the farmers have to education is that the labourer becomes able to understand his rights, and thus instead of being a mere piece of machinery or a slave, as he was formerly, forgetting his sorrows or cares in the beer pot, he becomes a reasonable and properly independent labourer, a sober and respectable man.[47]

Sections of the labourers themselves shared this view. George Rix, a Norfolk labourers' union leader, wrote,

> . . . unite for mutual intercourse, instruction and information. Knowledge is power. Leave off smoking and tippling and get reading, thinking and acting and there is for the working classes of old England a brighter and better day.[48]

In 1870 this potentially disruptive force became available, in theory at least, to all labourers' children with the passing of the Education Act. This was designed to provide elementary education for all children and authorized the building of rate-aided schools. In reality, the problems of getting children to attend remained, even after compulsory attendance, backed by the 'truancy man' and the courts, was introduced in 1880. But the change had come. Gradually the labourers became more literate and thus had access to new ideas. The effects of this were slow in becoming visible but they were real enough. Education remained a powerful source for the inculcation of middle class and urban ideas of respectability and worth but it always had another side which encouraged independence.

Education was simply one of a number of changes in the consciousness of the rural poor. These manifested themselves in the decades after 1870 in a whole range of labourers' movements, the most obvious of which were trades unions. The unions were not, however, the only such movements. Predating them, essential to them, but also enormously important in its own right was the growth of religious nonconformity. This gave the labourers a belief in themselves, a language of protest but, above all, experience in organization.

Religious nonconformity or 'dissent' was usually taken to mean those groups of Protestant churches which refused to accept part or all of the 39 Articles of the Church of England. Before the Methodist revival of the mid-eighteenth century, most dated from the period of the English Republic of 1649–60. The main groups were the Congregationalists (sometimes still referred to as Independents); various kinds of Baptists, some of whom were Calvinists; Presbyterians, whose strength lay mainly in the north; and Quakers. In addition there were an almost endless variety of tiny groups, like the Muggletonians, who held on to minute congregations and one or two chapels.

In the years before the 1830s nonconformity seems to have made little headway in rural areas. Following a period of growth in the seventeenth century rural nonconformity languished. England was dotted with communities of what Wesley called 'Godly people', existing outside the Church of England and rejecting its tenets, but they were isolated and inward looking, often concerned with the minutae of theological difference. Samuel Drew, a working man who became a famous preacher, remembered these disputes with affection. 'About this time disputes ran high in St. Austell between the Calvinists and the Arminians, and our shop afforded a convenient place for discussion.'[49] Joseph Parker remembered similar discussions in early nineteenth century Hexham.

> The subject was generally theological, and ranged most fiercely around the ninth chapter of Romans . . . The chief care of the

> kitchen academicians was to prove that few people could be saved, and those that were not saved would wallow in fire and brimstone eternally.[50]

To others it looked less alive. Phillip Dodderidge, the great Congregationalist divine of the mid-eighteenth century, took a more sanguine view.

> Soon we shall have the pleasure of being entertained with the echo of our own voices, and the delicacy of our discourses, in empty places, or admidst a little circle of friends, till perhaps, (like some of our brethren) we are starved into a good opinion of conformity.[51]

Dodderidge's judgement is probably a little harsh. Davidoff and Hall have shown in their excellent study of small family fortunes in the period up to 1850 just how important the support networks and families of East Anglia nonconformity were, as has Clyde Binfield's study of rural dissent in the same area.[52] Similarly in many small country towns nonconformity found a home among the middling sort. What 'Christopher Crayon' wrote of his Suffolk boyhood in the 1820s was true of many areas. 'In our chapel . . . we had a good congregation, especially in the afternoon, when the farmers and their families . . . put in an appearance . . . '[53] Places like Lewes in Sussex or Banbury in Oxfordshire nursed long-established and powerful dissenting congregations who influenced the countryside around.[54] Even some large county towns supported dissenting congregations although these tended to be composed of the urban elite. East Anglia, Ipswich, Bury and, centrally, Norwich supported a rich and powerful dissenting culture.

Yet the majority of the population in the rural areas, the labourers and small farmers in particular, remained outside the influence of nonconformity. In the rural south and east especially rural dissent was, and remained well into the nineteenth century, isolated and often ineffectual. However, even here there were regional exceptions. Dissent flourished at the margins, among independent small tradesmen, farmers and artisans. On the High Weald of Kent and Sussex, as Alan Everitt has shown, dissent kept alive an honourable and Godly tradition from the days of the Republic.[55] Cade Street Chapel, near Heathfield, an example of such a cause, still stands, isolated and beautiful, a late eighteenth century building which is a tribute to those who built it and those who have sustained it. The congregation was never large – in the 1820s they could attract only about 70 people to an anniversary meeting; and as their minutes somewhat gloomily say 'the company . . . principally from Lewes and Battle.'[56]

As Calvinists they could not evangelize and so recruitment seems to have been very much among established chapel families and to draw on the immediate area around the chapel. Names which occur in the 1780s, most notably the Harmer family, are still there in the twentieth; the Lade family who were among the first trustees in 1833 were still in the chapel a century later. The occupations of those involved as trustees show how close this little Bethel was to its Wealden community. In 1833 there were nine trustees and if we leave out two ministers the remainder were all from the Sussex High Weald and all involved in agriculture – five were farmers and two were farm servants. John Harmer, a central figure in the late eighteenth and early nineteenth century, was a potter and maker of terra cotta plaques and there seem to have been other rural artisans involved in the running of the chapel.

Cade Street was a strict and disciplined society. Throughout the eighteenth and nineteenth century it eschewed any kind of evangelism. Even the Sunday School, often a source of recruits even in Calvinist sects, was rigidly controlled, excluding children 'of those Parents who are Grossly Immoral in their lives . . . those Children who are begotten before Wedlock . . . [and] the Children of those Parents who Seldom or Never Attend the Worship of God . . . ' (spelling etc as original).[57] Doctrine was strictly adhered to, in this case the Westminster Creed, and those like the Rev. Jacob Martel who in 1809 'embraced the doctrine of Adult Baptism by Immersion' were ejected by the congregation.[58] Yet it was democratic. The new rules drawn up in 1833 vested power 'in the hands of such persons as are Actually Members of the Church at Heathfield'. This power was absolute, including the right to 'dispossess the Minister'.[59] In 1844 when the rules were changed this principle was preserved.

> 10- Should Questions Arise on any given subject that Cannot be satisfactorily decided by the Committee, a Meeting of the Church shall be called and the Question or Questions Shall be decided by the members that are present.[60]

Chapels like Cade Street existed all over rural England but their total effect was slight. Membership was small and their intense and internal theological bickering often alienated potential supporters. More importantly, before the 1820s and 1830s, the social order seems to have held firm in most country districts. This is not to say that all was calm. Rather, as James Obelkevich says, there still existed 'a society of ranks, in which there survived many *gemeinschaftlich* paternalistic (though not idyllic) elements from a still older order'.[61] However, the suppression of Swing and the bitterness created by the New Poor Law, plus the casualization of labour which marked the second agricultural revolution, destroyed the faith of many in the old order, or more precisely in the old order's values. In this situation new values were sought. As Brian Wilson says, 'particular groups are rendered marginal by some process of social change; there is a sudden need for a new interpretation of their social position or for a transvaluation of their experience'.[62] That new interpretation was provided in many areas of rural England by a revival of religious dissent, and especially by Methodism in its various forms.

The great revival of the lifetime of the Wesleys had, by and large, not touched the rural areas. However, after the mid 1820s and 1830s this began to change. The main group responsible were the Primitive Methodists whose origins lay in the proto-industrial areas of Staffordshire. They were formed as a separate sect after being expelled from the main (Wesleyan Methodist) body in 1811. In the years after 1817–18 they moved out from their Black Country base into the rural areas of Derbyshire, Nottinghamshire and Leicestershire. In May 1820 the first connectional conference was held at Hull and by 1824 William Clowes, one of the connection's founders, wrote, 'our circuit extended from Carlisle in Cumberland to Spurn Point in Holderness . . . '[63] However, it was in the rural areas that the greatest impact of the Primitive Methodists was to be felt. Here, in the aftermath of the ideological dislocation of the 1820s and 1830s Primitive Methodism, and its sister church the Bible Christians in the south-west, moved in providing a new framework through which to interpret the world.

In many a country cottage the Bible and the preaching of the Word inspired a generation of labourers as they had in the seventeenth century. A Buckinghamshire labourer described the coming of Methodism to the village of Slapton in the late 1830s.

> In the summer-time the Methodists walked backwards and forwards through the village on Sundays singing hymns, and as no room could be obtained, . . . the preaching and praying were conducted in the open air . . . They talked familiarly about Jesus Christ, as if he were a labourer keeping a family on nine shillings a week . . . It had been rumoured that these prayer meetings were more political than religious. The landlords and some of the farmers were prayed for by name. 'Cursed is he who removeth his neighbours landmark, and opresseth the poor and needy and joineth land to land' . . . these sentences always met with hearty amens.[64]

In Norfolk ten or fifteen years later young George Edwards, who became one of the leaders of the Norfolk labourers, learned to read painfully and slowly with the Bible and his wife's aid, and came to the conclusion that 'the social conditions of the people were not as God intended they should be'.[65] Ten years later, a thirteen year old Oxfordshire farm boy, Joseph Ashby, looked and saw that 'the labourers who could and dared make claims for themselves and their children were the Primitive Methodists'.[66]

It was not an easy road that village nonconformists followed. Not for nothing were the first Primitive Methodist class tickets headed by a quotation from Acts XXXVIII.22, 'but we desire of thee what thou thinkest; for as concerning this sect, we know that everywhere it is spoken against'. In Slapton, Buckinghamshire, the village shoemaker, who was one of their leaders and allowed the Methodists to meet in his house, found himself evicted; as did John Kent, a Methodist labourer from north Norfolk.[67] Kent's family also felt the sting of authority. His wife's work as a tailoress was taken away and the family were refused charity. Finally the vicar of his parish sent a letter to all the neighbouring farmers urging them not to employ Kent.[68] The records of the Maidstone Circuit of the Primitive Methodists record the more 'subtle' persuasion of paternalism aided by the harshness of winter.

> 7.12.1857. The reason of there being no collection or (?) very little class monies at Braybourne Lee (?) is owing to clerical intolerances and want of firmness in the man at whose house

> we preach, the clergyman of the above named place has offered the man at whose house we preach Coals, Blankets and soup if he would turn us out and although he and his wife are members with us we are not allowed to preach in his house. [spelling etc as original][69]

Individual persecution or the collective use of hired mobs made little difference; indeed they may have aided the growth of rural nonconformity by convincing those persecuted of their own godliness. By the time of the religious census of 1851 rural nonconformity was a powerful reality.[70] In the highland areas of small farms and where the influence of industry was greater nonconformity had effectively won. In no county north of a line drawn from the Wash to the Severn were Anglican attendances more than 40 per cent of all church attendances on census day. In vast areas of the north, Northumberland, Durham, Cumberland, Westmorland, Lancashire was much of Yorkshire, the Church of England had less than a quarter of all attendances, as they did in Cornwall. Even in counties where Anglicanism was strong, for instance Kent and Sussex, nonconformity was moving towards 40 per cent of the actively religious community. Elsewhere, for instance Norfolk and parts of Suffolk, the balance had gone even further with over 50 per cent dissenters.[71]

Yet it was not only numbers. Within most villages the truly active remained a minority. The Ashbys, the Edwards's or the Kents were always, 'the faithful few'. Yet their influence was enormous and chapel had given them a training and a base from which to work. Augustus Jessopp put it clearly.

> Explain it how we will, and draw our inferences as we choose, there is no denying it that in hundreds of parishes in England the stuffy little chapel by the wayside has been . . . the only place where the peasantry have enjoyed the free expression of their opinions, and where, under an organisation elaborated with extraordinary sagacity, they have kept up a school of music, literature, and politics, self supporting and unaided by dole or subsidy – above all a school of eloquence, in which the lowliest has become familiarized with the ordinary rules of debate, and has been trained to express himself with directness vigour and fluency.[72]

The labourer, self taught, brought via chapel to read and preach, to organize evangelizing and fundraising, to conduct a service or a quarterly meeting, was a formidable figure. Further, chapel connections or some primitive version of the 'Protestant ethic' often led to slight advancement – George Rix from Norfolk who became a higgler or dealer eventually getting his own small farm, as did John Kent.[73] In these cases economic independence was added to spiritual strength and organizational ability.

In the decades after 1870 the slackening hold of sections of the village elite opened the way for the chapel. Convinced by their own experiences of the injustice of rural life, armed with the rhetoric of the Bible and trained in Jessopp's 'school of eloquence', the lay preacher of the Primitives, Bible Christians and even the Wesleyan Methodists, or the 'old' dissent, became powerful advocates of social and political change. In their advocacy of freedom of religious belief and practice they challenged the dominance of the Church of England in the countryside. In their proud and fierce independence they cocked a snook at charity and undermined paternalism. 'Dare to be a Daniel' they sang, 'Dare to stand alone,/Dare to have a purpose firm,/Dare to make it known'.[74]

The first battles for the right to preach and hold meetings were usually over by the early 1860s but they had bred a deep distrust of the rural elite which, while it was not revolutionary – indeed was deeply contradictory in its politics – was potentially threatening to the social order. Joseph Ashby remembered a Primitive Methodist preacher putting it like this:

> 'Men are not equal', said the preacher, as making a quotation. 'No! but they are brothers! Our neighbours on the farms and in the great houses be lucky, and selfish and proud, and they expect you and me to put up with a lot of nonsense, but they be our brothers. Bitter in our hearts we are, but we can remember it: they and and we be brothers.[75]

In 1872 this confused mixture of religion and personal bitterness came together in another form – agricultural trades unionism.

There had been unions in the rural areas before the foundation of 'Arch's Union' (the National Agricultural Labourers Union) in 1872. Apart from the famous case of the Tolpuddle Martyrs there is some evidence of rural unionism in 1830–31 although very slight. However in the

1850s and especially the 1860s rural unions appeared in many counties in southern England, including Herefordshire, Buckinghamshire, Norfolk, Kent, Staffordshire and Warwickshire. They remained localized and were short lived.

In the winter of 1871–72 that changed. In January 1872 a group of labourers in the Warwickshire village of Harbury formed a local union and in February approached Joseph Arch to assist them.[76] There is no doubt that Arch was a good choice and he became an able leader. He was a skilled speaker and organizer, the product of the Primitive Methodist chapel, and he seems to have had local and powerful Liberal friends. He led a successful if limited local strike and, at Easter 1872, founded, in the bright lights of publicity from a sympathetic Liberal press, the first national union of labourers. At the end of the year it had spread over much of the midlands and was moving into East Anglia and had upwards of 40,000 members. In addition there were 'federal' unions in Lincolnshire (The Lincolnshire Labour League) and Kent and Sussex (the Kent and Sussex Labourers' Union) and an unknown but probably large number of truly local unions.

The success of the 'National' was striking and deeply shocking to contemporaries. The labourer, known derisively as 'John Hodge', had been regarded for decades as hopelessly backward by urban radicals while to the elite, he was seen as stupid but contented, the far end of the chain of paternalism. The unions struck at the heart of both these myths, but it was the attack on the latter which was most disturbing. By 'interfering' in the sacred relationship between master and man the union hit at the core of the paternalist social structure. As chapel denied the parson, so the union denied the farmer and the squire. Arch himself put it with great bitterness in his evidence before the Royal Commission in 1881.

> However impracticable it may be for the landlord, or however impracticable it may be for the farmer, the labourer has as much right to live as any of them . . . Do not talk about the good feeling (between master and man); it is a mockery to the agricultural labourer to talk about it so much; because the farmer has got all he could out of the labourer.[77]

Initially, the gains of trades unions were impressive, in the south at least. A temporary drop in real wages in the late

1860s was recovered by strike action or by the threat of it, and it seems likely that in some areas gains of up to 20 per cent may have been made by the spring of 1873.[78] Certainly those who gave evidence before the Royal Commissions of the 1889s and 1890s believed a rise of this order had taken place. More worrying to them though was the new spirit in the men, the 'independence' we have already come across. Henry Overman, who farmed 1,300 acres in Norfolk, told the 1881 commission that his men did not work so well now and were 'dissatisfied'. Characteristically it was blamed on outsiders, those who stood apart from the sacred bond of master and man, 'the agitators in the villages, and the men appointed to see that there is not too much work done . . . '[79] In Devon, according to a small hill farmer, Mr T. S. Carter it was the same.

> Are the labourers, generally speaking, in your part of the world contented? – No they are not.
>
> What are they discontented about? – I do not think they know. They get the low prints and read about these nasty agitations in the papers, and so on, and that has a bad effect upon them.[80]

These changes were to remain. The union movement certainly raised the consciousness of the labourer even when he or she was not directly involved. In many areas, especially in the east of the country, linked with the chapel and growing awareness of urban life, it created a new, aware and even politically astute section among the labourers.[81]

However, the farmers, usually supported by the landowners, began to organize in response and to sack and blacklist trades unionists. As a result, in the spring and summer of 1874, a protracted 'set piece' battle was fought out in Essex, Cambridgeshire and Suffolk between the National Agricultural Labourers Union and the organised farmers of those counties.[82] Beginning in the Newmarket area on 10 March 1874 the farmers locked out all men who refused to give up their union membership. By the middle of April the union claimed to be supporting something in the region of 6,000 men who had been locked out. Public outcry and support was widespread. Most famously the Bishop of Manchester, the Rev. James Fraser whose reports on the employment of women and children in agriculture are by far the most sympathetic to the workers, wrote to the *Times*: 'the most frightful thing that could happen for English society would be a peasants' war. Yet that is what we are driving to if insane counsels of mutual exasperation prevail.'[83]

Despite such sympathy and a good deal of support from urban unionists the lock-out succeeded. The weather in 1874 was good, widespread use was made of machinery and the farmers co-operated with each other, as they were to in every dispute up to 1923, in sharing blackleg labour brought into the area. Further, although in many villages in East Anglia union membership was all but total in many others there was virtually no membership at all. As a result there was always a supply of labour in many districts.

Harvest came and went, the only time the labour market moved absolutely in the labourers' favour. In mid-August, its funds depleted and with growing opposition to the strike from less militant areas, the National stopped paying strike pay to those still locked out. The Lincolnshire Labour League, which was also involved in the lock-out, followed suit. The lock-out broke the union movement in Essex, Cambridgeshire and much of Suffolk – but it had much wider effects. Psychologically it was disastrous. Coming after nearly two years of success it was a massive and unexpected setback. However, that could probably have been borne were it not for the fact that the cost of the lock-out was so high and the onset of the depression in 1874–75 weakened the labourers' position still further.

The lock-out exposed above all the fragility of the union's 'national' union even more so. Its real strength lay in East Anglia and the south midlands, on large or medium sized farms employing a large labour force. Here, where living-in was a thing of the past, relations between master and man were anyway less close than the idyllicist model suggested. It was also these areas where religious nonconformity was strong and where therefore certain kinds of organizational models and skills were available to the labourers.[84] Outside these areas union strength was either non-existent or based on local allegiances – the *pays* of the worker. Kent and Sussex, for instance, refused to join the National from the start, relying instead on the locally-based Kent and Sussex Labourers Union. Here, in an area of smaller farms and the persistence of living-in, unionism took on a much more ameliorative form with many aspects of a friendly society.[85]

There was another problem which seems to have affected most areas which was that all the unions, officially at least, excluded women from membership. Arch's position is made very clear in his autobiography where he writes of women's work in agriculture: 'the women should have been minding their houses, or should have been in domestic service, or working in some trade suited to women.'[86] In this Arch was not only echoing the dominant ideology of the elite but giving voice to a growing feeling within the male farm workforce. As the Swanton Morely Branch of Arch's Union put it in 1872, women were not to be allowed in the Union 'unless they united to put down field work and set an example by desisting from it themselves.'[87] This was the other side of respectability, as constructed by chapel and union, which placed a crucial emphasis on the family as a centre of the labourer's life. Women simply should not work and a major indicator of a respectable working man was that his wife did not work after marriage. The fact that many country women had to work was ignored; the fact that women were more than capable of such work was forgotten in the south at least; above all the opinion of country women as to whether they preferred wage slavery in the fields to domestic drudgery in service was never sought.

Nevertheless, women were involved, even in Arch's Union. Probably the most famous cause of that Union was that of the 'Ascott Women'. These were seventeen women from Ascott-under-Wychwood in Oxfordshire, labourers' wives and daughters, even if some of them certainly worked 'a'field'. They were summonsed for preventing blacklegs from working in 1873. They were defended by a Union solicitor and the Union raised a fund for them. However, sixteen of them were found guilty and imprisoned, seven for ten days, all with hard labour. There was a massive national outcry but throughout it all it was the fact that these were 'sixteen honest and respectable labourers' wives' who had been imprisoned that was stressed.[88] We do not know about the involvement of the Ascott women in branch life but there are sufficient indications from Norfolk, admittedly a strong Union district, to suggest that at rank-and-file level women did play a part in Arch's Union despite the Swanton Morely branch. At Beetley in Norfolk just over a year after the Swanton ban it was reported that there were three new members, one a woman. 'She insisted upon joining and this caused a good deal of merriment and many good humoured remarks.' What she felt is not recorded – but a member she became.[89] By 1878 this had changed further when the report from the Mileham branch ended, 'a number of Union females were present, a sure sign of a good branch . . . '[90] A year later the Sparham branch had a woman secretary.[91]

By this latter date though, things had changed significantly. In 1878, the East Dereham District, which included both Sparham and Mileham, split from Arch's Union and formed the Norfolk Federal Union. No rules survive of this union but it does seem that women were active in it, albeit very few of them. In 1890 there was more change when the remnant of the Norfolk Federal Union amalgamated with a Norwich general labourers' union to become the Norfolk and Norwich Amalgamated Labourers Union. Here at last women agricultural workers received some recognition when Miss M. L. Burgess of Norwich was appointed as women's organizer. Although her work was mainly with women in the urban and sweated trades she did speak at rural meetings, starting at Foulsham in March 1891.[92] How effective her work was we simply do not know as no records of the union survive but at the very least her existence was some recognition of the central importance of women in the southern English workforce.

Elsewhere there is even less information. Women were certainly active in the informal bargaining which characterized northern, and especially north eastern agriculture. They were involved in hiring bargains and on occasion could go further. There were strikes of women workers at Haydon Bridge in Northumberland in 1873 and in Fife in the same year, both over harvest payments.[93] It is not clear at this time whether or not women were allowed as members of the short-lived local Northumberland unions but it would seem more likely here than in the south, given the relative importance of women's work. However here, as elsewhere, the National Agricultural Labourers Union campaigned against women's work, particularly the 'bondage system'. The reasons given were familiar, home and family, as well as the fear that women were lowering men's wages, a fear repeated elsewhere.

The failure to gain women members was probably minor though compared to the almost total failure of the unions to gain a foothold in the north of England. Given the weakness of the unions in areas of small farms we would not expect much support in the north-west. However, in the north-east and parts of Yorkshire with their large farms and farm workforces one might expect some form of union organization. Certainly there were moves in that direction. A local union was formed in Northumberland quite separately from the Warwickshire agitation in February 1872 and this, or part of it, later joined with the National Agricultural Labourers Union. However, it only ever managed to form a dozen branches in the county.[94] There seems to have been an equal lack of success in the East Riding of Yorkshire.

The reasons for this failure lie in the specific local conditions. As we saw earlier, the hiring arrangements on northern farms often created close ties between master and man. Where this was not the case, for instance in the East Riding, yearly hiring and close supervision of young workers substituted control for identification. In addition, the labour market in the north was constantly under-supplied which gave the labourer a good deal of bargaining power. In this situation annual hiring, and the hiring fair, took on a special importance. We saw earlier how this worked year after year and all the movement of the 1870s seems to have done is given a slight edge to this bargaining process. For instance, the agitation of 1872 was deliberately timed so that some kind of united front could be presented at the March hirings. What evolved were demands for an increase in wages and reduction in hours with no 'member' agreeing to hire for less than these demands. The movement met with some success as did a similar campaign the following year. However, since there is good evidence that, at local level anyway, hiring fairs frequently performed this function it is difficult to know whether unionization, at this stage at least, made any difference. Clearly local workers did not think so given the very low level of unionization, and even Arch was forced to admit that the fairs of the north were not simply the 'slave markets' of the poorer southern districts. As he wrote in his autobiography, 'we could not do much in the north; about Newcastle and those northern districts the men were much better paid, and they said "The Union is a good thing, but we are well off and can get along without it."'[95]

After the eastern counties' lock-out this localization tendency increased as district after district reverted to the older models of organization based on the *pays*. In Norfolk George Rix led the most powerful of the East Anglian districts into a separate union, declaring, 'centralism is Toryism rank and rife. Federation is Radicalism pure and simple.'[96] In Oxfordshire the county split, with many branches following the district committees lead 'that this Committee is of openion that the Central Sistem of Government . . . has completly failed . . . and is conviced that Federation is the only effectual means to remedy the evil . . . ' (as original).[97] Elsewhere, in Kent, Surrey, Sussex and Lincolnshire, existing federal or local unions benefited from the National's problems.

Such moves were ambiguous. Certainly they represented in some ways a step backwards – a retreat into the known world of the locality – as a reaction to the failures of a new departure. However, that was not always the case. The Kent and Sussex Union may have been less progressive than Arch's but the Norfolk Federal Union under George Rix was an uncompromising and militant organization which used a real base in the locality to great effect. The local unions also had much greater staying power largely because their local base recognized the crucial reality of a world divided into small units. Their outgoings were also much lower than the National's, especially when Arch's personal autocracy led it in a number of disastrous schemes, including trying to run a national friendly society and a national newspaper.[98]

In the years after 1874 union membership plummeted. In that year total membership of all unions was about 116,000 or some 11 per cent of all farmworkers, male and female. However, since most of the unions excluded women from membership, as we have seen, it is probably more realistic to compare membership with male farmworkers. In this case, in 1874 116,000 represented about 12 per cent of full-time male farm workers. By 1891 total national membership was only just over 37,000, slightly less than 5 per cent of male farmworkers. Within these figures regional concentrations continued the same pattern. Indeed a revival in fortunes, probably caused by the first county council elections in 1889, strengthened existing regional distribution with an estimated 48 per cent of all members in East Anglia, and probably over a third in Norfolk.[99]

The decline in membership and influence in the 1880s was temporarily halted by the revival of 1889 and the granting of the franchise to most of the male farm labourers in 1884, but the unions' days were numbered. A series of bitter and disastrous winter strikes in 1891–92 and 1892–93, plus a revived and aggressive farmers' organization was too much. The Royal Commission on Labour, when it reported in 1892, told a grim tale for unionists. From Thakenham in Sussex it was reported, 'there are no trade unions among the agricultural labourers . . . and no strikes have occurred . . . during the last ten years.'[100] The Thame area of Oxfordshire was more disturbed. There had been attempts there in 1890 to establish branches of the Dockers Union, and some strikes but by 1892 these were over and the movement finished. Mr Chapman however noted, 'the men look back with regret to Arch's Union of 1874', and went on 'in most places . . . the relations between farmers and their men are somewhat strained.'[101] Dorchester, like Thakenham, showed no signs of unions but again it was commented that relations between master and man were 'not quite so friendly as they used to be.'[102] The end came in 1896 when Arch's Union, the National, was wound up, as was the Norfolk and Norwich. Only the old 'Lincolnshire League' staggered on with a handful of members until 1900.[103]

The unions were gone but 'not forgotten'. We have already talked of the legacy they left in terms of strained relations between master and man and we shall return to those points, but there was more than that. For a minority of labourers, but enough, the experience had changed their whole world. Their names are now forgotten but in many villages throughout England a combination of chapel and union had taught this group that subservience and deference rewarded by soup and coals were not the inevitable lot of the labourer. They had learned to organize themselves and because of franchise reform had a political voice which was to be vital in the next few decades. The collapse of the unions was for these 'faithful few' only a temporary setback.

Rural England began, very slowly at first, to emerge from the depression in 1898–99. In 1898 Rider Haggard noticed that wheat prices had risen again in his local market and in March of the same year the Board of Trade's journal *The Labour Gazette* noted that 'the better price of corn' was inducing farmers 'to undertake work which otherwise would have been left undone.'[104] For the next three years labour shortages were reported from many areas of England especially at harvest, a sure sign that things were improving as farmers returned to old ways and old standards. Yet it was a changed world. For the rural poor, the days of casual labour and laying off were over even in the south. For the farmer, the dominance of wheat was gone on all but the best lands. For the landlord, ever increasing agricultural rents were a thing of the past. For all, an apparently stable and ordered society had been shaken.

Its own mythology had given the 'golden age' of high farming a permanent character although it was of recent date. The depression challenged and shook that myth, opening to contemporaries a world in which commercial forces were going to produce a desolate and depopulated countryside. Suddenly, in the 1870s and 1880s, urban phenomena like trades unions appeared to disrupt what had been pictured by many as a separate and protected world. Commercial pressures challenged the notion of a classless and united agriculture, with labourer and farmer living harmoniously together under the benign gaze of parson and squire. That myth was to be re-established, but in the late 1890s that would scarcely have seemed possible.

NOTES

1 *PP 1893–4 XXXV*, Maldon, op. cit., p. 76.
2 *PP 1893–4 XXXV*, Driffield, op. cit., p. 53.
3 *PP 1893–4*, 'Royal Commission on Labour. The Agricultural Labourer. England. Report of Mr. James Wilson Fox . . . upon the Poor Law Union of Swaffam', p. 67.
4 *PP 1893–4 XXXV*, Glendale, op. cit., p. 101.
5 *PP 1900 LXXXIII*, 'Earnings of Agricultural Labourers. Report of Mr Wilson Fox on the Wages and Earnings of Agricultural labourers in the United Kingdom', p. 633.
6 ESRO SAS Acc 1276 Q (1851) and SAS Acc 1276 V (1894), Courthope estate, Wages Book.
7 *PP 1893–4 XXXV*, Maldon, op. cit., p. 76.
8 Haggard, *Rural England*, Vol. II, op. cit., p. 100.
9 Street, *Gentlemen*, op. cit., p. 54.
10 *Journal of the Folk Song Society*, Vol. VII, part 27 (1923), pp. 85–6. My thanks to Roy Palmer for correcting this reference from the first edition.
11 Street, *Gentlemen*, op. cit., p. 54.
12 *PP 1893–4 XXXV*, 'Royal Commission on Labour. The Agricultural Labourer. England. Report by Mr. Cecil Chapman . . . upon the Poor Law Union of Thame', p. 53.
13 *PP 1894 XVI, pt.1*, op. cit., p. 15.
14 Collins, *Orsett*, op. cit., p. 67.

15 *George Meek. Bath-Chair-Man*, By Himself, [London, 1910], p. 53.
16 Michael Winstanley, *Life in Kent at the Turn of the Twentieth Century*, [Folkstone, 1978], p. 79.
17 Haggard, *Rural England*, op. cit., p. 53.
18 ibid., p. 54.
19 Perry, *British Agriculture*, op. cit., p. xx.
20 *PP 1893–4 CVI*, op. cit., p. 333.
21 E. J. T. Collins, 'The Diffusion of the Threshing Machine in Britain, 1790–1880', *Tools and Tillage*, Vol. II, 1972.
22 Collins, *Labour Supply*, op. cit., pp. 470–2; E. J. T. Collins, 'The Rationality of "Surplus" Agricultural Labour, Mechanization in English Agriculture in the Nineteenth Century', *AHR* Vol. 35 pt.1 1987, p. 41.
23 J. R. Walton, *A Study of the Diffusion of Agricultural Machinery in the Nineteenth Century*, School of Geography, University of Oxford Research Papers, no. 5 1973, p. 12.
24 ibid., p. 11.
25 Alistair Mutch, 'The Mechanization of Harvest in South West Lancashire 1850–1914', *AHR*, Vol. II, 1981, p. 129.
26 Henry Rider Haggard, *A Farmers Year*, [London, 1899], pp. 273–4.
27 NRO T.56, Acc no 1051, Interview Mr A. R. Robson, b. 1891, pitman, Alnwick.
28 NRO T.34, Interview, Bob Thompson, b. 1896, farmer, Seaton Sluice.
29 Collins, 'Rationality', op. cit., p. 45.
30 Augustus Jessopp, D. D., *Arcady. For Better for Worse*, [London, 1887], pp. 108–9.
31 Interview Dixon, op. cit..
32 Flora Thompson, op. cit., pp. 162–3.
33 *PP 1881 XVII*, op. cit., p. 20.
34 *PP 1893–4, XXXV*, op. cit., p. 133.
35 *PP 1893–4, XXXV*, Crediton, op. cit., p. 99.
36 F. E. Green, *The Awakening of Rural England*, [London, n.d. but 1912], p. 311.
37 Pamela Horn, *The Victorian Country Child*, [pb. ed. Gloucester, 1985], pp. 39–42.
38 Hassall, op. cit., pp. 98–9.
39 *MC*, 8th December 1849.
40 ibid..
41 *PP 1867 XVI*, op. cit., p. 176.
42 ibid., p. 177.
43 *PP 1867–8, XVII*, op. cit., p. 203.
44 *PP 1867 XVI*, op. cit., p. 174.
45 *PP 1867–8, XVII*, p. 203.
46 ibid., p. 71.

47 *PP 1867 XVI*, op. cit., p. 175.
48 *EWP*, 15th May 1880.
49 *Samuel Drew, M.A., The Self Taught Cornishman. A Life's Lesson*. By his eldest son, [London, 1861], p. 65.
50 Joseph Parker, *Tyne Childe: My Life and Teaching*, [London, 1886], pp. 4–5.
51 Quoted in A. D. Gibert, *Religion and Society in Industrial England*, [London, 1976], p. 16.
52 Davidoff and Hall, op. cit., pp. 99 *ff*; Clyde Binfield. *So Down to Prayers. Studies in English Nonconformity 1780–1820*, [London, 1977] Ch. 3.
53 *Christopher Crayon's Recollections*, op. cit., p. 37.
54 On Lewes see Colin Brent, [ed] *Lewes in 1871. A household and political directory*, [Brighton, University of Sussex, 1978]; on Banbury, J. R. Hodgkins, *Over the Hills to Glory: Radicalism in Banburyshire 1832–1945*, [Southend-on-Sea, 1978], Chs. 1 & 2.
55 Alan Everitt, *The Pattern of Rural Dissent: The Nineteenth Century*, [Leicester, 1972].
56 ESRO, NC4/1 Minute Book of Heathfield Independent Chapel, 23rd June 1825.
57 ibid., 'Resolutions of Church, 1812'.
58 ibid., Minutes 1809 meeting.
59 ibid., 'New Rules', 4.12. 1833.
60 ibid., Minutes, 10.1. 1884.
61 James Obelkevich, 'Religion and Rural Society in South Lindsey, 1825–1875', Unpublished Ph.D thesis, Columbia University, 1971, p. 2.
62 Brian R. Wilson, 'An Analysis of Sect Development' in Brian R. Wilson (ed), *Patterns of Sectarianism*, [London, 1967], p. 31.
63 Quoted in John T. Wilkinson, 'The Rise of the Other Methodist Traditions' in Rupert Davies, A. Raymond George and Gordon Rupp (eds) *A History of the Methodist Church in Great Britain*, Vol. 2, p. 310, [London, 1978]. This is the only basic modern account of the Primitive Methodists. The best account is still H. B. Kendall, *The History of the Primitive Methodist Church*, [London, 1912].
64 J. C. Buckmaster, *A Village Politician. The Life Story of John Buckley* [1897, new ed, Horsham, 1982], p. 38.
65 George Edwards, *From Crow Scaring to Westminster* [London, 1922], p. 36.
66 Mabel K. Ashby, *Joseph Ashby of Tysoe 1859–1919. A Study of English Village Life*, [Cambridge, 1961], pp. 79–80.
67 Buckmaster, op. cit., pp. 41–5; Rev. D. Newton, *True to Principle: The Story of John Kent. An Agricultural Labourer in the County of Norfolk*, [London, n.d. but *c.* 1880], p. 56. My thanks to Mike Pickering for a photocopy of this pamphlet.

68 ibid., pp. 57–9.
69 KCRO N/MC/2/1, 'Maidstone Station of the Hull Circuit Quarterly Minutes' (Primitive Methodists).
70 W. R. Ward, 'Church and Society in the First Half of the Nineteenth Century' in Davies, George and Rupp, op. cit., p. 26.
71 Alan D. Gilbert, 'The Land and the Church', in G. E. Mingay (ed) *The Victorian Countryside*, op. cit., Vol. 1, p. 45.
71 Jessopp, op. cit., pp. 77–8.
73 For George Rix see 'The Autobiography of George Rix' in *EWP*, 7th April 1906, 14th April 1906, 21st April 1906; for Kent, op. cit., pp. 90–3.
74 'Daniel's Band' in Ira D. Sankey *Sacred Songs and Solo's*, [London, n.d. but 'Cheap Edition' *c.* 1875], Hymn no. 7.
75 Asby, op. cit., p. 80.
76 There are several accounts of agricultural unionism. Two articles remain basic, both by J. P. D. Dunbabin, 'The Revolt of the Field' in *Past and Present* no. 26, 1963 and 'The Incidence and Organisation of Agricultural Trades Unionism in the 1870s' in *AHR* Vol. XVI. Joseph Arch's autobiography, *From Ploughtail to Parliament*, op. cit., is an important if biased account. Other local studies are mentioned below.
77 *PP 1882 XIV*, op. cit., p. 69.
78 Alan Armstrong, *Farmworkers. A Social and Economic History 1770–1980* [London, 1988], p. 109.
79 *PP 1881 XVII*, op. cit., p. 742.
80 ibid., p. 734.
81 For an elaboration of this in relation to Norfolk see Alun Howkins, *Poor Labouring Men* [London, 1985].
82 The basic account of the lock-out is in Reg Groves, *Sharpen the Sickle*, [London, 1948]. The main contemporary account is in F. Clifford, *The Agricultural Lock Out of 1874*, [Edinburgh and London, 1875]. See also F. E. Green, *A History of the English Agricultural Labourer 1870–1920*, [London, 1920]; A. J. Peacock '"The Revolt of the Field" in East Anglia' in Lionel M. Munby (ed) *The Luddites and Other Essays*, [London, 1976]; J. P. D. Dunbabin, *Rural Discontent in Nineteenth Century Britain*, [London, 1974].
83 Quoted in Green, op. cit., p. 55.
84 See Dunbabin, *AHR* op. cit., especially pp. 120–5.
85 See Rollo Arnold, 'The Revolt of the Field in Kent', *PP* no. 64. For a more detailed treatment, Felicity Charlton. '"A Substantial and Sterling Friend to the Labouring Man": the Kent and Sussex Labourers Union.' Unpublished M. Phil thesis, University of Sussex, 1978.
86 Arch, *Ploughtail*, op. cit., p. 250.
87 *EWP*, 20th December 1873.

88 The Quote is from Arch, op. cit., p. 143. For another account see Groves, op. cit..

89 *EWP*, 20th March 1875.

90 ibid., 11th May 1878, p. 1.

91 ibid., 1st March 1879, p. 1.

92 ibid., 21st March 1891, p. 1.

93 Dunbabin, *Rural Discontent*, op. cit., pp. 161–2.

94 ibid., pp. 155–65.

95 Arch, op. cit., p. 221.

96 *EWP*, 22nd February 1879, p. 1.

97 'Minute Book of the Oxford District of the National Agricultural Labourers' Union' reprinted as Pamela Horn (ed) *Agricultural Trade Unionism in Oxfordshire, 1872–1881*, Oxfordshire Record Society, Vol. XLVIII [Oxford, 1974], p. 104.

98 See F. E. Green, *History*, op. cit., pp. 70–1.

99 The membership figures come from Dunbabin, *Rural Discontent*, op. cit., pp. 80–1.

100 *PP 1893–4 XXXV*, 'Royal Commission on Labour. The Agricultural Labourer. England. Report by Mr. William E. Beer on the Poor Law Union of Thakenham (Sussex)', p. 63.

101 *PP 1893–4 XXXV*, Thame, op. cit., p. 56.

102 *PP 1893–4 XXXV*, 'Royal Commission on Labour. The Agricultural Labourer. England. Report by Mr Aubrey Spencer upon the Poor Law Union of Dorchester', p. 31.

103 Howkins, *Poor Labouring Men*, op. cit., pp. 78–9.

104 *LG*, March 1898, p. 78.

8

A New Rural England

The late 1890s saw the end of the worst of the depression. Prices began to rise again, albeit slowly, and even in the hardest hit areas signs of prosperity began to return. In 1902 Henry Rider Haggard toured 'rural England', or more accurately 27 counties of rural England, and recorded 'what he saw and heard'. His conclusions were gloomy. 'The impression left upon my mind by my extensive wandering is that English agriculture seems to be fighting against the mills of God. Many circumstances combine to threaten it with ruin, although as yet it is not actually ruined.'[1]

Yet we must beware of taking these conclusions at face value. I grew up in the countryside and it was always said that you never met a poor farmer or one who hadn't just been ruined. Even Haggard saw this.

> The farmers . . . do no more than make a hard living . . . Still one fact must be remembered which farmers themselves are apt to forget – they do for the most part live, and, in comparison with the rest of the world, not at all unpleasantly.[2]

In fact the picture was complex, and as we would expect regionally varied. Wheat remained, as Haggard argued, 'the foundation of our food supply' and the most important of all crops.[3] The acreage under wheat began to increase again after an all-time low in 1895–96. Although this was to drop again in 1903–4 the overall trend was upwards. Similarly, yield per acre, which had dropped quite dramatically in the depression as farmers 'farmed dirty', began to recover in the 1890s.[4] This tendency was accelerated by the abandoning of marginal grain lands in the depression and this led to a concentration on the drier and lighter soils of the south and east.[5] The story of other cereal crops was similar although oats, which were grown almost entirely for cattle and especially horse fodder seemed less susceptible to foreign competition.

Added to this, increasing urban demand ensured the acreage under oats continued to rise.

Yet wheat had been dethroned as the monarch of English agriculture. As Edith Whetham writes,

> The census of production taken in 1908 showed that two-thirds of the output of British farms consisted of livestock and their products, for a high proportion of the crops was destined for consumption by animals, which also consumed the output of the grassland.[6]

This is seen clearly by looking at the relative values of the different sectors of British agriculture in 1908.

As this table shows though it was not only livestock which was important. All the 'new' farming, the 'alternative husbandries', as Joan Thirsk calls them, of the depression, have found a permanent place. It is striking for instance that poultry, once the despised product of women's labour, and fruit and flowers, have overtaken wool, once England's pride. Moreover it was these areas that were growing. For example, the acreage under small fruit rose from 52,969 in 1891 to 76,331 in 1914, an increase of nearly 50 per cent.[7] More importantly, milk and dairy production has all but caught up with farm crops, a further testimony to urban demand for the one, and the continuing imports of the other. In the years 1909–13 Britain produced only 21 per cent of its wheat and flour against 100 per cent of its fresh milk, 38 per cent of its butter, 25 per cent of its cheese and 46 per cent of its condensed milk.[8]

In general terms, the farming regions of England remained much as described in Chapter 1, since soil type, settlement

Table 8.1 Output of British agriculture, 1908[7]

	£ million
Farm crops	46.6
Fruit and flowers	4.6
Timber	0.6
Livestock	61.4
Wool	2.6
Milk and dairy produce	30.0
Poultry and eggs	5.0
Total	150.8

pattern and landscape do not alter much in fifty years. The division of England by a line from the Severn to the Wash, first noted by Caird in 1851, into highland/lowland, pasture/arable, still held good even if Northumberland and the East Riding of Yorkshire had great arable areas and Devon was certainly not a lowland arable county. The main changes were probably on the borders between the regions.

> The lack of profits from arable farming in the last twenty years of the nineteenth century had seen . . . corn production shrinking back on to the eastern and southern areas of lighter soils and drier climate, while grass and rough grazings occupied more of the valley sides, the wetter fields, and the heavier soils in all areas.[9]

As a result, in the last years before the Great War only East Anglia had more arable than grass land although the east midlands were very nearly equally divided.

Overall, the agricultural population continued to decline, although the steepness of that decline levelled out. Indeed in 1911 the trend to rural depopulation was reversed, at least as far as labourers were concerned.[10] This seems to have been a result of more accurate recording rather than significant change. However, as we shall see below, there were certainly areas of employment, for example market gardening, where real increases in employment took place.[11] This ever smaller workforce was also a changed workforce. Central to this was the continuing decline in the number

Table 8.2 Numbers (male and female) engaged in agriculture 1901–21 in England and Wales

Year	Landowners	Farmers	Labourers	Total
1901	25,431[a]	475,633[b]	621,068	1,124,701
1911		383,333[c]	656,337	1,065,101
1921		351,857	560,129[d]	911,966

[a] As before a problematic figure simply carries over from 1871.

[b] As before I have added a proportion for farmers' wives and daughters, assuming them to be economically active members of this group.

[c] In 1911 farmers' daughters 'and other female relatives' were included again. If this figure is accurate it fits in very well with my earlier projections.

[d] This number is arrived at by going through the revised classification for 1921 and finding the comparable groups.

of casual workers in most of arable England at least. This process had begun in the depression, as we saw above, and was regionally very uneven, but throughout the late 1890s and early 1900s, of the great wheatlands of East Anglia, the *Labour Gazette* continued to report labour shortage at harvest and other periods of high labour demand. At corn harvest in 1898 it was said of the Walsingham District of north Norfolk, 'not a man, woman, or child who is willing to work need be in want of a job,'[12] while a month later, looking at arable England generally, the same paper wrote, 'extra hands for harvest difficult, and sometimes impossible to obtain'.[13]

In one sense, these extremes were to be relatively short-lived. The season still ruled all and wet harvests like those of 1902 or 1904 could still lead to casual workers being unemployed.[14] Equally importantly, the state of the weather was crucial to a whole range of trades other than the agricultural labourer, and large numbers could be released on to the agricultural labour market. Winter always brought hardship except in very unusual years like 1900. More common were months and years like January 1902 when it was reported from Smallburgh in Norfolk, as well as elsewhere, that 'owing to building operations along the coast being slack, a good many labourers are spread over the various parishes in the Union looking for jobs.'[15] In February 1908 bad weather prevented the fishing fleet putting to sea and as a result 'a number of fishermen were seeking employment on the land.' As a Northumberland fisherman put it, 'going back before there was any self-binders or anything you could always get a job harvest time, getting the harvest in, because it was generally cut with scythe and sickle.'[16]

Yet in the medium term the position really had changed. These recurrent shortages of casual labour led the farmers to adopt different strategies, especially at hay and corn harvests. Most obvious was the increasing use of machinery. As we saw above, mechanization was slow to come to English agriculture, but when the depression lifted and the real extent of the casual labour shortage became clear, the reaper and the reaper binder appeared in large numbers. These machines largely replaced casual workers. As the *Labour Gazette* noted of Suffolk in 1899, a year of generally severe labour shortage, 'the supply of labour for harvest in this county has been, generally speaking, sufficient, owing in great measure to the large use made of self binding machines.'[17] Regionally, two key groups of workers were affected by this change, the travelling harvesters, especially the Irish, and women.

As we have already seen, the number of Irish migrating seasonally to England went into decline in the aftermath of the Great Famine of 1845–50. As E. J. T. Collins has written, 'the famine . . . was a watershed in the history of Irish seasonal migration, and its decline thereafter was as dramatic as in the previous half century had been its rise.'[18] The depression in England and changing patterns of landholding at home, which became established by the 1870s, added to the increasing tendency for Irish men and women to move permanently rather than follow a seasonal pattern of migration. Nevertheless they continued to come, especially to the midlands and the north of England. About 30,000 came in 1900 and although the spread is impossible to chart with any detail, evidence from memoirs and farm books shows the continuing importance of such workers. This was particularly so in the north where competition from industrial employment created constant labour shortages in the agricultural sector. The labour records of Castle Heaton Farm in north Northumberland show regular use of migrant Irish workers up to the Great War and even afterwards.[19] Interview material from Northumberland supports this.

> When the turnips were to be hoed, then singled, gangs used to come over from Ireland . . . and they were employed by most people, and there again you see . . . hoe the turnips on one farm then move on to the next farm. And they also of course helped with hay work, or helped with harvest work and . . . with threshing work.[20]

Similarly it is clear that Irish workers were still regularly visiting the Yorkshire Dales and the agricultural areas of Lancashire right up to the Second World War although numbers had decreased considerably.[21] Further south, travelling Irish workers were still a regular part of Flora Thompson's Oxfordshire in the early 1900s, 'who came to her neighbourhood for a season, as the swallows came, then disappeared across the sea . . . '[22]

The position of women is more complex. In many areas, mostly in the north and to a lesser extent the west of England women were not only or mainly casual workers but full-time members of the farm workforce, and we shall return to these groups later. Also, as I have said before, census data and official reports certainly underestimate the number of women employed at any one point. However, in the south and especially the eastern counties the casualization of all farm work in the 20 years after 1850 particularly affected women. They became, like the migrant workers, a 'reserve army of labour', called when needed, laid off when not. As a result women workers were increasingly marginalized within the production process and particularly susceptible to technical change. This is demonstrated brilliantly by Eve Hostettler in her short study of the illustrations for Henry Steven's *The Book of the Farm* which shows the mechanization of the harvest process. In three illustrations we see 'Reapers in a Bandwin' with four women reapers, 'Mowing Corn with a Scythe' with three women gathering and stooking the corn, and finally 'Brigham and Bickertomns self-delivery reaper at work' where there is one woman gathering stooks.[23] As Hostettler points out, the movement from sickle, to scythe, to reaper, was the path followed by nineteenth century arable production and the reduction in labour demand that went with it is clear.

Yet caution is needed. By 1905, when Wilson Fox wrote his second report on wages and conditions in agriculture, the decline in causal field work for women was far advanced. 'The practice of employing women and children on the land', he said, 'largely declined in the early "seventies" and by the early "eighties" it had almost entirely ceased in many districts.'[24] Yet his own detailed material points out the extent to which arable agriculture still relied upon seasonal inputs from women workers. On a Lincolnshire farm of 4,000 acres of which 2,800 acres were arable, 'a good deal of extra labour is employed at certain seasons of the year, including a number of women; sometimes 70 or 80 women are employed mainly at picking and sorting potatoes and weeding.' In Warwickshire, 'ten women are frequently employed on the farm at such work as weeding, root clearing, potato cropping and hay and corn harvest.'[25]

Even in the most advanced counties where machinery was widely used, like Norfolk, farm books show that casual employment of women continued up to the Great War.[26] It is possible that it may even have increased as the decline in migrant workers and rural depopulation left many farmers short at crucial times of the year. For example, the wages books quoted above *appear* to show that no women were employed either as full-time or casual workers between 1903 and 1907, although women do appear on the list of those getting Christmas 'boxes'. In 1907, however, women are listed for payment for threshing, where hitherto men's names only had appeared. From 1907–14 women's employment seems to increase and by the latter date to include many of the tasks like weeding, stone picking and work at hay and corn harvest which many thought they had abandoned in the depression.[27] One series of wages books obviously cannot prove very much but it is instructive and is a counter to the view that women's work was in terminal decline from the 1870s onwards.

Casual work did decline, but it declined for both men and women. What this meant was that on each farm the core workforce stabilized, and possibly even grew slightly in number, and that they were regularly employed all the year round even in those districts, like East Anglia, where hiring by the day had been the practice for many years. This process was helped by the gradual introduction of machinery; as a Devon farmer put it, 'since I have availed myself of the machinery that there is I can comfortably complete my harvest with my regular labourers alone.'[28] Henry Rider Haggard felt the same. His reaper, bought in 1898, paid 'its cost twice over' because it dispensed with labour and worked much faster.[29]

Probably more important though, were obvious but usually local changes in the nature of production. For example, the widespread complaints by workers to the various commissioners from the *Royal Commission on Labour* in 1894 that farmers were using fewer and fewer workers were probably exaggerated but are too widespread to be dismissed out of hand. Even if farming standards, in terms of weeding, hoeing, stone picking, hedging and ditching and general cleanliness, did improve again in the Edwardian period there is no suggestion anywhere that the massive inputs of labour required for the old system of high farming returned with this improvement. This process continued for the rest of our period until our own day and the number of workers per unit became smaller and smaller. By the 1900s, in the arable regions at least, it seems that there were probably three or four regular workers for every one casual. By the 1920s it was five to one.[30]

At the other end of the social scale the changes brought about by the depression were equally difficult to see with much precision. To Lady Bracknell land may have ceased to be either 'a profit or a pleasure' but a country house remained an essential part of a 'gentleman's self definition. As Jack Worthing in *The Importance of Being Earnest* says, 'I have a country house with some land, of course, attached to it, about fifteen hundred acres, I believe; but I don't depend on that for my real income.'[31] Rents certainly fell, as we saw earlier, but again regions, or rather types of agriculture were of vital importance. On the bad or indifferent wheat lands substantial rent reductions did affect landowners' fortunes but as F. M. L. Thompson points out, 'such a fall . . . seemed to make little difference to a landowner's style of living.'[32] Some great landowners maintained their fortunes by judicious agricultural change. The Third Earl of Carrington, for instance, suffered a drop in rental income of around 40 per cent between 1873 and 1897 on his lands in Buckinghamshire and Lincolnshire. Nevertheless, by reorganizing his estate affairs and selling land on the periphery of his core estates, he maintained 'a personal expenditure of over £10,000 a year without recourse to borrowing' or to urban or commercial speculation.[33] Thompson also notes precise geographical distinctions between the 'sheep/corn' areas of the estates of the Marquis of Bath where 'arrears mounted sharply after 1878, farms fell into hand . . . and rents were ultimately reduced by about a quarter' and those areas given over to dairying where 'there were few signs of strain.'[34]

However, for many great landowners, sources of income from other than agricultural land became increasingly important. We saw earlier that it was those landowners who did not rely solely on rents who fared best during the depression and there was certainly a switch away from rents into other sources of income, especially investment overseas and through the Stock Exchange. This was not entirely new and is still not well documented, but it is clear from a number of different accounts that sections of the elite began to adopt new strategies from the mid-1890s onwards. Thompson points to the Earls of Verulam. The 2nd Earl's fortune suffered badly from the depression and falls in rents, but his son, the 3rd Earl, who inherited in 1895, 'was altogether more businesslike, as befitted one who became something of a businessman'. He controlled his expenditure with great care and invested cautiously in a number of ventures. By 1913 over one-third of his income came from director's fees and share income.[35] Nor was Verulam alone. In the 1890s the Earls of Fitzwilliam and Durham 'undertook large-scale conversions of their assets into stocks and bonds' while the Duke of Portland 'invested in a wide range of industrial debenture and ordinary shares.'[36]

Some however did suffer. The Marquess of Ailesbury succeeded in 1894 to a neglected estate at Savernake and was forced to live in a small house on the estate leaving Tottenham Park empty. The shooting was let and until 1911 the land yielded no personal income to the Marquess. Until the Great War he 'continued to lead the frugal life of a modest country gentleman, with no attempt to resume the grand manner of aristocratic living.'[37] In general terms then, the pattern established in the 1880s continued. It was the smaller landlords in the arable districts who suffered most and their ill fortune tended to be, as Thompson puts it, 'self perpetuating'. Reduced rents led to less reinvestment in the estate and therefore made it more difficult to let farms to good tenants when the times began to improve in the 1900s.[38]

An alternative in this situation was land sale but after twenty years of apparent depression the land market was stagnant. The 1860s had seen the land market buoyant with high prices, a situation which continued until the late 1870s. Thereafter the volume of sales and price of land fell dramatically. As rents continued to fall this situation got worse.[39] However, in the 1900s land sales began to pick up as agricultural fortunes began their slow improvement and by 1910–11 'a flood of land sales started, continuing through to the outbreak of war in 1914.'[40] These sales pointed to a new and changed situation and for the first time there was talk of the break up of estates. The key factor was that it was tenant farmers who were buying up their 'own' holdings. They often bought with some reluctance, but with agriculture reviving the alternative of a new landlord who might well raise the rent and reimpose farming and cropping covenants which had been abandoned during the depression was too serious a threat. Purchase by tenants, like the gradual disappearance of casual workers and the overall reduction in numbers employed per unit, was the beginning of a trend which was to come to dominate in the post war years.

To contemporaries though sale to tenants was little noticed compared with a fear of new 'men of property' – the businessman and the banker buying into the gentry. Between Alex

D'Urberville, the villain of Hardy's *Tess of the D'Ubervilles* who has 'bought' the Norman name with the family mansion, and Galsworthy's Forsyths, stretch a range of parvenu gentry. The 'purple of commerce' and, more rarely, the grime of industry bought their way into rural England and some at least of the great houses of Victorian England found themselves with new owners. Apethorpe in Northamptonshire was bought by one of the Brasseys, the family which made its fortunes as railways contractors, as was Battle Abbey in Sussex. Hengrave Hall in Suffolk was sold to a cotton spinner from Lancashire, while Gilling Castle in Yorkshire was sold to a colliery owner.[41] Elsewhere national and racial pride were damaged when the German-born diamond magnate Sir Julius Wernher bought Luton Hoo, while others who made their fortune in South Africa, the 'Randlords', offended simply by ostentatious shows of wealth.[42]

We must beware of trusting this contemporary picture too easily, for there was an important distinction between 'country life' and a 'country' house, and being a landlord. W. D. Rubenstein's work has shown quite clearly that in the second half of the nineteenth century, despite popular ideas, relatively few of those who had made money in the city or in industry bought into land. Even fewer bought enough land to qualify among Bateman's 'great landowners', mainly because, even at its lowest price land in England (as opposed to Ireland and Scotland) was simply too expensive to enable the purchase of large enough estates.[43] Yet the desire to live in the country and to adopt 'country ways' was widespread even if it more often resulted in the purchase or renting of what was essentially a country house rather than an estate. As Clive Aslet says of houses built in the countryside after 1890:

> [they] were designed for a semblance of landed life, but the estates were rarely more than a thousand acres, and even then they were often bought for sport rather than farming. Virtually none was big enough or profitable enough to justify the size of the house it was apparently designed to support. In many cases, it was the form rather than the reality of landownership that appealed to the generally self-made men who built new country houses . . .[44]

There were other changes within the elite which amazed and even titillated contemporaries. The aristocracy had been for most of the nineteenth century 'a self-contained and largely self-demarcated group.'[45] This was especially marked in the symbolically key areas of social relationships, particularly marriage. The process of self-demarcation relied ɒoth on precise codes of inclusion and exclusion and knowledge about who to include or exclude. Both these areas were becoming more of a problem in the years after 1890. Marriage, for example, had always been a way of dealing with financial problems but the arrival of American money made the whole process somehow more blatant.

> The novelty of glamour of these moves to call in young and vigorous dollar stock to refresh the old, and sometimes decaying, English aristocracy naturally attracted attention, but they were in fact no more than a striking new version of the old established practice of marrying into new wealth.[46]

Yet these matches, along with the even more 'scandalous' habit of peers marrying actresses (there were 19 such marriages between 1894 and 1914 as opposed to only ten in the hundred years before[47]) did indicate change. Society was broadening its self-definition even if the aristocracy remained in many ways a closed group. As Leonore Davidoff writes:

> the amount of wealth became as important a criterion of entry to society as its source. This shift in emphasis was increased by the introduction of foreign-made fortunes . . . The whole basis of Society was growing wider and these new very wealthy groups only helped to 'raise the ante' for the material base of operations.[48]

Widening the group created other problems – who was now in the social elite? Definitions became crucial if difficult. Books like Walford's *County Families* which listed, with photographs, the county elite for each county were as John Lowerson says, 'a sign of growing uncertainty' among the county ruling class.[49] Even the London season, once a clearly demarcated area, became more complex and *The Queen* ran a regular column called 'The Upper 10,000 at Home and Abroad' so that the newcomer could identify the elite and be identified in turn. *The Times* also performed a crucial role as 'the local paper of the national elite' while by 1910 the semi-annual *Boyle's Court Guide* provided lists of 'At Homes'.[50] By this date advertisements were appearing regularly in the elite press offering the services of well connected 'Ladies' as chaperones and guides, especially for Americans. The world though was truly 'upside down' when the future King Edward VII chose to stay in the home of an American self-made man at West Dean rather than with the Duke of Richmond at Goodwood House for Goodwood Week in 1899.[51]

Between the labourers and the great society families lay the great mass of what earlier times had called the 'middling sort'. Their fortunes in the aftermath of the depression are difficult to trace mainly because, at the most basic level, the census does not distinguish, for example, between an urban shopkeeper or solicitor and their rural counterparts. However, the continuing decline in numbers of those engaged in agriculture concealed the fact that the population of the rural areas was increasing for the first time since the 1850s. In 1911 the census looked at 105 Registration Districts which were entirely rural from 1801–1911. This showed steady population growth until the ten years 1851–61 and then decline. In 1901 the population started to increase again and this continued in 1911.

What we see here in part was the appearance of a new countryman and woman since most of the growth was attributable, according to the census, to 'residential development owing to proximity to towns, increased travelling facilities, & c.'[52] We will return to this group in more detail in the next chapter but in the most basic terms these were the first generation of urban dwellers who fled the city, first for the suburbs, but ultimately for the countryside itself, especially the countryside of the south and south-east. In 1877 the Rev. Benjamin Armstrong, travelling from his Norfolk home to the area of his birth south of London, 'was surprised to find London almost extending to Croydon, and also at the little army of city clerks and men of business who got on at the various stations.'[53]

However, there were other groups who were growing, partly as a direct result of this suburban spread, but also because of changes within agricultural production and, less clearly, changes within the broad social and economic structure.

Urban and suburban growth produced not only 'newcomers' but a whole range of trades which catered to them. The most obvious examples of this were, as we have already seen, the growth of small-scale agricultural and horticultural units producing 'luxury' foods, and, newest of all, plants and flowers. At its most simple, increasing urban concentration and incomes, especially among the middle and upper working class, coupled with falling wheat prices, made intensive agriculture in areas with good access to urban centres a sound financial option. This was not of course new. As we said above Joan Thirsk has noted this kind of switch in the seventeenth century as well as the nineteenth century, and in many of the same areas.

A central difference was the scale of the change and the fact that it was permanent rather than a temporary expedient to get through bad times. Again numbers are difficult to trace over time since the category of 'gardener' before 1881 was confused by the fact that many 'domestic' gardeners were included in a category designed to cover essentially commercial operations. The census of 1881 dealt with this in a fairly haphazard way but ended by estimating that in the previous decade the number of persons employed in non-domestic garden work had increased by about 24 per cent.[54] Ten years later the change, now recorded more accurately, showed only a slight slowing down with an increase of 20.9 per cent over 1881. However, the area of land used as 'market gardens and nursery grounds' had increased by 65 per cent in the same period. In the next decade a similar increase was recorded.[55] Between 1901 and 1911 it is possible to make accurate comparisons. In a period when the agricultural population as a whole was declining those employed in market gardening and nursery work increased by a further 13 per cent. This slowing down may well be a reflection of the gradual return of prosperity to arable farming. Thus, between 1870 and 1911 when the total population involved in agriculture had declined by something in the region of 44 per cent, those involved in market gardening and nurserying had increased by something in the order of 75 per cent. The numbers involved were still relatively small, 140,103 in 1911, but by this date this represents about 10 per cent of the total 'agricultural population'. In addition, it is certain that a sizable part of the 'farmer' category, especially those farming less than twenty acres, need to be added to this group. Finally there were those 'poultry farmers' who were not clearly distinguished as a separate category until 1921.

Without detailed census work it is impossible to locate this group geographically, but it seems certain that they tended to cluster around the great cities, especially those of southern England. London in particular attracted market gardeners and nursery men as well as enabling larger, established farmers to capitalize on their nearness to the market. At this end of the scale was Mr G. F. Hempson of Ardleigh near Colchester. He farmed 400 acres, some of it on conventional arable lines but also supplied flowers, good chickens 'dressed but not pulled' and beef to the London market.[56] In the middle range, but still a substantial man was Mr Hamilton of Waltham Cross who Henry Rider Haggard spoke to in 1902. Mr Hamilton was a Scots 'settler' who had taken an unprofitable small farm in the mid-1870s. When Haggard visited it there were 20 acres under glass growing tomatoes, cucumbers, grapes and peaches for the London market. All his produce went to London by road, the waggons returning not empty but filled with stable manure, 'which he found more valuable than any artificial fertiliser'.[57] At the extreme end were holdings in Kent of three and four acres which provided a 'good living growing plums, cherries and soft fruits although their owners worked twice as hard as any hired labourer'.[58]

Moving away from London other urban conurbations provided the same conditions, if sometimes in a modified form. The reliance of small farmers in Durham and Northumberland on pit villages has already been mentioned as has the continuing prosperity of Lancashire farming which was based on an urban/industrial market. Similarly Cheshire, according to A. D. Hall in 1911, was 'a most productive and intensively farmed county, for nowhere else is there such an area of good land close to one of the densest and richest town populations in the world'.[59] The county produced cheese, milk, 'magnificent' potatoes, fruit and vegetables for industrial Lancashire and the 'seaside' trades of Southport and Blackpool.[60]

Where communications were good the influence of a great conurbation spread far. The Sandy district of Bedfordshire, although poor soil for cereal, was 'flat and easy to work in any weather', according to Hall, and responded well to intensive cultivation. Here, market gardening was on the increase and plots were getting smaller and smaller at high rents. Yet growing early potatoes, carrots, turnips, sprouts, onions, marrows, runner beans and asparagus provided a good living on 20 acres or less. The key factor here was the Great Northern Railway. 'London dung and the railway facilities for sale northward and southward have made the district.'[61] These factors were also important in parts of Norfolk and Lincolnshire where the considerable distance from an urban centre was made up for by excellent transport.

Additionally, there were some areas, the Vale of Evesham, the Tiptree District of Essex or the Penzance area of Cornwall for example, where particular local circumstances had enabled communities of smallholders to develop far away from urban areas although still very much as a response to urban demand. Tiptree, like Histon in Cambridgeshire, developed on the back of the 'jam revolution' although for most of the smallholders the real source of income was seed growing. In 1907 one Tiptree man had five acres devoted to seed growing on which he had nasturtiums, mangolds, turnips and cabbages for seed, 'a few' vegetables for sale at Colchester market, an acre of outdoor tomatoes and some glass houses.[62] The Vale of Evesham developed quite differently. In 1907 there were, in the Evesham District, about 10,000 acres of land in holdings of between one and eight acres and the numbers were growing. Here, as in Cornwall, a mixture of favourable climate and good soils created an ideal site. Two crops dominated in Evesham, although there was a great variety, plums, especially Pershores, and asparagus. Selling was well organized at Evesham. Most of the producers were too small to sell direct and so sold to the larger growers who in turn sold mostly 'in Birmingham and other northern towns.'[63] What is striking about Evesham, and even more so about the growth of vegetable-based smallholding in the Penzance area, was the importance of luxury production for the home market. Evesham 'grass' sold on purely 'gourmet' grounds as did the 'new' broccoli and potatoes of the Penzance District. The key to them both, and many others, was the impossibility of foreign growers competing, in an expanding market, because of transport costs. It was to be short-lived though, for Cornwall at least. In 1912 French broccoli from Roscoff and potatoes from St. Malo were beginning to threaten Cornwall's position.[64]

The final area of expansion of this kind was directed at 'urban' growth within the countryside itself. When Haggard visited Sussex he commented gloomily on the eastern part of the county that but 'for the fact that many rich men from London occupy large houses, which absorb much produce at a good price, it would go very hardly both with tenants and landlords'.[65] Elsewhere, for example on the Surrey Sands, a curious double process took place whereby new housing destroyed some aspects of agriculture by taking land but supported other aspects by the demand for produce. In the Woking area for instance, suburban development reduced the arable acreage from 2,300 acres in 1870 to a mere 500 by 1930, while maintaining meadow land for milk at much the same level.[66]

Nor was it only what the urban and suburban world ate that created new kinds of agriculture. Seed production for agriculture was a long established 'industry' but the growth in urban interest in gardening and especially flower gardening increased demand enormously. Haggard noted that around Witham in Essex were, 'hundreds of garden plots devoted to the cultivation of various seeds, among them those of Shirley poppies, mangold, parsley, swede, nasturtium, and pansy.'[67] In the Bagshot Sands region it was more striking still.

> . . . growing demand for shrubs such as azaleas and rhododendrons (the so called 'American plants') could be satisfied from the careful cultivation of local soils, and the products found ready sales in the villa suburbs of London.[68]

As a result of these demands, nurserymen in Woking parish increased from three in 1854 to 19 in 1911 and 30 by 1938. By 1930 18 per cent of Woking's farmland was nurseries.[69]

While the great towns contributed to important changes in farming, their industrial products also directly affected the rural areas. We saw in Chapters 1 and 2 how a market town created around it a *pays*, an area on which it depended but which it in turn serviced. This relationship remained crucial, certainly until the Great War and probably for the rest of our period, but changes were again taking place within the system. The second half of the nineteenth century saw mass production extend into new areas, especially articles of domestic consumption. This process, which began in the 1830s, accelerated as the century progressed. From the 1850s and 1860s, factory-made clothing, boots and shoes became widely available, while the factory products of Stoke-on-Trent replaced the local potteries. Franklin's 'Field Town Chiney' (actually slip decorated earthenware) which had once been famous all over West Oxfordshire finally stopped producing in the 1890s while Alfred Grove and Sons of the same village made their last pots in 1906.[70] William Smith, the farmer/potter from Surrey, found problems even earlier when the railway brought the 'better ware' from Doultons at Lambeth into the Surrey countryside.[71] This move away from local production spread into most country crafts; as Chartres and Turnbull say, 'employment in virtually all crafts and in most of the selected counties dropped consistently from the 1861 or the 1871 census . . . '[72]

This opens up the whole question of industries in the countryside. It is clear that much of what we think of as 'industrialization' in the first part of the nineteenth century and earlier was actually rural in its character and situation. Areas like the West Midlands, Staffordshire and even parts of the north-east retained a distinctively rural character in the midst of industrial growth. Some of the industries, based essentially on hand craft technology, collapsed, like Franklins in Leafield, when faced with mechanization elsewhere in England.[73] Others though had a remarkably long existence, particularly where machine technology was not obviously cheaper or easier. This was especially the case where the majority of the workforce were women. Hand work gloving, for instance, survived well into the twentieth century in West Oxfordshire; hand bombazine weaving survived in rural Norfolk long after the complete eradication of other types of hand loom work; so did straw plait making in Buckinghamshire and Bedfordshire. There were also settlements, like Allendale in Northumberland where agricultural employment and 'industrial' employment co-existed. Here, as for the free miners of the Forest of Dean, common land, industrial employment in mining and small farms enabled a proto-industrial social formation to survive into the twentieth century.

There were also 'new' industries in rural areas which appeared throughout the nineteenth century. The most obvious of these were coal mining and other forms of extractive industry. New pits were being opened throughout our period and often within firmly rural areas. The Deerness Valley in Co. Durham was opened up as a mining area between the mid-1860s and the mid-1890s. Before that date the area had been entirely agricultural but for some drift mining beginning in the 1850s.[74] A similar situation existed in many areas of northern and even midland England. One thinks here of D. H. Lawrence's Nottinghamshire with its mixture of pits and farms, miners and labourers. The opening of railways could have a similar effect. Wolverton in Buckinghamshire stood out even in my childhood as an industrial town, with its rows of cottages built by the Midland Railway for the men who worked in the carriage works. Wigston in Leicestershire had an almost identical history with something like 600 cottages built by the railway company between 1883 and 1890.[75]

Nevertheless, in general terms, the last years of the nineteenth century and early years of this century saw a process of 'de-industrialization' in the countryside as mechanization and factory production grew. Indeed by the 1900s the 'decline of rural industry' was one of the great worries of reformers and advocates of the 'back to the land movement', and its restoration, in carefully controlled terms, was one of their panaceas for rural decay.

Hand in hand with the growth of mass production and the erosion of local manufacture went the decline in the market and its replacement by regular shops. In 1888 it was said of Helston in Cornwall, the 'market is decreasing very much, the trade being diverted to the shops'.[76] This was the countryside's share of the late nineteenth century 'retailing revolution'. Trade through shops, even of foodstuffs, especially imported ones, became the norm after the 1870s. Markets as such did not actually disappear, it was more that they themselves became more specialized. 'New' cattle markets, often custom built and away from the old market place became more and more common in the last decades of the century and this led to a division between 'shopping' and 'marketing'. Now the farmer would go off to the market leaving his wife and daughters to go round the shops.[77]

However, the decline in markets and in local production did not mean a reduction in goods available at this stage, rather the opposite. By the 1900s the range of shops and services available in most country towns was impressive. A detailed 'trade and industrial' directory of the eastern counties published in the late 1880s gives an idea of what the countryman or woman could expect from the 'retailing revolution'. In Colchester, Essex, Barritt and Sons 'Dispensing and Family Chemists' boasted that it was 'on three stories' with 'two fine windows on each street, in which an attractive display of goods is always maintained'. As well as all 'the usual drugs and medicinal preparations' customers could easily get all their needs since the company was in 'daily receipt of parcels from London'. Frank Chapman, a greengrocer also in Colchester always had 'a fine show of game, poultry, vegetables, fruit (both foreign and English) etc., etc.' and A. E. Hammond informed his customers that he sold 'teas, coffees, spices, dried and candid (sic) fruits, sago, rice, oatmeal, sugar, sauces, pickles, condiments, tinned or preserved fish, fruits, meats etc. . . . ' Colchester also had shops selling cigars, pianos, artists' materials, children's clothes and cycles as well as all the more usual goods and services.[78]

The country town, like the *pays* around it, had also become a more complex society, meshed into a national market, a national system of government, and a national legal and financial system. All this subtly changed rural social structure by enlarging the size and increasing the importance of the rural middle class. For example, as property law hardened in the eighteenth century and the old manorial tenures were gradually replaced by leases, both estate agents and lawyers grew in importance. The growth of local government and bodies like the Boards of Health brought the nineteenth century revolution in government down to village or at least small town level and produced a new class of local administrators. Medical changes and gradual professionalization in the 1840s and 1850s created a class of county doctors and apothecaries.

Local figures are difficult to obtain but nationally (urban and rural) the numbers in professional occupations more than doubled from 162,000 in 1851 to 413,000 in 1911; and commercial occupations increased by more than seven times from 91,000 to 739,000 in the same period during a time when the male workforce had barely doubled. If we look at North Walsham in Norfolk in 1890 some idea of how these changes translated themselves at local level can be gained.

In 1890 North Walsham had a population of about 4,000 who relied for their livelihoods essentially on the surrounding rural hinterland. According to *Whites Directory* signs of a new middle class presence were to be seen in the 'suburbs' where 'many neat houses' had been built in 'recent years' and in the town centre 'some of the old houses . . . have been rebuilt with handsome fronts'. Its middle class was not large but in 1890 the area supported six banks or bankers' agents, five firms of solicitors, five private schools as well as the Grammar School and the Board School, two pharmacists, two firms of auctioneers, three farm stewards, an Inland Revenue Inspector, a Sanitary Officer, four clerks, two managers, and a vet. Moving out of the 'professional and commercial class' there was a huge array of shops and small businesses. In some cases one person combined a variety of roles although Josiah Sadler Empson was exceptional and sounds like a character from a Gilbert and Sullivan opera. In 1890 he lived in one of the new middle class houses 'The Limes' and was 'solicitor, commissioner in all courts, perpetual commissioner, clerk to the magistrates for Tunstead and Happing Division, clerk to the commissioner of taxes, clerk to North Walsham Local Board, clerk to Paston United District School Boards, Conservative Agent for the districts of North Walsham, Coltishall, Stalham, &c., and agent for the Phoenix Fire, Pelican Life, Commercial Union Fire and Life and Guarantee offices, Grammar School Road.'[79]

People like this constituted a coherent and respected group within a country town. R. H. Mottram was a junior in Gurney's Bank in North Walsham in the 1900s and was a fringe member this of this group. Its core was, according to Mottram,

> a distinguished incumbent, whose influence was, however, more obvious in social, than in business circles. A long-established firm of lawyers belonged to both worlds, for one of its partners was a cricketer of county standing. While a very well known doctor completed the powers that ruled the place.[80]

The middle classes of North Walsham bound themselves together and excluded those below by their own social round and rituals, such as bowls and tennis, whist parties and dances. Their place was known, respected and assured. It was also increasingly set and professionalized. As G. E. Mingay writes.

> By the opening of the twentieth century the most important of the specialized services – law, medicine, veterinary science, education, land agency, the valuing and auctioning of property – were largely in expert and trained hands . . . and their especial reward was the great fund of respect which was theirs in the small, and still personal, rural community.[81]

In this chapter we have outlined some of the changes which we now need to fill in with more detail, for it is within these great regions and nationally-registered changes that both the alterations to the basic farming and social systems and their persistences are most striking. We must not forget that England was still a local world, although that was changing as we shall see in the next chapter, and the experiences of those who lived in that world are our concern. Thus the local world continued to mediate, structure and give value to change and to continuity. In this process what hardly registers on the annual return of agricultural statistics could be traumatic within a particular *pays*. Yet the local world was being threatened. For the first time for generations economic change in the form of the depression had shaken agricultural society. In addition urbanization and industrialization had changed the nature of the non-rural world and were now about to begin to change the countryside.

NOTES

1 Haggard, *Rural England*, op, cit., Vol. II, p. 536.
2 ibid., p. 543.
3 Mitchell and Dean, op. cit., pp. 78–90.
4 Haggard, op. cit., p. 556.
5 Edith M. Whetham, *The Agrarian History of England and Wales, Vol. VIII 1914–1939*, [Cambridge, 1978], p. 3.
6 ibid..
7 Derived from Whetham, ibid., and *PP 1912–13 X*, 'Report in Connection with the Census of Production Act . . . ', p. 25. Prothero, op, cit., p. 465a.
8 W. H. Beveridge, *British Food Control*, [London, 1928], p. 359.
9 Whetham, op. cit., p. 29.
10 *PP 1914 XLIV*, 'Census of England and Wales, 1911, Vol. X, Occupations and Industries', pp. 112-15.
11 ibid., p. 38.
12 *L.G.*, September, 1898, p. 246.
13 ibid., October, 1898, p. 300.
14 ibid., September 1902, p. 258 and October 1904, p. 291.
15 ibid., January 1902, p. 16.
16 ibid., February 1980, p. 56; NRO, NRO T/95 Interview with Mr. Jack Stewart, fisherman, Alnmouth.
17 ibid., October 1899, p. 291.
18 Collins, 'Migrant Labour', op. cit., p. 50.
19 NRO, NRO 302/172 Wood Ms., Castle Heaton Farm, day books 1909–1914.
20 NRO, NRO T 135, Interview Mr. E. C. Spence, farmer, Stannington area.
21 For example the fiddler Michael Gorman worked in Lancashire and Yorkshire in the years before 1939. Information from Reg Hall. See also Kightly, op. cit., pp. 121–2.
22 Thompson, *Lark Rise*, op. cit., p. 471.
23 Eve Hostettler, 'Gourlay Steell and the Sexual Division of Labour', *HWJ* no. 4 [1977], pp. 95–100.

24 *PP 1905 XCVIII*, 'Second Report of Mr Wilson Fox on the Wages, Earnings and Condition of Employment of Agricultural labourers', p. 12.
25 ibid., pp. 401-3.
26 NNRO R 154D, Labour Books Ditchingham-Hemphall Area.
27 ibid..
28 Quoted in Armstrong, op. cit., p. 112.
29 Haggard, *A Farmers Year*, op. cit., p. 274.
30 Collins, thesis, op. cit., pp. 35 *ff*.
31 Wilde, *Importance*, op. cit., p. 304.
32 Thompson, *Landed Society*, op. cit., p. 313.
33 Andrew Adonis, 'Aristocracy, Agriculture and Liberalism: The Politics, Finances and Estates of the Third Earl of Carrington', *HJ*, Vol. 31, 4 [1988], pp. 881–3.
34 Thompson, *Landed Society*, op. cit., p. 312.
35 ibid., pp. 303–6.
36 ibid., p. 307.
37 ibid., p. 314.
38 ibid., pp. 315–6.
39 F. M. L. Thompson, 'The Land Market in the Nineteenth Century', in W. E. Minchinton, [ed] *Essays in Agrarian History*, Vol. II, [Newton Abbot, 1968], pp. 29–54.
40 Thompson, *Landed Society*, op. cit, pp. 321–2.
41 Mark Girouard, *Life in the English Country House*, [New Haven and London, 1978], p. 300.
42 Clive Aslet, *The Last Country Houses*, [New Haven and London, 1982], esp. Ch. 1.
43 W. D. Rubinstein, 'New Men of Wealth and the Purchase of Land in Nineteenth Century England', *P&P* 92 [1981], pp. 125–47.
44 Aslet, op. cit., p. 4.
45 Rubinstein, 'Wealth and Land', op. cit., p. 147.
46 Thompson, *Landed Society*, op. cit., p. 302.
47 ibid., p. 302.
48 Davidoff, *Best Circles*, op. cit., p. 59.
49 Lowerson, in Wanklyn, op. cit., pp. 121–2.
50 Davidoff, op. cit., p. 62.
51 Aslet, op. cit., p. 19.
52 *PP 1914 XLIV* 'Census of England and Wales 1911, Vol. X, Occupations and Industries', p. 39.
53 Armstrong [ed], *Further Passages*, op. cit., p. 155.
54 *PP 1881 LXXX*, op. cit., p. 38.
55 *PP 1893–4 CVI*, op. cit., p. 44 and *PP 1904 CVIII pt. 1*, 'Census of England and Wales. 1901, General Report with Appendices', p. 24.
56 Rider Haggard, *Rural England*, op. cit., Vol. I, pp. 450–2.
57 ibid., pp. 470–2.

58 ibid., pp. 146–7.
59 A. D. Hall, *A Pilgrimage of British Farming, 1910–1912*, [London, 1913], p. 222.
60 ibid., pp. 233–5.
61 ibid., p. 424.
62 L. Jebb, *The Small Holdings of England. A Survey of Various Systems*, [London, 1907], pp. 111–12.
63 ibid., pp. 52–68.
64 Hall, op. cit., p. 346.
65 Haggard, *Rural England*, Vol. 1, op. cit., p. 135.
66 Michael Henry Ferguson, 'Land Use, Settlement and Society in the Bagshot Sands Region, 1840–1940', Unpublished PhD thesis, University of Reading 1979, p. 568.
67 Haggard, *Rural England*, Vol. 1, op. cit., p. 460.
68 Ferguson, op. cit., p. 73.
69 ibid., p. 568.
70 Christine Sibbit, '. . . *bells, blankets, baskets, and boats.' A Survey of Crafts and Industries in Oxfordshire*. [Oxford, 1968], pp. 24–6.
71 Sturt, *William Smith*, op. cit., pp. 221–2.
72 J. A. Chartres and G. L. Turnbull, 'Country Craftsmen' in G. E. Mingay [ed] *Victorian Countryside*, op. cit., Vol II, p. 320.
73 David Hey, 'Industrialized Villages' in ibid., pp. 352 *ff*.
74 Robert Moore, *Pitmen, Preachers and Politics. The Effects of Methodism in a Durham Mining Community* [Cambridge, 1974], pp. 64–7.
75 On Wigston see W. G. Hoskins, *The Midland Peasant*, [London, 1957], pp. 261–82.
76 Quoted in C. W. Chalklin, 'Country Towns' in Mingay [ed], op. cit., p. 279.
77 See St George Cramp, op. cit., pp. 112–14.
78 *Industries of the Eastern Counties*, [Birmingham, n.d. but *c*. 1885], pp. 175 *ff*.
79 *White's Norfolk*, op. cit., pp. 868–72.
80 R. H. Mottram, *Bowler Hat:*, op. cit., pp. 141 *ff*.
81 G. E. Mingay, *Rural Life in Victorian England*, [London, 1977], pp. 167–8.

9

The Rural Social Structure 1895–1914: Continuity and Discontinuity

In Chapter 3 we talked of aspects of the rural world as characterized by stability and harmony. This was not a 'natural' state but an achieved balance of great complexity. Until the 1880s this relatively short-lived system managed to convey a sense of permanence and longevity, which it simply did not have, through a set of personalities and institutions at village and *pays* level. This balance was threatened fundamentally in the years between 1875–95. The threat came from changes originating outside the rural world which could not be controlled by those in it, especially the agricultural depression; and by forces created by the contradictions within that rural world, especially low wages combined with a growth in 'consciousness' among the poorest sections of the community. What emerged in the first years of this century was a changed social structure, but one which was changed more in perceptions of the world and its hierarchy of status than in any real redistribution of social or economic power. Yet we must stress that such change was not automatic – 'men make their own history'. The changes we have talked about and those we shall look at in this chapter were the result of often conscious and collective agency.

A central change, but one which is extremely difficult to document, was the 'modernization' of social relations. The 'old order' predicated a quasi-feudal structure of rank in which all had duties and obligations to those above and below them. In reality this was an idyllicist representation of a world which was exploitative and structurally unequal. However, as we saw in Chapter 3 in the recreation of paternalism in the years after 1850 it had some basis. The depression threatened this system not simply by increasing its monetary costs beyond the level where social reward was worthwhile but by publicly subjecting what was supposed to be a sacred, permanent and non-cash social order to crude economic considerations. Landowning and farming were shown to be what they had always been in reality – profit-making economic activities. This was not the first time this had happened in English rural history for it was also true of the period from *c.* 1790–1830. It was simply different.

The main reason for the different outcome in social terms was that the 'recipients' of the hierarchy, 'the poor and middling sort' were different and that in the processes of social change which characterized the years up to the mid-1920s they were not passive but were agents in their own transformation. We have already seen key aspects of this in relation to the growth of radical nonconformity and trades unionism. Also important was the continuing urbanization of English society which further marginalized the rural areas both in terms of productivity and ideology. That is, the dominant image of England was increasingly urban/commercial/industrial. As we shall see below this was to be challenged, but the key element was that the urban world was coming more and more to define, in a positive way, the aspirations and ideas of the rural.

However, we are not talking about a social revolution. 'Modernization' of social relations did not, in England at least, mean the creation of an antagonistic class culture except in some few areas at particular times. This does not mean such a culture could not have developed, or even that it was not developing in the last years of peace. What it does mean is that the new social aspirations and ideas and the re-evaluation of social structures was taking place within a framework – the chapel, the friendly society, the village club or Parish Council – which were limited in their possibility for social criticism and change. What was emerging was a society in which 'respectability' was as much a keyword of working class organization and culture as it was of the middle class. Indeed, the aspiration to respectability, towards a 'family' wage paid to the male 'breadwinner', the right to vote, temperance and legal honesty, was a powerful incentive to social change and frequently lay at the core of the working class side of 'modernized' social relationships.

In addition, there were real continuities. As we saw in the last chapter, farming practice was intimately linked to regionality which could be tinkered with but not easily changed, no matter how serious the economic problems of an old system. Similarly, social relationships which were produced by these regions, the village structures of the south and midlands or the farmstead settlement patterns of the north, could not be quickly altered, although within them there could be substantial changes, as we shall see below.

The core of the rural social structure was an axis of landed wealth or at least tenant wealth, and control of the means both of representing and governing the rural areas. The first of these, landed wealth, was not seriously challenged before the late 1910s, although there were serious problems in some areas as we saw above. As fortunes began to recover from the worst of the depression, investment in land again became worthwhile and land sales began to increase. It was however, politics, and politics from outside the rural world, that caused most problems. In 1906 a Liberal government was returned to power with an overwhelming majority. Although not at this stage committed to an 'anti-landlord' policy, there was no doubt in the eyes of many that major land reform was to come. In 1908 the first signs of such a change came with a strengthening of tenants' rights and the granting of powers to County Councils to enable them to compulsorily purchase land for allotments. The 1909 Budget augured worse to come with an Increment Value Duty and Undeveloped Land Duty and the provision for the greatest land survey in England since 1066.

That 1909 Budget was the work of David Lloyd George. Lloyd George had a deep and abiding hatred for the English rural ruling class born of his own Welsh childhood. In July 1909 he had made his feelings on the future of the landowners absolutely clear in his famous speech at Limehouse. In this he argued that the landlords had systematically avoided contributing to the national wealth for generations, simply drawing ever increased rents from both rural but especially urban land, without any input on their part. The logic of Lloyd George's position was clear – the taxation of land values in some form, but it was his language that chilled the rural elite and *The Times*. 'Who is the landlord', he cried to his largely working class audience,

> the landlord is a gentleman – I have not a word to say about him in his personal capacity – the landlord is a gentleman who does

> not earn his wealth. He does not even take the trouble to receive his wealth . . . He does not even trouble to spend his wealth . . . His sole function, his chief pride is stately consumption of wealth produced by others,[1]

The landed class had always been a traditional Liberal/Radical enemy but in the past the attack had been tempered by a need to retain the support of the 'whig' peers. From 1886 onwards this group declined rapidly as more and more of them switched their allegiance to the Tories. By 1910, although there were some Liberal landowners, they were few in number and declining in importance to the party.

This political attack, coupled with rises in land prices, led to a wave of selling. 'Not for many generations has there been so enormous a dispersal piecemeal of landed estate as in 1911 and 1912', wrote *The Estates Gazette*, 'and the supply of ancestral acres in the provinces is apparently unlimited'.[2] For the first time talk of the 'break-up of the great estates' had some foundation in reality, and by 1915 it was estimated that 800,000 acres, worth about £20 million, had changed hands.[3] Yet we must beware simply 'blaming the radicals' as many an owner did at the time. As F. M. L. Thompson points out, and as we have seen, changes had been slowly coming since at least the late 1870s. Lloyd George's budgets 'provided self-justification for a course which had long seemed wise, the realization of some of their landed assets so soon as a favourable market should appear.'[4] The break up of estates in the years after 1910, coupled with the growth of business activities among the aristocracy and even the gentry, which we looked at in the last chapter, was beginning to undermine the economic bases of landed power and prestige by 1914. Additionally, newcomers, especially middle class newcomers, were confusing the class structure in rural areas as well as introducing new ideas and problems.

'Back to the Land' had become by 1911, according to no less a figure than the great imperialist Viscount Milner, 'a watchword which . . . is beginning to appeal to serious men of every hue of political thought'.[5] This notion, of returning to a purer, better and more natural life, was, of course, not new. 'Agrarianism', the idea of small producer units supported by some form of co-operation or communal production was a powerful part of English radical thought throughout the nineteenth century. At the other extreme, the great merchant buying into landed society by the purchase of an estate and title has been a stock figure of English imagination if not English reality since at least the sixteenth century. From the 1880s however these ideas took on a new urgency and attractiveness.

The problem was in origin urban and lay in notions of 'racial degeneration' derived from Social Darwinism.[6] This argued, crudely, that 'pure' country stock, migrants from the rural areas, degenerated racially within three generations into inferior 'city' types. The idea is set out clearly by Henry Rider Haggard in 1899 and is worth quoting at length.

> Look at the pure bred Cockney – I mean the little fellow whom you see running in and out of offices in the City, and whose forefathers have for the last two generations dwelt within a two mile radius of Charing Cross. And then look at your average young labourer coming home from his day's field work and I think that you will admit that the city breeds one stamp of human being and the country breeds another . . . Take the people away from their natural breed and growing grounds, thereby sapping their health and strength in cities such as nature never intended to be the permanent homes of men, and the decay of this country becomes only a question of time.[7]

The cities also created poverty. The Victorian dream had been that urbanization and industrialization led to ever-increasing wealth which, via the mechanism of the free market, would pass to all classes of the community. Nobody expected this distribution to be equal, but all were supposed to benefit. In the late 1880s and early 1890s this was fundamentally challenged when H. M. Hyndman, an early socialist, claimed that a quarter of the population of Britain lived below the poverty line. His challenge was taken up by Charles Booth, whose massive study of the London poor was begun in 1887. The study proved Hyndman's figure was wrong. He had underestimated. According to Booth's calculations, which were not generous, about a third of London's population lived below the poverty line. In the next twenty years study after study of urban England confirmed Booth's findings.

So urban England not only created an inferior race but urbanization and industrialization had failed to deliver the English out of poverty. To a generation of young, urban and largely intellectual men and women the conclusions were inescapable – the system having failed, alternatives had to be found. For many the alternatives were found in the vision of William Morris. His *News from Nowhere*, published in the early 1890s, became a Bible of 'back to the landers'. In *News from Nowhere* Morris draws a picture of a rural Utopia with London reduced in scale and 'greened'. Production is in small-scale workshops and craftsmanship is elevated by the destruction of the factory. Although few who followed Morris possessed his critical sense or revolutionary socialism, his picture of a perfect and rural future inspired thousands, including High Tories like Henry Rider Haggard. What they took from it, as well as a powerful anti-urbanism, was a romantic worship of all things rural and simple. It was a short step from this position to one where rural England now, or in the recent past, became the basis of a future society and the values and practices of that society became the basis of a new or revived England and Englishness.[8]

This movement took two routes which were powerfully mutually reinforcing: a practical one – literally moving back to the land or the countryside at least; and an intellectual one – the revival of, and interest in, things rural. Initially, both these strands were restricted to a few. However, by the mid-1890s, both had widespread support. At the practical level, some literally went back to the land, following Morris's vision of 'little communities among gardens and green fields'.[9] Most went individually, and many of those survived; some went to live and work collectively and most of these experiments were failures, like so many Utopian schemes before them. The largest colony of the 1890s was the Purleigh 'Tolstoyans' in Essex which was established in 1897. By February 1898, there were seventy-five colonists living in Purleigh, some working the land and some continuing to follow urban trades. They attempted, very sensibly in view of the markets, to grow vegetables, including tomatoes and grapes under glass. The first crops under glass in the autumn of 1897 were encouraging but the outdoor ones failed. Nevertheless, they persisted planting apples, pears, plums, gooseberries and currants as well as 1 3/4 acres of winter wheat.[10] However dissent within the colony led to its break up in 1899. The most 'pure' of the Purleigh group set up another, anarchist, colony at Whiteway in Gloucestershire. Here communal living and cultivation went hand in hand with sexual radicalism, much to the horror of the local population. But in 1901, after several bad years, the Whiteway colonists moved to individual cultivation of their own plots, although retaining elements of communal living and still rejecting the 'contamination' of the outside world. This saved the colony and by the 1930s it was selling milk, butter, cheese and bread to the surrounding villages. The colony still survives.[11]

Slightly different, though still ruralist, or at least Morrisite in inspiration, was C. R. Ashbee's Guild of Handicrafts. Ashbee was a friend and follower of Morris who had set up his Guild in Whitechapel in 1888, to revive and encourage craftsmanship on the Morris model. In 1902 he took most of the Guild's members, about 150 in all, to the decayed woollen town of Chipping Campden in Gloucestershire because, according to Ashbee, 'Good honest craftsmanship is better done the nearer the people get in touch with the elemental things of life.'[12] Ashbee's aim though was also to revive the rural craftsmanship of the past and to recreate the situation in which it had flourished. His unlikely move worked for about seven years but even when it failed in Campden many of his craftsmen remained in the town, working on their own account. Ashbee was not alone either in Gloucestershire or in his wish to revive the rural crafts of the past. In Sapperton, also in Gloucestershire, Ernest Gimson and the Barnsley brothers revived the traditions of rural furniture making, basing their designs and methods on 'old English' models. Their venture was even more successful than Ashbee's and they established a tradition of recreating traditional furniture which survived well into the 1980s at the workshops of Geoffrey Lupton at Steep in Hampshire.[13]

Those who returned to the land in the sense of the Purleigh or Whiteway colonists were few but many more sought to revive interest in, and give value to, 'things rural'. This took two routes. The first, and numerically the most important, was that which sought access to the countryside and rural areas for reasons of health or aesthetics. The second was the giving of value to aspects of rural life or craft, for example, the revival of English folk song.

Going into the countryside for recreation had a long history from the Romantic movement onwards. However, from the late 1860s there is evidence that rural excursions, especially in the areas around large towns, were becoming a part of life for more and more people. In 1869, when a Select Committee of the House of Commons looked at the working of the parliamentary inclosure of 1845, they returned, time and again, to the use of land for recreation. One commissioner for inclosure reported that he had set land aside near Bath 'to be set apart for exercise and recreation' because, 'people had been in the habit of walking (there) especially on Sundays, and the most beautiful views were obtained from it'.[14] Worstenbury Hill outside Brighton was also a place where 'many persons go upon the Sunday or whatever day is convenient'.[15]

Behind evidence like this lay the first attempts to organize the protection of open spaces. In 1865 the Commons Preservation Society was founded with the object of securing 'for the use and enjoyment of the public open spaces, situate in the neighbourhood of towns, especially of London, still remaining unbuilt on.'[16] This was followed in 1884 by the National Footpaths Preservation Society. The two organizations merged into the Commons and Footpaths Preservation Society in 1899. In 1894, another organization, the National Trust, had been created with the aim of securing, permanently for the nation, land and buildings threatened by development.

By the outbreak of the Great War, the record of these organizations was impressive and every person who loves the English countryside owes them an enormous debt. At the most spectacular level they had saved commons such as Wimbledon Common and Hampstead, the area of the Chilterns around Burnham Beeches and protected public access to Epping Forest and prevented its development. At a more mundane level, countless footpaths were kept open by local legal action and occasionally, as at Honour Oak in London in 1897, by something that looked more like an enclosure riot. In this case the NFPS felt unable to support the cases since no right of way actually existed.[17] The National Trust's activities also preserved the countryside. In 1895 its second acquisition was the land at Barras Head around Tintagel in Cornwall. It is surprising in view of the Trust's image now as a preserver of great country houses that its most famous and successful campaign in the years before the Great War was to acquire parts of the Lake District, a campaign which lasted nearly ten years and secured forever land around Derwentwater, Gowbarrow, Ullswater and Borrowdale.[18]

These movements were, in origin, middle class and urban, which created problems to which we shall return. However, by the 1900s, the unorganized pleasure seeking of the working class Sunday walk had taken on a more organized form. Like the preservation societies, rambling and cycling clubs were middle class, even aristocratic to begin with but, especially in the north of England both had, by the 1900s, a strong working class element. Vital here was the *Clarion*, a socialist weekly paper founded by Robert Blatchford. Blatchford, like many followers of Morris, equated capitalism with urbanism. Hence the destruction of the former would automatically destroy the latter. To Blatchford and his followers however, it was not simply a matter of waiting – one had 'to make that future now' and so every weekend, urged on by Blatchford's love of nature, *Clarion* supporters took to the hills and fields on foot or on bicycle. Their aim was theoretically to spread the socialist message to the countryside, and many did that, but for most it was the escape from the urban world that mattered. By the outbreak of war the Clarion Cycling Club and its various rambling and social organizations took thousands into the countryside every weekend.

Less numerically important than those who 'went out' into the countryside were those who tried to give it value. Like the active 'back-to-the-landers' these often rejected city life and the values of urban capitalism in favour of what they saw as a purer, prior set of values. Like Ashbee, they sought to restore craftsmanship although their attempts to revive lace making or the making of Sussex 'trugs' smack more of paternalism than a real sense of the needs of a rural world. Perhaps more importantly, they saw these 'prior' values as restructuring the whole of the nation, urban as well as rural. This was put clearly in 1910 by Mary Neale, ruralist, folk song collector, and folk dance teacher.

> This revival of our English folk music is . . . part of a great national revival, a going back from the town to the country, a reaction against all that is demoralising in city life. It is a re-awakening of that part of our nation's consciousness which makes for wholeness, saneness and healthy merriment . . . We can never, as a nation, go back to the days when country life sufficed for everything. The town has come too near the country for that. But an interchange between town and country is what we must look for in the future.[19]

It was, however, not the 'purists', those who set up land colonies or collected folklore or designed gardens 'in the cottage manner', that were the most important. Rather, it was the thousands who followed them to the new suburbs beyond the suburbs to live, or rather invent, English country life, who were the real new country men and women. It was this group which reversed the decline in the rural population in the 1900s by moving out, especially in the south and east, into new developments linked by rail to London where they could, in the evenings and at weekends, live a rural life.

This influx of largely middle class families into the rural areas caused problems. The 'old order' had always seemed clear – the squire, the parson, the farmer and the labourer stood in precisely defined socio-economic positions in relation to the wider world and to one another. The newcomers in some senses challenged that. Their wealth was obvious, but did not fit into the old structure. In some places they directly challenged or replaced old owners or ways of doing things. In Ferguson's study of Berkshire, he shows how about 36,000 acres of large local estates built up between the 1840s and the 1870s, that is about 20 per cent of the land in the Bagshot Sands region, changed hands between 1905 and 1922, with the vast majority of it going to building.[20] This development was carefully controlled by class. Prices of houses were high and at Sunningdale for instance, controlled by the developers, as were the materials used and the housing density. Purchase of one of these houses entitled the owner's name to go to the top of the waiting list for membership of the exclusive Sunningdale Golf Club.[21] Housing and social amenities went together here to create a new strata of bourgeois/urban wealth in an essentially rural/traditional setting.

The newcomers usually did little directly to challenge the old order in terms of social relations. In fact the opposite was often the case. The reasons behind the movement out of the city were as much ideological as physical – the new country man and woman were not simply leaving a crowded or insanitary urban area, they were going to a rural myth which they were recreating. Central to that myth were ideas of a 'natural' or 'organic' social order and society. When the first generation of suburbanities moved to the new 'village' of Bedford Park they built a village inn, suitably half timbered and called it 'The Tabard' and erected a Maypole to celebrate their village festivals in Tudor dress.[22] Fifty years later, George Orwell's world weary ex-countryman George Bowling found that similar pseudo-ruralism had spread to the Thames Valley.[23] It was an 'incomer', Janet Blunt, the daughter of an Anglo-Indian family, who collected folk songs and revived the

May Day customs in the Oxfordshire village of Adderbury.[24] Similarly, Morris dancing was spread far outside the areas of its recent existence (essentially West Oxfordshire) into most of the south of England by enthusiastic stockbrokers.

Both the economic bases and the political and cultural representations of power were changing. Landed property was being gradually eroded before 1914 and especially after 1910 as we have already seen. The new middle class incomers confused social relations with their wealth and status which could not be related to the old model of society in the longer term. Even the revival of 'rural England' had ambiguities. Those who bought £1,000 houses in Sunningdale in 1906 may have had little real interest in the rural world but the members of the Clarion Cycling Club did. They 'knew' a history in which the commons had been stolen from the poor and the labourer driven from the land. Their vision was of a proud and free countryman and woman whose songs and culture were the basis, not of a pastoral revival but of a new, better and socialist world.

There were chiller winds still. Although the trades unions of the 1870s finally collapsed in the late 1890s what appeared to be more fundamental changes were taking place. Local government reform in 1889 and 1894 created County, District and Parish Councils on an elective basis. At times, in many places those elected tended to be the same members of the county elites who had served on the bench, the Quarter Sessions and vestries which preceeded the elective bodies. However, this gradually began to change and politics, even the politics of independent working class representation, began to appear in the late 1890s. By the mid-1900s, in some areas of rural England, East Anglia and Lancashire for instance, Independent Labour Party candidates were standing at all levels of local government. Perhaps even more startling was that some of those elected were working women, for example Mrs George Edwards, who was elected as one of six 'labour' representatives to Erpingham RDC in Norfolk.[25]

In some ways the importance of this was more symbolic than real, but it did mark the end of the formal institutional links between landownership and the complete control of local government. I also indicated that sections of the rural working class no longer accepted without criticism the structures imposed on them by their betters. As the *Eastern Weekly Leader*, a radical Norfolk paper, put it on the eve of the first

Parish Council elections in 1894: 'the finger of the labourer has stopped an inch short of his cap when the parson has passed . . . '[26]

None of this was lost on the local elites and in some counties, most noticeably counties where the unions of the 1870s had been strong, like Norfolk, there was a backlash against labourers and their supporters who dared to stand for election. Although the County Council elections of 1889 produced little real change in the type of person running local government, the very presence of working men candidates led to men who supported them being dismissed at Shipdham in Norfolk.[27] At Wroxham, in Norfolk in 1894, a working class candidate found himself evicted and sacked form his job, while at Wisbech in Cambridgeshire a schoolmaster was sacked after chairing a parish meeting at which he ruled the vicar out of order.[28]

In 1906 came yet more startling evidence that the labourers had changed in their attitudes. In that year the Liberals won the greatest electoral victory in English history up to that point. At the core of that victory were the substantial numbers of county seats where the labourer's vote returned Liberal and radical members. R. H. Mottram watched the labourers going to vote in North Walsham in 1906.

> They poured into the booth, recorded their 'wut', and streamed of to the lesser public houses. There was no stopping them. Something influenced them . . . something left over from Litester's Rebellion and Kett's Rebellion . . . (they) recorded their 'wut' and felt that they had 'got back' at all the rest of the world, for all the pheasants they had not poached, for all the beer they had not drunk, for all the money they had not spent.[29]

For whatever reason, the labourer voted Liberal, and the 1906 results in rural England were a shock to all. In East Anglia not one of the sixteen county constituencies returned a Conservative whereas eight had in 1900. In the rural north, that is Cumberland, Westmorland Northumberland and Durham, out of eighteen county constituencies only one returned a Conservative compared with six in 1900. Perhaps most striking, if not so spectacular, were the isolated victories throughout rural England. East Grinstead, in Sussex, returned a Liberal, the only time in its history and the only time a Liberal won a Sussex county seat in our period. The Liberals also won Hardy's Wessex by gaining three out of four Dorset seats from the Conservatives.

Many of these gains, it must be said, were short term, but they were enormously important as indicators of that new 'spirit of independence' which was noted, as we saw in Chapter 6, by many observers in the 1870s and 1880s and was now finding real expression. This was given further strength by the refounding of the Labourers' Union in 1906 in Norfolk. Although, at first, the 'new' union was controlled by largely outside, middle class sympathisers, by 1911–12, it had become independent of that group and was affiliated to the TUC. In 1913, the union's new paper, *The Labourer*, carried as part of its masthead the slogan 'Workers of the World Unite' and in 1914 it voted to affiliate to the Labour Representation Committee.[30]

Problems of landownership, a new middle class and increasingly independent labourers were added to by a crisis in aspects of the paternalism which had so successfully governed much of rural England until the 1880s. Local government passed into elected hands, as we have seen, which at least opened up the possibility of questioning the nature of local power. George Rix, the only working man elected to the new Norfolk County Council in 1889, shocked the county by demanding at his first meeting that the police should be removed from game protection, 'because he did not like police being turned into gamekeepers. Those who preserved game should employ gamekeepers and pay them.' Looking deliberately at his largely plutocratic fellow councillors he said 'he hoped that gentlemen who preserved game would pay an instalment towards (police) expenses.'[31] By the 1910s, people like Rix on the County Councils and Mrs Edwards on the RDCs and Boards of Guardians had done more than attack gentry power, they had actively altered things. Allotments Committees, Sanitary Committees, Emigration Committees as well as a humanising of aspects of the Poor Law, represented real curbs on the elite's ability to manipulate local institutions for paternalist ends. Equally, the gradual reform of the magistracy throughout the century had the effect of reducing the direct power of the elite in criminal matters.

This temporary weakening of local power was compounded by continuing problems within the Church of England. The revival in the Anglican Church in the 1850s and 1860s had some success. New churches were built, especially in remote areas or areas where settlement postdated the old parish structure. The quality of the clergy as a whole seems to have improved. E. N. Bennett wrote in 1913,

> The vitalising influence of the Oxford Movement . . . left its mark also on our rural parishes. The improved discipline of the Anglican Church . . . has at least helped to weed out many notorious cases of worthless clergymen . . . while infinitely greater care is exercised in Church patronage than was the case fifty years ago. Services are brighter and more numerous, and the connection between the Church and the social and intellectual life of the parish becomes daily more close.[32]

Yet in terms of numbers, Anglicanism had really done little more than hold its ground in the years after the 1870s, although it does seem to have entered a period of growth in the 1900s. Bennett estimated that in the 1910s only about 30 per cent of the rural population of Oxfordshire attended any kind of religious worship on a regular basis and that, of these, a majority were probably nonconformists.[33] Nationally, it has been argued that, 'active nonconformists must have outnumbered active Anglicans at the turn of the century'.[34] Yet in the villages just as in the towns, casual infidelism and simple non-attendance was more important than either.

The reasons for the failure of the Church of England in the villages are not far to seek. Throughout the nineteenth century the Church had been closely identified with the rural elite. 'The clergy', wrote Bennett,

> have always identified themselves with one political party – the party which, more especially in rural districts stands for the defence of property, privileges and social influence. Mr. Masterman's dictum that no established Church had ever been on the side of the poor is supported by ample testimony from our country parishes.[35]

For many areas in the years up to the 1870s this identification worked to the advantage of the Church, as we saw in Chapter 3. In the 'new' rural world of the 1890s and 1900s it became more and more of a problem. It was not that organized anticlericism was a strong movement in rural areas, rather that the changes of the depression years disturbed the Church's position. For many farmers, for example, the drop in wheat prices made the payment of tithe an issue again and led in some areas to a real antagonism between Church and farmers.[35] In John Moore's novel about Tewkesbury, *Portrait of Elmbury* we find Mr Jeffs, who loathed the Vicar because he 'thought he was immensely rich, and that he waxed and grew fat at the expense of agriculture, out of the tithe. So, whenever he met him Mr. Jeffs would shake his whip angrily and cry out in a loud voice: "Let them as wants Parsons pay for them!"'.[36]

It was the rural poor who were probably most affected by changes after the 1870s and 1880s. Clearly there had always been some villagers whose Anglicanism was honest and sincere but for many their religion was forced on them as the price of charity. The unions, rural depopulation and the growth of political ideas all contributed to undermining this position as did the Church's widespread hostility to any form of change. Arch's Union as well as the many local unions of the 1870s were more or less universally condemned by the Church of England. This was pointed to by an Anglican clergyman, Rev. A. H. Baverstock, in an influential pamphlet, *The Failure of the Church in the Villages*, published in 1913, as explaining much of the hostility to the Anglican Church.[37] Nor did it end there. The clergy's identification with the Poor Law and the bench had been a source of power, and remained so, but now it was an additional reason for dislike. Further, their commitment to a paternalist ethic led them to oppose many aspects of the Liberal social reforms of the 1900s and 1910s. As E. N. Bennett wrote, 'measures like the Small Holdings Act, the Old-Age Pensions Act, the Insurance Act have, alas, been received by the vast majority of the rural clergy with either open hostility or sullen acquiescence.'[38]

Of course not all the clergy fitted these stereotypes. Baverstock was a High Churchman and a supporter of the 'rural revivalist' Peasant Arts Fellowship which sought to encourage rural industry. Bennett was also sympathetic to High Anglican ideals and urged the creation of 'brotherhoods of unmarried clergymen, working several parishes from a common centre' as a way of restoring the best of church influence to the villages.[39] Others went further still. The Rev. Conrad Noel at Thaxted in Essex combined High Church beliefs and a re-creation of village life, complete with Morris dancing and folk song, with trades unionism and rural socialism. At Walsingham, in Norfolk, the revival of the pre-Reformation Catholic shrine produced the kind of group Bennett seemed to have in mind, one of whom, Father McNab, was an active supporter of the labourers' union in the bitter strike of the spring of 1923.[40] Additionally, there were many unsung and decent village priests who sympathized with the poorest of their parishioners and carried on the best traditions of rural religion – but they remained a minority.

Above and beyond these changes were others which are still less easily documented, perhaps crucially the secularization and nationalization of local cultures and belief structures. Secularization, the decreasing importance of religious or even magical beliefs and their replacement by those of civil society, is easy to assert but much more difficult to document. Church attendances as a proportion of population were declining probably from the 1870s but this was concealed, up to the Great War, by increasing actual attendances and membership. Simply statistically, England, including its rural areas, was becoming a less religious society. Even within this real changes were occurring. James Obelkevich's study of Lincolnshire notes subtle changes in Primitive Methodism even before 1870, 'for example evangelism yielded to entertainments, the community of "saints" to "fellowship" and soul-making to character building.'[41] In Eastbourne in Sussex, admittedly not a typical rural area, the minister of Pevensey Road Wesleyan Church complained to the class leaders in 1912 'that the church was being deluged with a flood of amusements, social gatherings and Musical Evenings and pleaded with the members, to throw their weight on the side of the Spiritual Life of the Church.'[42] At one level his complaint was certainly justified given that there were events almost every night of the week whose 'spiritual' side is not obvious, but the Wesleyans were competing, in Eastbourne as elsewhere, with an increasingly organized and sophisticated range of social activities.

There were other ways in which chapel societies had altered. 'Everywhere Methodists grow rich' John Wesley had said in the 1780s. By the 1900s, village Methodism, even if it was not rich, had a powerful secular, although usually informal, side to it. Business connections were reinforced by marriage within the chapel to create chapel families and chapel employment networks. Partly as a result of this growing respectability, the automatic connections made in the 1870s and 1880s between chapel and radicalism began to fade. When the farm labourers were given the vote in 1884 George Rix, the Norfolk trade unionist and Primitive Methodist preacher, could boast, 'three fourths of the new voters are in principle Nonconformists . . . and as such must for the very nature of things be advanced Liberals.'[43] Only eleven years later one of his successors, George Edwards, saw things very differently. 'I will admit at once that Nonconformists have not moved along so fast these few years . . . and that they have far too much ignored the fact that Christ came to redress social wrongs as much as to prepare the way for a higher life.'[44]

The Church, because it had made less exalted spiritual claims for its membership at least, probably dealt with the problems of secularization better than the chapel. Indeed it could be argued that by accepting or even creating a secular role for itself within the power structure from at least the 1850s the Church could hardly be damaged by a shift in that direction in rural society as a whole. Either way, the direct influence of both Church and chapel was decreasing and becoming more private. Especially in relation to the chapel, religious belief seems to have been 'increasingly regarded as an individual, even private matter, of no concern to other people.'[45] In 1908 this view was given powerful support in a book written by a Congregational minister, *Nonconformity and Politics*, which argued, like the minister at Eastbourne, that political activity was detracting from the spiritual aspects of nonconformist life.[46] The move into spirituality may have encouraged many into the chapels who had been alienated by the social Christianity of the 1870s and 1880s but it handed over local leadership in town and village to an essentially secular group.

The 'nationalization' of rural culture was less clear. We saw above how the physical tentacles of urban England had begun to reach into the rural areas. However, it was internal change as well as external since, by the 1890s and 1900s, the combination of the kind of changes in rural social structure we have talked about in the last four chapters were beginning seriously to weaken local identities. Movement to and from urban areas, especially by the young, contributed more than a general feeling of discontent to those 'left behind'. We have already talked about politics and trades unionism but equally significant were less obvious cultural changes. Flora Thompson's *Lark Rise to Candelford* is a remarkably (and self-consciously) perceptive account of these gradual shifts. Her account of singing in the pub, for instance, where three different generations sing three quite distinct groups of songs, each one closer in time and space to the urban world, clearly shows how the urban and national were beginning to creep into the local world of the rural. Oldest were the 'folk' songs of 'Old Master Tuffrey' with his singing of 'The Outlandish Knight', the song his grandfather had sung, and had said that he had heard his own grandfather sing it . . . but David was fated to be the last of them. It was out of date, even then . . . ' Next in age were the middle aged men who sang a range of songs. Some of them would have graced the pages of a folk song collector's notebook, most were the product of early and mid-Victorian commercial popular music, 'long and usually mournful stories in verse of thwarted lovers, children buried in snowdrifts, dead maidens and motherless homes'. Youngest in age and nearest to the town were the young men, the 'boy chaps'. When the singing began 'they came into their own, for they represented the novel'. Their songs were the product of recent times which 'arrived complete with tune from the outer world'. This 'curious mixture of old and new' as Flora Thompson calls it, catches the extent to which an outside, 'national' world was beginning to reach even into remote country areas not as a rumour or a garbled message but as a concrete reality.[47]

Flora Thompson also writes about fashion, a concept which arrived in North Oxfordshire with the 'daughters of the hamlet' going into service. In the 1830s and 1840s women's style of dress, among the poor at least, changed slowly and was the product as much of local custom and the availability of materials as any notion of fashion. In the 1880s and 1890s that began to change with parcels of clothes sent by a daughter away in service.

> . . . the Sunday best had to be just so. 'Better be out of the world than out of the fashion' was one of their sayings. To be appreciated, the hat or coat contained in the parcel had to be in fashion, and the hamlet had a fashion of its own, a year or two behind outside standards, and strictly limited in style and colour.[48]

In adopting 'fashion', even if out-of-date and muted in colour, the women of the hamlet were doing no more than their middle class and gentry counterparts had done before, yet the spreading of such 'national' cultural notions downwards to the rural poor created change of a more fundamental kind, if only because there were more of them.

We can see a similar, and equally important change in relation to reading and reading matter. The Education Act of 1870 had only just begun to have real impact in the 1890s and 1900s, but literacy was now assumed, even if that assumption was sometimes optimistic. Again, women were important. In Lark Rise, 'most of the younger women and some of the older ones were fond of what they called "a bit of a read" and their mental fare consisted almost exclusively of the novelette'. These were bought weekly by the slightly better off women and circulated among their friends.[49]

More obvious in impact, if of no greater cultural significance, was the change in newspaper reading. The old county papers, like *Jackson's Oxford Journal*, which were founded in the eighteenth century, were essentially weekly versions of the London press, carrying a good deal of reprinted material for the benefit of the county gentry. By the 1840s these had been added to or modified to appeal to the farmers and the rural middle class by carrying a considerable amount of local news. In addition, national newspapers like *The Times* and the *Morning Chronicle* were reaching out into the rural areas although still only to the elite. In the 1860s, a new generation of 'penny papers' aimed at the rural artisan and even the labourers began to appear. *The Eastern Weekly Press*, for example, was founded in 1867 according to its owners 'to guide the working-classes politically and morally'. By 1873 it was selling 12,000 copies per week, mainly in Norfolk.[50]

There followed some thirty years which have been called 'the golden age of the local newspaper' in which these papers consciously strove to create a local identity and culture as the basis of their power and appeal. However, even by the 1890s that was starting to change. In Lark Rise, Sunday newspapers, especially *Reynold's News* and *Lloyd's News*, had begun to appear in the hamlet, although they existed alongside 'that fine old local newspaper, the *Bicester Herald*'.[51] By the 1900s, the new popular daily papers of Alfred Harmsworth, especially the *Daily Mail*, had reached the country towns. They were to be followed by a rush of others including, by the 1910s, 'illustrated' papers like the *Daily Mirror* and *Daily Sketch* which used the new technology to reproduce photographs.

These papers had a distinct nationalizing tendency. Harmsworth himself said in 1894 that he wanted to create 'a circle of morning papers centring on London and looking to London for their news and opinions.'[52] Gradually these papers reached out into the rural districts along with other Harmsworth productions like the weeklies *Tit-Bits* and *Answers*. As they spread they either destroyed the old local press or modified it beyond recognition. *The Eastern Weekly Press*, for example, ceased publication in 1918, while *Jackson's Oxford Journal* had become *The Oxford Journal Illustrated*, a direct *Daily Mirror* copy, by 1914.

Against these changes we must set some fundamental continuities. Central to these, as we have already indicated, were the persistence of the social structures which rested directly on the productive relations of agriculture. The depression modified these rather than fundamentally changing them, and that modification was more noticeable in some areas than in others. Crucially, for all the moves towards a 'national' culture or market, regional differences remained, and were to remain, until well after the 1920s.

In John Moore's Tewkesbury the local press still dominated the local scene with 'freedom, integrity and independence'.[53] Flora Thompson's *Bicester Herald* survived the Great War and its rival the *Bicester Advertiser* was still much like a nineteenth century newspaper in my own youth, written, printed and distributed from the 'Advertiser Offices' in the Market Square. It was also still avidly read, and, as it probably had been for a hundred years by then, sent to sons and daughters who had 'gone away' to keep them up to date with the local world of 'hatched, matched and despatched'.

Nor did the central institutions of rural society vanish, even if they were modified. The elite sought to maintain the show of paternalism in the face of the modernizing world even if it was an increasingly hollow show. For example, the Hunts suffered under the depression as the minor gentry and sections of the tenant farmers could no longer afford to ride to hounds. In 1891, John Simpson Calvertt recorded in his dairy 'Grand opening meet at Heythrop . . . small attendance of hunting men'.[54]

Yet we must beware. Hunting was incredibly expensive but there were always members of the elite, old and young, to whom riding to hounds was worth it. Furthermore, outside the elite there were always those willing to replace the newly impoverished who could no longer afford to hunt. The young Siegfried Sassoon, certainly not old, but nor really 'new' gentry, used his life of leisure almost exclusively in pursuit of the fox when he could barely afford it. After his final season (1914) with the Atherstone, one of the great midland hunts, he wrote,

> .... when the afternoons began to lengthen and I had just paid another bill for forage I was forced to look ahead and to realize that the end of the winter would find me in no end of a fix ... I was £300 in debt ... It was certain that I should be obliged to sell two of the horses at the end of the season.[55]

In the north of England, which was to some extent cushioned from the worst of the depression, as well as more remote from London, a combination of horse breeding for the wealthier south and 'love of sport' helped 'to bind the farmers and yeomen to the land' and kept up hunting, according to Rider Haggard in 1902.[56] Even if there weren't any hard-riding squires or squires' sons, the new elite saw hunting as one of the aspects of rural Englishness which they had bought, or at least could buy. *The Field* wrote in 1908, 'in these times two-thirds of every field are business men of sort',[57] while Sassoon remembered 'a newly-rich manufacturer who lived in a gaudy multi-gabled mansion' and hunted with the Atherstone and a 'formerly none-too-successful stockbroker' with the Southdown.[58]

Institutionally, attempts were made to restructure paternalism via a range of organizations and create a sense of continuity through the years of change. In 1893, as we have already mentioned, Lord Winchelsea founded The National Agricultural Union as 'a society uniting landowner, tenant and labourer – a three fold cable'.[59] This was aimed directly at 'bringing-in' the rural labourer and according to a sympathetic account it had some success. It was however, shortlived and certainly in some areas of England, especially East Anglia, it met with widespread hostility from the labourers at least. To men like George Edwards and Zachariah Walker who had seen the combination of farmers and landowners destroying the labourers' unions such schemes, no matter how well meant on Winchelsea's part, were unthinkable.[60]

Much more successful was the Primrose League. Founded in 1883, urban in origin and seen at first as a kind of alternative 'rank-and-file' Tory organization, it quickly became a kind of political charity, and a highly successful one. Through it, funds raised essentially among the elite, were channelled into a variety of events and activities whose aim was to win working men and women for the Conservative Party.[61] Its core membership 'Knights and Dames' paid a guinea a year membership which automatically excluded the rural poor from full participation and even when associate membership was introduced the League remained an organization of recipients rather than participants in the rural areas.

Nevertheless, the Primrose League was a mass organization. By 1910 it claimed over two million members, and was probably most successful in terms of its work in rural areas. As Henderson Robb writes,

> the Primrose League's most conspicuous achievement was its success in penetrating and taking root in the rural areas. The *Primrose League Gazette* estimated that of its reported membership at least 57% were either agricultural labourers or persons living in small towns.[62]

The Primrose Fête, the tea meeting, the Primrose circulating library and the heavily subsidized outings and dinners perpetuated aspects of the myth of paternalism. In addition, the League adopted many of the forms of the friendly societies with an invented tradition of signs, ranks, badges and banners, all of which came together in the 'Habitation', as local branches were called. Village meetings played on all these aspects, including dancing and singing as well as political speeches. 'It is, in short a return to Merrie England's traditions for the village folks' said the *Illustrated London News* in 1887. 'But mark! It is politics all the same.'[63]

This powerful combination of paternalism, ruralism, charity and Toryism had both short-and long-term effects. In the short term, up to 1906, it successfully fought political radicalism in many rural areas and, according to one of its historians, helped turn the sweeping Liberal gains of 1885 in the shires into the safe Tory majorities of the 1890s. Certainly it worried the rural radicals. To George Rix in 1885 the Primrose League ladies were 'Tory Delilahs' who, having dandled the labourers on their knees to find their strength, the union, would destroy it. In 1886 they were worse still, now they were 'about as bad as the serpent that beguiled Eve' and well into the 1890s 'Primrose Dames' with their charity in exchange for votes were one of the folk-devils of rural radicalism.[64]

In the long term, the effects of the League in rural areas were less spectacular but still important. The 1906 election, it has been argued, marked the beginning of the end for the League. Certainly, although its membership kept growing, there was a very marked slowing down in recruitment after 1900. This was, according to Henderson Robb, because the League was left behind by class politics. Further, its appeal to 'reverence for tradition, and the impulse to escape reality into a world brilliant with aristocracy and titles and fête in great parks' was increasingly marginal. However true this may be for the urban areas, in many rural districts this was precisely the appeal of the League. More importantly, it was the idea behind this world, of a society of order and ranks, of charity and natural inequality, that the League carried through a difficult period in which the very basis of the paternalist interpretation and representation of power seemed doomed.

Vital to continuity in many areas was the persistence of locally based farming systems. As we saw in the last chapter, depression forced modification to farming techniques rather than fundamental changes. Crucially, in rural terms the north and west probably changed less than the south and east. This is not only because these areas were less hard hit in the depression, but also because they were less directly able to take advantage of suburbanization and especially the growth in power and importance of London and the Home Counties. When A. D. Hall visited North Northumberland in 1910 he reacted to the distinctive nature of this region's agriculture in much the same way as Coleman had 30 years earlier. It was still different and strange. The farms still stood isolated and alone, almost villages in themselves. To the stranger, he wrote 'the most striking feature of Northumbrian farming . . . is the magnitude and excellence of the farm buildings – great blocks of well-built stone structures, dominated by a very factory like chimney.'[65] The farm accounts of Northumberland farms show that this was not simply physical continuity but that older hiring practices, especially family hiring, remained common until the Great War and after. Castle Heaton Farm, which we looked at in Chapter 2, for instance, still hired in this way, with the male head of household drawing wages for all the family group each month. As a result, women made up just under a third of the regular workforce in 1913. This was also true of another, larger, Glendale farm investigated by Wilson Fox in 1905 where there were 10 women regular workers out of a total workforce of 38.[66]

Other 'old' practices continued, like payment in kind. In 1900, according to Wilson Fox, a hind in the Glendale Union got a cottage and garden, 1,200 yards of potatoes and coals led, just as his father would have done in the 1850s.[67] Another farm investigated five years later showed a yet more generous and complex system where the farmer kept a cow for the men all the year round and gave straw for pigs. Additionally byremen, those looking after cattle, got six bushels of barley and a free pig because of Sunday work.[68] On Castle Heaton Farm, although allowances remained, subtle changes had taken place. At harvest, for instance, workers were given an allowance in money instead of beer, a practice which was becoming more and more common throughout the northern and western areas.[69] In Devon, where there was also a wide range of payments in kind, the practice of giving free cider was vanishing in the 1890s and being replaced by money payments. This was objected to by the labourers who argued that cider was worth 2s a week whereas when payment was substituted the farmers paid only 1s or 1/6d.[70]

Slight changes like these had an importance which was more than simply monetary. Payment in kind represented the 'special' relationship between farmer and labourer, a gift which showed that the worker had a share in the product of the farm. It was like living-in or eating in the farmhouse on a lesser scale and its abandonment also marked the abandonment of certain idyllicist ideas and their replacement by a pure cash nexus. The extreme was to be found, not surprisingly, in the highly capitalist regions of East Anglia, especially Norfolk and parts of Suffolk. Here true payment in kind was non-existent even in the 1890s when it was noted that 'practically no perquisites given to ordinary labourers.'[71] In some parts of East Anglia it went further still and labourers were actually forbidden to keep pigs, chickens or even rabbits.[72]

Returning to the north, other aspects of employment and workplace relationships had little changed since the 1850s. In these areas, as we have already seen, casual workers, especially the Irish, remained as a vital part of the farm workforce. The seasonal arrival of these workers is recorded in the day books of Castle Heaton Farm up to 1916. Thereafter their names vanish, replaced initially by extra women workers, and after the war by men.[73] As we also saw above, women continued to be a vital part of the casual workforce in Northumberland until the 1920s. The much smaller farm at Dinnington farmed by the Rutherford family continued to hire women from the colliery community around for potato picking and hay harvest until after the end of our period.[74]

In other parts of the north and west there were similar continuities. Lancashire, having weathered the depression well, retained its characteristic structures. In the small farm areas in the north of the county family labour and living-in service for a small number of single labourers remained normal, certainly up to the Great War. In the North and East Ridings of Yorkshire the hiring system persisted with single men living-in, especially on the large farms of the Wolds. Yet within the system there were changes which are difficult to be precise about. In the East Riding, for instance, although hiring by the year remained normal the hiring fairs gradually declined as they did all over the north. In 1905, Wilson Fox wrote that although the fairs continued 'there has been a marked tendency in recent years for the best men to get re-engaged by their old employers, or by new ones, without going to the fairs'.[75] This change was partly a result of moral pressure by those who saw the fairs as disorderly and threatening but it marked, on the part of master and man, a change in attitude to a more 'modern' and rational system. Interestingly, at the same period, the folk custom overwhelmingly associated with 'plough-boy' service, the Plough Plays, also appear to go into terminal decline.

In southern Lancashire, where wage relations had always been more straightforwardly capitalistic than elsewhere, the change was yet more obvious. The continuing success of the vegetable trade and increasingly intensive cultivation had bought prosperity to the farmers who were, by the 1900s, a well organized force. The other side of this was the final demise of living-in service and the increased capital needs of a new agriculture which meant that the chances of a labourer climbing the farming ladder were increasingly remote. In this situation trades unionism, which had been virtually non-existent in Lancashire in the 1870s and 1880s, appeared as a powerful force.[76] In 1912 George Edwards and James Coe from Norfolk visited the area to start a union. It was, however, 'new countrymen' in the shape of the rural railway workers who were the key. As Mutch points out, 'they were free from the constraints on farm workers, but at the same time an integral part of the local economy, which relied heavily on rail transport'.[77] In June 1913 the railwaymen were a key element in a brief but bitter strike when they refused to move farm produce out of the strike area as well as using their contacts through the 'Triple Alliance' of railwaymen, miners and transport workers, to prevent Irish goods and labour being imported through Liverpool.[78] It was perhaps a small and local affair but it showed, like the growth of unionism and even socialism elsewhere in rural England, that things were changing even within what seemed like immutable social formations.

In the south and east, farm structure and perhaps village structure had changed more. We have already looked at the growth and effects of mixed and specialist farming, especially in the area around London, as well as the longer-term switch away from cereal production. By the mid-1900s for most of the south and east, living-in service for men and most women had vanished except in a residual way in Cornwall and Devon. Additionally, any form of payment in kind was increasingly rare, even outside East Anglia. In these terms southern and eastern agriculture had entered a fully capitalist stage where the labourer and farmer stood in a purely cash relationship to one another. This was added to by the fact that the workforce on many of these farms was large, larger indeed than those of many small factories and workshops. A 560 acre mixed farm in Warwickshire in 1902 employed twenty-nine regular workers; an 888 acre mixed farm in Northamptonshire employed twenty; a 580 acre arable farm in Suffolk employed twenty-six; a 265 acre arable farm in Kent employed twenty-four and a 690 acre mainly pasture farm in Sussex employed thirty-one.[79]

While there were, of course, still many small farms, the majority of hired workers were increasingly concentrated on the large holdings of the south and east. However, there were countervailing tendencies which were to have fundamental effects in the long term. We saw above that the workforce as a whole was getting smaller and more regularly employed partly because of demographic factors and partly because of the gradual introduction of machinery. What this meant was that the numbers per unit decreased, even on the large farms. Although within our period this had little real effect it was the basis of the post-Second World War situation described so well by Howard Newby.[80] Here the 'size effect' meant that because each unit employed so few workers, and because agricultural work was relatively isolated, contact with the 'master' became more frequent than with other workers on the farm. In this situation the face-to-face relationship of paternalism in the workplace could be revived – but that was still a distant future in 1914.

On the surface, the village structure of the south and east, particularly away from London, retained many features from the 1850s. The nucleated village remained as a centre, surrounded by farms drawing their labour mainly from the village. In many areas these settlements were virtually 'occupational communities' with the vast majority of the inhabitants working in agriculture, as they had been for many generations. There were other continuities. The Church had been modified rather than wiped out, unlike in parts of Wales, and the parson remained a key figure, as did his opposite, the publican.

Yet there were changes, as well as continuities in village society. These are less easy to summarize, especially given that ruralism and nostalgia were already combining in the 1900s to create an aura of permanence around the villages of southern England. The impact of 'newcomers' has already been looked at briefly, as have some of the changes in local government and landownership. These, combined with other factors, altered and possibly eradicated the dominant model of village structure in the south and east, that of 'open' and 'close'. Although, as late as the 1890s, Wilson Fox continued to use the notion, it had already received its death blow. Central to this, although their impact was delayed, were changes to the Poor Law brought about by the Irremovable Poor Act of 1861 and the Union Changeability Act of 1865 which between them gave the right to settlement after one year's residence. These also made the Poor Law Union as a whole both the place of settlement for each person and rated the Union as a whole rather than parish by parish. This removed the need to prevent population growth because of fear of the poor gaining a settlement and thus becoming the responsibility of the parish in sickness, old age or infirmity, one of the main reasons for the existence of 'close' parishes. In the longer term, population decline made the model increasingly irrelevant. By the 1900s, although some features of the 'open/close' model remained, especially in the extreme case of estate villages, labour shortage had done away with the problem just as surely as labour surplus had created it.[81] It is significant that central books of social criticism published in the 1900s and 1910s like Bennett's *Problems of Village Life*, or F. E. Green's *The Awakening of Rural England*, and above all the Liberal Land report, either simply do not mention the 'problem' of open/close or give it very little attention.

In *Lark Rise to Candleford* Flora Thompson writes of her village in the 1880s, 'all times are times of transition; but the eighteen-eighties were so in a special sense for the world was at the beginning of a new era . . . Values and conditions of life were changing everywhere. Even to simple country people the change was apparent.'[82] Allowing for some simplification, of which Flora Thompson is aware, there is a good deal of truth in this. Certainly, the rural world had changed in many ways since the 1850s, and many of those changes occurred after 1880 or at least their impact was felt mainly after 1880. The depression and continuing rural depopulation, coupled with urban demand both for land and new, and more varied diet, forced the countryside to adapt, especially the south country. Yet, at the same moment, there were those, coming out of the towns, who wanted to hold the process still and to do that created a nostalgic and idyllicised view of a world that was vanishing before them, giving it a permanence in elite and even popular culture which it never had in reality.

NOTES

1 David Lloyd George, *Better Times*, [London, 1910], pp. 156–7.
2 Quoted in Thompson, *Landed Society*, op. cit., p. 322.
3 ibid..
4 ibid., p. 325.
5 Introduction to Christopher Turnor, *Land Problems and National Welfare*, [London, 1911], p. vii.
6 For much of what follows see Alun Howkins, 'The Discovery of Rural England' in R. Colls and P. Dodd [eds] *Englishness: Culture and Politics 1880–1920*, [London, 1986]; also Martin J. Wiener, *English Culture and the Decline of the Industrial Spirit*, [Cambridge, 1981].
7 Haggard, *Farmers Year*, op. cit., p. 466.
8 For what follows see Colls and Dodd, op. cit.; Jan Marsh, *Back to the Land*, [London, 1982]; Peter C. Gould, *Early Green Politics. Back to Nature. Back to the Land, and Socialism in Britain 1880–1900*, [Brighton, 1988].
9 Quoted in Gould, op. cit., p. 15.
10 On Purleigh see Marsh, op. cit., pp. 105–7 and Gould, op. cit., pp. 51–2.

11 Marsh, op. cit., pp. 107–11.
12 Quoted in Fiona MacCarthy, *The Simple Life. C. R. Ashbee and the Cotswolds*, [London, 1981], p. 31, also for what follows.
13 Marsh, op. cit., pp. 152–7.
14 *PP 1868–69 X*, op. cit., p. 65.
15 ibid., p. 109.
16 Quoted in Marsh, op. cit., p. 39.
17 ibid., p. 51.
18 ibid., pp. 58–9.
19 Quoted in Vic Gammon, 'Folk Song Collecting in Sussex and Surrey 1843–1914' in *HWJ*, no. 10 [1980], p. 81.
20 Ferguson, op. cit., p. 67.
21 ibid., pp. 495–7.
22 Margaret Jones Bolsterli, *The Early Community at Bedford Park*, [London, 1977], pp. 76 *ff*.
23 George Orwell, *Coming Up for Air*, [Harmondsworth, 1962], pp. 212-15.
24 On Blunt see Michael Pickering, *Village Song and Culture*, [London, 1982], pp. 3–4.
25 Hollis, *Ladies Elect*, op. cit., p. 379.
26 *EWL*, 1st December 1894.
27 Hollis, op. cit., pp. 363–4.
28 *EWP*, 23rd February 1889.
29 Mottram, op. cit., pp. 159–60.
30 For this see Howkins, *Poor Labouring Men*, op. cit., Ch. 5.
31 *EWP*, 20th April 1889.
32 E. N. Bennett, *Problems of Village Life*, [London, 1913], p. 124.
33 ibid., p. 122.
34 D. W. Bebbington, *The Nonconformist Conscience. Chapel and Politics 1870–1914*, [London, 1982], p. 2.
35 Evans, *Contentious Tithe*, op. cit., pp. 163–4.
36 John Moore, *The Brensham Trilogy: Portrait of Elmbury*, [pb. ed. Oxford, 1985], p. 35.
37 A. H. Baverstock, *The Failure of the Church in the Villages*, [London, 1913].
38 Bennett, op. cit., pp. 129–30.
39 ibid., p. 140.
40 Reg Groves, *Sharpen the Sickle!*, [London, 1949], p. 191.
41 Obelkevich, op. cit., p. 324.
42 ESRO NMB/15/5/3 Minutes, Leaders Meeting, Eastbourne Pevensey Road Wesleyan Methodist Church.
43 *EWP*, 27th December 1884.
44 *EWL*, 9th February 1895.
45 Obelkevich, op. cit., p. 327.
46 Bebbington, op. cit., pp. 157–9.
47 Thompson, *Lark Rise*, op. cit., pp. 69–75.

48 ibid., p. 102.
49 ibid., p. 109.
50 Rex Steadman 'Vox Populi: The Norfolk Newspaper Press 1760–1900', Unpublished FLA thesis, 1971, p. 282.
51 Thompson, *Lark Rise*, op. cit., p. 111.
52 Quoted in S. Koss, *The Rise and Fall of the Political Press in Britain*, [London, 1981], Vol. 1 p. 357.
53 Moore, op. cit., p. 167.
54 Calvertt, op. cit., p. 176.
55 Siegfried Sassoon, *The Complete Memoirs of George Sherston*, op. cit., p. 215.
56 Haggard, *Rural England* Vol. II, op. cit., p. 283.
57 Quoted in Raymond Carr, *English Fox Hunting. A History*. [London, 1976] p. 136.
58 Sassoon, op. cit., pp. 201 and 155.
59 Turnor, op. cit., p. 263.
60 See for example *EWP*, 4th February 1893.
61 There is no account of the Primrose League in its local manifestations but see J. Henderson Robb, *The Primrose League 1883–1906*, [New York 1942, rep. 1968] and more recently M. Pugh, *The Tories and the People 1880–1935*, [London, 1985].
62 Henderson Robb, op. cit., p. 173.
63 Quoted in ibid., p. 166.
64 *EWP*, 11th July 1885; 10th July 1886.
65 Hall, op. cit., p. 129.
66 *PP 1905 XCVII*, 'Second Report by Mr. Wilson Fox on the Wages, Earnings and Conditions of Employment of Agricultural Labourers in the United Kingdom', p. 394.
67 *PP 1900 LXXXIII*, op. cit., p. 601.
68 *PP 1905 XCVII*, op. cit., p. 394.
69 NRO Woods MS, op. cit..
70 *PP 1893–4 XXXV*, Crediton, op. cit., p. 201.
71 ibid., Swaffam, op. cit., p. 69.
72 ibid., p. 71; also interview AJH/Jack Leeder, op. cit..
73 NRO Woods MS, op. cit..
74 NRO Rutherford MS, op. cit..
75 *PP 1905 XCVII*, op. cit., p. 362.
76 Mutch, thesis, op. cit., p. 336.
77 Mutch, *Rural Life*, op. cit., p. 57.
78 Groves, op. cit., pp. 140–3, also Mutch, thesis, op. cit., Ch. 8 *passim*.
79 *PP 1905 XCVII*, pp. 403–8.
80 See Howard Newby, *The Deferential Worker*, [Harmondsworth, 1979].
81 For some of these points see Banks, op. cit., pp. 193–4.
82 Thompson, *Lark Rise*, op. cit., p. 69.

10
The Great War

Rural England in the early summer of 1914 had an atmosphere of modest prosperity. In general, farming had adapted well to the new patterns of demand and supply created by the depression and continuing urban growth. When A. D. Hall finished his three tours through England in 1912 he wrote 'we must recognize that the industry is at present sound and prosperous . . . To the man who takes the trouble to learn and attended to his business, farming now offers every prospect of a good return on his capital.'[1] There were however, costs. As L. Margaret Barnett writes, 'In 1872 the United Kingdom had 24 million acres under crops, or 51.3% of the cultivated area. By 1913 this had shrunk to 19 1/2 million, or 41.6%'.[2] The most serious declines were in cereal production for, by the outbreak of war, imported wheat accounted for over 70 per cent of British consumption.[3] But few worried and they were usually regarded as eccentric, bellicose or simply gloomy. To the majority Britain's command of the seas and the universality of free trade were sufficient guarantee of continuing imports.[4]

To others who looked at England that summer things were less straightforward. As Barbara Tuchman says 'all statements of how lovely it was in the era made by persons contemporary with it will be found to have been made after 1914.'[5] The strikes in Lancashire in 1913 had been followed by other, more bitter disputes in Norfolk in the spring of 1914 and in June and July there had been further strikes in Northamptonshire and Essex.[6] In London, Lloyd George was laying plans for the culmination of his great land campaign which was to divert the interest of the urban working class away from its struggle with capital on to an older enemy, the landlord, and thus ensure a Liberal victory in the 1915 election. But the hay harvest was good, even if disrupted by the strikes in some areas, and although the elite might claim to fear 'radical land seizure' it was a long way off and rents were going up again as were land prices. At the end of July the prospects for the cereal harvest looked good and in some southern counties, for instance Wiltshire, they had begun cutting by 1 August.[6] In Trunch in North Norfolk the harvest was nearly ready at the end of July but on Mr Buck's farm, the biggest in the parish, young 'Billa' Dixon led the men out on a strike for £7 harvest money. After four days the farmer's son came round and offered the £7.

> We were always two or three days nearly longer than anyone else on a big farm . . . we were always three week three day or a month . . . then the war come out just as we started harvest, on the 4th of August, and so I joined up, soon as we finished harvest, they were calling like for volunteers, and several of us in the village, I should think about 10 of us, went that morning down to Mundesley and joined, took the shilling.[7]

Siegfried Sassoon, about the same age as 'Billa' Dixon but a world apart, was at Weirleigh and was alerted by a family friend and by 4 August was in khaki, albeit 'ill-fitting', as a trooper in the Yeomanry Cavalry.[8]

Sassoon, like most who wrote afterwards, gave a significance to that August as the end of an old world. Although this may or may not be true in retrospect, 'Billa' Dixon's matter-of-fact account is probably nearer the truth for most who volunteered from city or country in the first months of the war. A. G. Street's 'imaginary' Wiltshire village, Sutton Evias, took it in much the same way.

> Like most country folk, although they were alarmed at the news England had gone to war, the inhabitants of Sutton Evias and the neighbouring district reckoned that such an event would have but little effect on their lives . . . The land waited for no man, either in war or peace. There was the harvest to finish, and a thousand and one other jobs to be done, all of which were far more important than any war.[9]

This attitude was also shared by those members of the government and Civil Service who had thought about the effects of war on agriculture at all. As Peter Dewey has written, 'the experience of the farming industry in the first half of the war was one of "business as usual" rather than any radical change to meet an emergency.'[10] Indeed it would perhaps have been surprising if there had been any other reaction. Government had little precedent for intervention in agriculture at any level, and in other respects the attitude of the villagers of Sutton Evias was widely shared. It was a continental war and likely to be limited in duration even if the 'over by Christmas' optimism was not as widely held by the military leadership as by the ordinary men and women of England. Most important though was an overwhelming belief that imports of foodstuffs would continue unabated. In February 1914, the Committee on Imperial Defence put this position clearly, 'by maintaining a general control of sea communications this country should, in the future as in the past, be able to bear the exhausting consequences of war.'[11]

Initially, this optimism was borne out. The gradual switch back to cereals in some areas, though still limited, continued, and yield per acre in 1914 was slightly up on the average for the four years previously.[12] Nor were there real problems in gathering it in. Many labourers, like 'Billa' Dixon, waited until after harvest before taking the shilling and in some areas, where enlistment had been too enthusiastic, recruits were sent on to farms. The main problem was horses where overly-keen requisitioning often took animals for army use which could be ill afforded. The number of farm horses was not to return to its 1914 level until 1917.[13] By the winter of 1914–15, problems began to appear. Grain imports from the Black Sea areas of Russia, Turkey and Rumania, which had accounted for 35 per cent of Britain's imports in 1911, were lost by the closure of the Dardenelles and Turkey's alliance with the Central Powers, the Australian crop failed and the government of India decided to keep most of its crop to deal with rising prices. On the 1911 figures this meant a potential drop of 57 per cent in England's imported grain.[14] Additionally, where grain was available, for instance in North and South America, prices were going up rapidly.

However, home supply was responding to some extent. Rapid price rises in 1914 encouraged British farmers to plant extra corn crops in the winter of 1914 and the spring of 1915 and the harvest of 1915 showed a 20 per cent increase in home grown wheat and 8 per cent in oats. The problem was that little of this increase was met by ploughing up since there was a 19 per cent decrease in barley production and, more worrying in terms of long-term fertility, farmers were reducing the root break in the rotation. These problems came home to roost in 1916. Although the area under food crops was still up on the prewar period there was a drop of 12 per cent in the acreage under wheat. Further, the North American wheat harvest of 1916 was bad which meant that Britain could not rely on relatively cheap food imports as it had in 1915. Suddenly in the summer and autumn of 1916 the problems of food supply took a more serious turn.

The government and farming itself gradually faced these problems and adapted to them at national and at local level. Even in the first months of the war the slogan 'business as usual' concealed, among some members of the administration, an unease at the workings of free trade. This led to a growing willingness to intervene in the purchase of food abroad and attempts to increase the home grown food supply.[15] Initially, however, little was done at a practical level and some government measures, like attempting to buy wheat in Argentina in the winter of 1915 which simply resulted in agents paying more than market price and selling below it, were disastrous. Nevertheless, a growing body of opinion at national level was convinced of the need for state intervention to maintain food supply. This was fuelled by rapidly rising prices. By December 1914, food prices were 22 per cent above the level of June 1914 and by mid-1916 it was estimated that the cost of food for a low-income working class family had increased by 68 per cent since the outbreak of war. As a result, by the spring of 1915, the government was intervening in the purchase of wheat, meat and sugar and had created 'a nucleus of administration that was to feed the future control mechanism.'[16]

At a local level significant changes occurred earlier with the creation, in the summer of 1915, of the War Agricultural Committees. These were attached to the County Councils to organize the supply of labour, examine food production in their localities and report on shortages of supplies. To start with, the impact of the committees was slight as they had no statutory powers and tended to be dominated by farmers who reflected opinion of the problems of production rather than created it. But, like changes at national level, the committees provided an important basis for firm government intervention after 1916.

The impact of the war on the rural areas and on rural society was initially muted. With hindsight, the events of August 1914 take on a tragic importance and even finality.

Mabel Ashby wrote what is the most moving of many accounts of this kind.

> The last week of July and the first days of August, my mother and I harnessed a pony every evening, and drove the five miles from the Lower Town to Kineton Post Office to read in its windows the latest telegrams . . . Each evening all the wide valley was bathed in golden serene sunset light, but on the third of August the weather changed. The sunset was more gorgeous than ever; but the valley was filled with mist of raucous purple. When my mother recited the messages we had brought home there was a long stillness that (my father) broke with the only possible words; 'Few things will ever be the same again'.[17]

Yet we should beware for 'business as usual', as we have already suggested, was not only a slogan of government. At the most basic level many farmworkers would have found an obvious conflict of interest between the needs of harvest or, in the longer term, animal care, and the demands of patriotism. The shepherd in Sutton Evias when asked if he is going 'list' replies, 'Not me! . . . I got me sheep to zee to . . . Our job be to do our work, and let the army do theirn.'[18] On Castle Heaton Farm in Northumberland the casual labour books record the annual arrival of John and Harry McFadden and James McGee, Irish harvest workers, and the employment of the same number of extra women workers as normal. Similarly, the annual hirings on the same farm in October show no change as compared with previous years in terms of those recruited.

These impressionistic accounts are given weight by Peter Dewey's careful work on the recruitment of farm labour during the war.[19] He argues that contemporary figures of the numbers recruited from the rural districts were greatly overestimated. In addition, skilled farm workers were exempted from recruiting form early in the war. This leads him to the conclusion that rather than a loss of about a third of the farm labour supply by 1916 it seems likely the figure was nearer a tenth, something in the order of 123,000 men, including juvenile labour. Given that skilled men were protected, the majority of these were ordinary labourers. This is borne out by surveys carried out in 1916 and early 1917. In Hertfordshire in 1916 there had been a loss of 1,623 labourers as against 1,022 ploughmen and 629 cowmen, while a report from West Sussex in early 1917 shows that twice as many ordinary labourers were required to bring the farm workforce up to its prewar levels as carters and ploughmen.[20]

The first to go from the villages were those who were peacetime members of the reserve. These were ex-regular soldiers who remained part of the battalion 'strength' after their regular service had ended. W. H. Barrett remembered 'most of the postmen and policemen' going away 'at a few hours notice' from the east coast town where he was living because they were reservists.[21] The next to go were the Territorials. George Hewins who, like many one suspects, had joined in peacetime more for a uniform and a few shillings than any desire to fight, found himself to his horror leaving Stratford-on-Avon for basic training.

> Fred Winter the draper on the High Street swore me in, and afore I knowed what was happening we was being marched through the streets to the station. It was Christmas 1914. The missus had had the babby about a week before – she was still abed. The little uns was waving flags, only our Flo was crying . . . [22]

But the greatest impact both in terms of numbers and emotions was the raising, and then going away of the New Armies – the nearly two million men who enlisted between August 1914 and March 1915. The reasons they went were many. Certainly the recruiting propaganda worked. Kitchener's pointing finger, or the posters which urged women to persuade their menfolk to enlist, as well as the despicable white feather campaign, started by a retired admiral in Folkestone but which soon spread over much of England, had real effects. As late as 1918, Mont Abbot, a sixteen year old Oxfordshire carter, felt their presence.

> The gwoost of Kitchener had been fading his finger at me for some time on they washed-out posters outside the Post Office, 'Your King and Country NEED YOU'. Being up to me eyes in the last few years in 'Rosy's rump', lone calves, mad bulls and hungry horses out at Fulwell I hadn't time to list to Kitchener. But by 1918 the old gwoost were cropping up a fresh, pointing at me from barn doors and tree trunks . . . I'd be sixteen in July. I only hoped the lads could hold out till I got there.[23]

A different form of 'compulsion' came from local pressure; either from your 'pals' or from your betters. Time and again, even before the recruiting authorities allowed men who joined together to form 'pals' battalions, accounts of enlistment have a collective air. Like 'Billa' Dixon going of with ten mates from Trunch after harvest, many a young man who would probably not have acted alone found himself swept along by the collective feelings of a crowd of friends. There was also pressure from 'betters'. Sassoon's bitter poem with its lines 'Squire nagged and bullied till I went to fight/ (Under Lord Derby's Scheme) I died in Hell – (They called it Passchendaele)'[24] found precise echoes time and again.

> Landowners frequently selected likely men from among their servants and farm labourers and transported them to the nearest recruiting office. Lieutenant-Colonel A. C. Borton, who owned an estate at Cheveney in Kent and was a local Justice of the peace, drove his butler, footman and cowman to Maidstone Barracks to enlist . . . The Royal Berkshire Regiment included one platoon of butlers and footmen and another composed almost exclusively of gardeners and workers from a peer's estate.[25]

In this, as in other respects, the war, to begin with at least, relied on prewar structures of paternalism. Men were urged to go as much as a part of their duty to the social structure of rural areas as to King and Country. In return, paternalism offered to 'look after' wives and children and, as the Norfolk Chamber of Agriculture agreed in September 1914, 'to keep open the places of all those employees who have joined the forces of the King.'[26] When things began to go wrong and casualties mounted this paternalist pressure was a source of great bitterness and anger among both those who had served and those who had sent family to the front.

To others, the war was an escape from poverty or unemployment. A private's pay of 6/8 1/2d a week was about half what a farm labourer got, even in the poorest paid areas, but they were fed and clothed and a separation allowance was paid for wives and children, although especially early in the war it was slow in coming. Not all were as lucky as George Hewins, who left a life of irregular casual employment and became an officer's servant with tips and perks. He and his wife had eight children.

> One thing was certain she was better off with me in the army! . . . She had money coming in regular, now, for the first time. It didn't matter that the rent was seven and six; with my officers and the allowance they'd started giving for

> the kiddies, she got two pound ten shillings a week – more money than a lot of us had ever brought in![27]

Economic reasons for enlistment, especially among the unemployed, are clearly shown by the fact that once trade began to pick up, largely as a result of wartime demands, recruiting fell.[28]

However, for most countrymen who joined the New Armies it is clear that a vague patriotism, personal or collective, was the overwhelming reason for taking the shilling. Their feelings were often inarticulate and low key once the shouting had stopped and, as Peter Simkins points out, their actions were often more considered than the mythology of 1914 suggests. 'Less than one-third of all volunteers were involved in the first rush to the colours in August and September 1914 . . . ' which suggests 'a sense of duty and obligation rather than missionary zeal.'[29] George Hewins put it neatly and clearly. 'If you'd asked me why I was going to fight I'd have said; "To save the country". If the Germans won we would be slaves!'[30] Equally striking was that those who enlisted came from all classes. The prewar army had too often been the 'last refuge of the scoundrel' but those who went in 1914 presented a very different picture. The 5th Oxfordshire and Buckinghamshire Light Infantry, according to Lieutenant-Colonel Cobb, drew 'a great many from most respectable homes and businesses. Some gentlemen, many indoor servants, grooms, gardeners, chauffeurs, gamekeepers, well-to-do trades, hotel-keepers, clerks etc . . . '[31]

The county elite had less objection to the army than the rural poor. In prewar years members of the elite held commissions in the county regiments and the Territorial Army. Most enlisted as, or quickly became, officers, which reinforced within the army the nuances of a class but also a paternalist structure of home. To many young officers, especially those who actually fought, 'my men' or 'my platoon' had the ring of 'my village' or 'my workers' even where the officers themselves came from urban backgrounds. In return, their men responded within the same framework. Young officers, when brave and willing to share danger, were worshipped. In stark contrast to more professional armies where the ethos was a military one this essentially 'civilian' ideology, especially of the Territorials and the New Armies, was a major element in preventing disaffection. The identification of the young officer, like Sassoon, with his men and vice versa often survived the war and turned the bitterness of the trenches into anger against those who had 'stayed at home' regardless of class.

As the men left for the army the countryside adjusted as needed. Up to 1916 'business as usual' covered many aspects of rural life. As we have already seen, recruitment into the army was probably not as serious in economic terms as many contemporaries believed. The harvest of 1914 was got in without substantial help from outside and winter was always a slack time. The hunting season began as normal and indeed was strongly defended by many as an essential training ground for young cavalry officers as well as a vital relaxation. 'What on earth are officers home from the front to do with their time if there's no hunting for them' said Lord Lonsdale, a main supporter of the Cottesmore.[32] The London season also continued, as did many other aspects of elite life yet already, changes, some of them trivial, some unbearably tragic, had begun. C. F. G. Masterman, a prewar critic of the elite, later claimed that the 'flower of the British aristocracy' was slaughtered in the retreat from Mons and the Battle of Ypres in 1914–15.[33] Certainly, losses among the aristocracy and gentry were high and their effects disastrous. Sir Edward Antrobus's only son was killed in action in 1915 and when Sir Edward died shortly afterwards the whole of the Amesbury Abbey estate was put on the market.[34] By the end of 1914, the dead included 'three peers and fifty-two peers sons, as well as a large number of baronets and their sons.'[35]

At the 'trivial' level, in terms of living standards at least, reduction in the supply of domestic labour meant changes. The number of gardeners at Aynho Park in Northamptonshire was cut from nine in 1914 to four by 1917, none of whom were of military age.[36] The great hunts, despite their insistence that the war effort required their continuance, were finding it increasingly difficult to hold on to servants.[37] Even where male servants didn't particularly want to go to was and where their employees were prepared to 'protect' them, other pressures were felt from their own class.

> Rufford Abbey had asked some of their more valuable staff to delay enlistment, but Arthur wasn't happy about it. He could see

that his parents were being persecuted and confided to George, 'It's all very well these people hanging on to our shirt tails, but they don't have to suffer the opinion of folk who don't know the truth.'[38]

Worse still, even women servants were leaving as wartime pressure as well as opportunity began to reverse the dominant ideology's insistence that a woman's place, whatever her class, was in the home.

At the 'top' of society the real effect of the war on women's position depends on perspective. Much work carried out by the wives and daughters of the gentry looks very like a continuation of the charitable and political work that their mothers had done for the Primrose League or some other worthy cause. 'Lady Orr Lewis was busy with knitting circles, jumble sales and anything else that would raise money for the Red Cross and comforts for the troops.'[39] Many aristocratic women's accounts of the war, like those of Sonia Keppel, Lady Diana Manners and Venetia Stanley show their lives almost as a chapter from a novel by Evelyn Waugh with a feverish social life, including, in Keppel's case, a full 'coming out' ball in 1918, interspersed with war work. But they were not the only ones. Some aristocratic and gentry women turned their homes into hospitals or convalescent homes for the wounded and the very fact that many of them were finding outside employment for the first time in their lives had a fundamental effect on them. 'Miss Dillon and they others of high born rank, who'd kept theyselves uppity on their high horse before the war, now seemed more natural, down-to-earth walking about among the villagers and inclined to stop and speak.'[40]

Below the elite, among the rural middle class and especially working class, the war had a fundamental, if ultimately short-lived, effect on women and women's employment. From early 1915 onwards labour shortages in industry, trade and even commercial occupations were tempting younger women out of the home and domestic service and even out of agriculture where the numbers permanently employed on the land fell by about a quarter between July 1914 and 1915.[41] As men joined up and the demands of war production, especially munitions, increased, whole areas opened up for women's employment, in urban areas and county towns, which had not only been closed before the war but were considered deeply unsuitable. In these trades wages were good, especially to a country girl whose father probably brought home about 14s a week in 1914. In Leicester by 1917 a girl could earn 52s for a 52 1/2 hour week as a tram conductress with a uniform and a week's paid holiday. In a factory in the same town she could earn up to 40s a week. Additionally many 'new' war orientated factories were prewar agricultural engineering works like Ransomes of Ipswich which meant it was relatively easy for a country woman to go into munitions without moving far from home. In Warwickshire, for instance, where munitions factories were widespread, 'there was great difficulty in persuading females to take on any kind of land work.'[42] It was probably these factories which provided work for the girls from Enstone in North Oxfordshire who taunted the under-age Mont Abbott.

> Worst of all were the 'canaries', the gals that worked in the Munitions Factories, defiantly flaunting their yellow skin and hair wreaked upon them by the TNT they was constantly having to handle. In some villages the Canaries was turning quite nasty, throwing white feathers, the symbol of cowardice, at chaps not in the war.[43]

In terms of rural society it was those who stayed at home, 'village women' as the reports call them, who were most important. From 1915 onwards there were a range of governmental and quasi-governmental interventions to get these women into the labour force. Early in 1915, the Board of Agriculture started training schemes on a county basis through the County Councils and the Agricultural Colleges, to train women in milking and light farm work. However, these schemes attracted very few women and they were mostly outsiders. There were also attempts to use prewar land settlement and ruralist organizations for women, and especially the agricultural branch of the Women's Legion. Again these were unsuccessful, except in recruiting and placing a limited number of usually urban and middle class volunteers on farms.[44]

As a result of these failures, and a growing belief among sections of government that a real labour shortage on the land was now a possibility, in February 1916, the War Agricultural Committees were ordered to set up Women's War Agricultural Committees. The main aim of these committees was to register village women who were willing to work on the land and put them in contact with farmers who needed labour. By the end of 1916 it was claimed that about 140,000 women were registered nationally. Of these, 72,000 women had received certificates saying that they were 'as truly serving (their) country as the man who is fighting in the trenches or on the sea'; and about 62,000 had received a 'bottle green armlet marked with a scarlet crown' to show the wearer had done 30 days' approved service.[45] However, the reality of even these low figures was a good deal worse since at harvest 1916 the Board of Agriculture reported that only about 29,000 women were at work under this scheme.[46]

As a result of these campaigns, as well as a range of informal economic and social pressures, Dewey has estimated that the loss of women to factories and other employment in the year 1914–15 had been overturned by 1916, and exceeded prewar figures, with 143,000 full and part-time workers as against 130,000 in 1914.[47] There were however, as there had always been, more women at work in the fields than this. Many country women refused to register for fear that they might be conscripted away or that they could be forced to take men's jobs and thus lower wages. Probably more never appeared in any of the returns because the arrangements made were essentially informal. Figures also conceal other changes. In some areas, where women had worked regularly, the war gave them increased status and importance. In Northumberland, Castle Heaton Farm shows some of these. In 1914 it was very much 'business as usual' as we have already said. In that year, extra work at harvest was taken by three Irishmen, five local women, all of whom were related to regular workers, and one extra man. In 1916 there were no Irish hired but six women were paid extra as were two men. By 1917 the situation had changed further. In that year, eleven women worked the harvest, no Irishmen and only one extra man. There were also more subtle changes. The amount of piece-work done by women increased at all seasons even in 1915. By 1916, at least one family group has a woman head, one assumes because of her husband's enlistment because her husband had been 'head' in 1915. In early 1917, two single women appear on the wages book, described not by their Christian names as normal but as 'Miss'. It seems safe to assume these are war workers of some kind, since all other women hired are referred to in the ordinary way. Finally, from 1917 the time honoured practice of paying the family head all the wages of his or her group disappears and all workers, including the women, are paid individually.[48]

Even given all this, the response of village women to the call to patriotic duty was slow. There were several reasons for this. Many women were better off, especially country women, than they had ever been. The value of allowances to soldier's dependants kept up with inflation until 1917. Additionally, billeting of soldiers provided valuable income in many areas. As well, many women simply couldn't work because of young children. Unlike some factories, there was no systematic attempt to provide crèches or to pay for child care although this was under discussion in the War Cabinet in July 1918.[49] Most important, though, was probably simple hostility to the work. For nearly fifty years country women had been told by their betters that field work was demeaning, unwomanly and immoral and although many had ignored this from economic necessity a good deal of this ideology had stuck. It could not be reversed overnight.

In those areas, which were growing throughout the war, where the trades unions were strong, this was reinforced by opposition to women's employment on the grounds that it cut men's wages. The unions had always opposed women's work in agriculture, even if it allowed women members, and it retained that position despite George Edwards, the president, who urged women to work as their patriotic duty.[50] Nor was this simply a union matter, for many women knew from bitter experience, especially in the arable areas, that 'going afield' was hard work for miserable pay. For example 'A Working Woman' replied to Edwards' appeal suggesting that he had better direct his advice to 'the middle-class and rich mens daughters' as 'some of them have never done a useful days work in their lives.'[51]

In a way her call was already being answered. Alongside the registration of village women, the Board of Agriculture began to 'encourage the recruitment of a more permanent and mobile force of female workers drawn principally from the middle classes.' Called initially the Women's National Land Service Corps, it had attracted, by the beginning of 1917, about 2,000 volunteers who, having received six weeks' training, went, usually in groups of two or three, to villages where there was a labour shortage. In January 1917 it was estimated that an extra 40,000 women workers would be needed in the next twelve months and, following meetings between Rowland Prothero, President of the Board of Agriculture, and representatives of the WNLSC, it was decided to create a Women's Land Army. The first appeal in March 1917 for 10,000 volunteers drew over 30,000 and by July 1917 2,000 WLA volunteers had been placed on farms.[52]

WLA volunteers were much better trained than the WLNSC predecessors, had free uniforms and were paid a national scale of wages of between 18s and 20s a week, with extra payments for those with skills like tractor driving and ploughing. Although most were middle class there is little doubt that generally they were skilled workers capable of doing the same work in many cases as the increasingly elderly workforce left on the farms by the recruitment of young men. This is borne out by the very low 'drop out' rate. For example, in Norfolk it was found that only 7 per cent of WLA volunteers were 'failures' and those who 'quit' were a very small proportion indeed.[53]

At the start, the WLA volunteers found it difficult to gain acceptance. Farmers were distrustful of them as were many village women and male workers. Their dress, which included breeches, was a source of horror although it did give *Punch* the chance to appeal to its male readership with drawings of shapely female legs. By the end of the war some of these attitudes had changed, although one cannot help but get the impression that the authorities remained at least as concerned about the morality of single women in trousers as about agricultural skills. By 1918 the WLA had a working strength of 11,529 in a wide range of farming jobs throughout the British Isles.

However, by this date, other changes of fundamental importance had taken place. By the end of 1916 a series of crises had first created a coalition and then ousted Asquith as Prime Minister. He was replaced by Lloyd George. 'Business as usual' in agriculture as elsewhere came to an end. One of Lloyd George's first acts was to bring in Rowland Prothero, whose long-term commitment to an interventionist policy was well known, as President of the Board of Agriculture. In December 1916 Prothero initiated what was dubbed the 'plough policy' with its slogan 'Back to the seventies'. It was the beginning of an organised food production policy – the first in British history. Its purpose, as Jonathan Brown writes, was twofold.

> This slogan applied specifically to the policy of ploughing up grassland, for in other respects the food production campaign had little relation to the agriculture of the 1870s. Besides increasing the extent of arable land with a view to growing more corn and potatoes, the principles of the food production policy were to direct farmers into more efficient practices through a survey of badly cultivated land.[54]

The first phase of this policy started in January 1917, under the direction of the newly-formed Food Production Department of the Board of Agriculture. This transformed the county agricultural committees into War Agriculture Executive Committees whose job was to survey land locally, urge farmers to switch to cereal production and bring land up to a higher state of cultivation. Their powers were mainly consultative but ultimately they did have powers of compulsion. In extreme cases, bad farmers could be dispossessed and the land 'determined' and placed under another tenancy or farmed through the Committee. These were very much last resorts and by the end of the war only 317 tenancies had been determined 'in respect of 20,197 acres, and the ECs took possession of 27,287 acres of badly farmed land.'[55]

More usual were ploughing orders and 'good husbandry' directives, and many thousands of these were issued in 1917 and 1918. Peter Dewey takes an example of one page from the Somerset War Agriculture Executive Committee special cultivation orders book for the early spring of 1918 which shows individual fields and even 'villa gardens' of a quarter of an acre subject to orders to 'cultivate, clean and crop with potatoes'; 'cultivate and clean, cut and burn the brambles' or 'plough crop to corn.'[56] Some of this had unexpected local effects as in the case of a Norfolk labourer, Charlie Barber, who, through an Executive Committee decision, realised his ambition to become a smallholder.

> That was during the war and three chaps come driving into the farmyard . . . they said 'Are you Mr Barber', I said, 'Yes'. They said 'Ain't there some land down here you would have hired'. 'Yes' . . . 'Would you still take it on', they said, 'Well yes', I said, 'on conditions' . . . Of course when we got down there that was 'havering', covered in haver, this old dead grass what had bin there for two years . . . They said 'that have got to be cropped, we aren't a-going to let the land lay here dormant.'[57]

Charlie Barber borrowed a team and plough from his employer and ploughed up his five acres, putting it down to wheat and potatoes.

The second stage of the policy, which marked both an intensification of the measures of January 1917 and a new departure, was the Corn Production Act. This was passed into law, under the shadow of unrestricted U-boat attacks, on 21 August 1917. It had four main provisions. Firstly, it guaranteed a minimum price for wheat and oats, though not barley which was mainly used for brewing. Secondly, it guaranteed a minimum wage for agricultural labourers which was to be set by an Agricultural Wages Board. Thirdly, it attempted to restrict rents and, finally, it strengthened the powers of the Board of Agriculture in relation to good cultivation. Thus, by August 1917, the government had taken to itself unprecedented interventionist powers in relation to vast areas of agriculture. Its success has been the subject of debate but at the most basic level the area under plough in England and Wales increased by 1.86 million acres by 1918, compared with 1916.[58] In more direct terms the policy of food control, both rationing and changing methods of extraction of nutrition – for instance raising the extraction rate of flour from wheat from about 70 per cent before the war to a wartime peak of 91 per cent – were probably more significant.[59] Nevertheless, the fact that bread was the only major foodstuff unrationed was widely believed to have been a result of government intervention in guaranteeing wheat prices, which was a considerable propaganda coup and was to have postwar repercussions.

Probably the most publicly important of the Corn Production Act's provisions was the guaranteed minimum wage. Since 1912 the labourers' unions had argued that agriculture, because of the 'special' nature of labour relations within the industry, should be governed by a trade board which would fix hours, wages and conditions. In 1917 this was conceded. County Boards were set up on which representatives of the labourers and the farmers disagreed about wages and were led to compromise by an independent member. These recommendations became the county rate which was then ratified by the main Agricultural Wages Board in London and given the force of law. Like the guaranteed price for cereals, the reality of the AWB was less startling than the theory. The Corn Production Act set a minimum national wage of 25s which operated until the county boards could be set up, and the first of these, in Norfolk, was in fact not fully working until May 1918. This 25s was an increase in wages in some areas, for instance much of the south and East Anglia. However, elsewhere, in the old 'high wage' areas of the north for example, it was well below what was already being paid.

Yet the principal, and the medium term change in practice was vital since it took bargaining for wages out of the paternalist relationship and placed it within the sphere of the state. In the long term, this may well have worked against the labourer's interest; in the short term it seemed like liberation, especially in those areas of the south and east where weekly or even daily hiring with a lot of piece-work had been the prewar norm. As Jack Leeder, a Norfolk horseman, put it, 'Men were afraid you see . . . That was understandable. But the union did away with all that sort of thing and that was a good job when they negotiated the harvest wages and your weekly wage.'[60] The Wages Boards marked the final phase in what was a transformation, albeit a temporary one, in the relationship between master and man. The prewar fall in the numbers employed in agriculture had given those left, especially the skilled men, a real sense of their worth. In many areas the unions had turned this sense of worth into positive action for change. Even where the unions were weak or nonexistent, the chapel and radical politics had spread similar ideas. The Wages Boards were in a curious way a recognition of this change, with the power and worth of the labourers at long last recognized by the state.

Partly as a result, between 1917 and 1921 union membership soared. Not since the heady days of the 1870s had the farm labourer had such organized power. In 1914 the National Agricultural Labourers Union had 350 branches and about 9,000 members; by 1919 it had over 2,300 branches and 170,000 members. The Workers Union Agriculture section had over 100,000 members by that date.[61] As early as 1915 there had been strikes in Norfolk, both to raise wages and against the use of soldiers on the farms, and there were further strikes in East Anglia in 1917 and 1918. By 1918, in some areas, the movement had gone further. Robert Walker, secretary of the National Agricultural Labourers Union, welcomed the Russian Revolution and argued that it held out great hopes for England and, in the 1918 election, for the first time, socialist candidates, backed by the unions, appeared in rural areas opposing both Conservatives and Liberals. Their successes were limited but it seemed to many that the mould was broken.[62]

Unionization and perhaps some growth in radicalism, even in the rural areas, were signs of deeper problems. By 1917 the war was draining England physically and emotionally. A sense of this comes through in A. G. Street's *The Gentlemen of the Party*. 'By now most people, even many of those who were making a lot of money out of it, were sick and tired of the war. Of what use was money or profit while such nightmare conditions of life obtained?'[63] Mont Abbot put it more concisely. "When the war ends . . . " were the only dream we had left.'[64] Conscription, introduced in 1916, gave the final lie to a volunteer army, although many of course did continue to enlist of their own will. Conscription also showed just how serious the decline in the normal supply of male labour was, a situation which had worsened by the harvest of 1917. According to Peter Dewey's estimates, conventional male labour supply had fallen by 13 per cent by 1918, while demand had increased because of changes in productive techniques. The government met these problems both by giving exemptions to those in agriculture and releasing soldier labour for key harvest operations. Mont Abbot from Oxfordshire tried to enlist in 1918 on his sixteenth birthday only to be told that 'we was fighting a more important battle [on the land] . . . with food so short and harvest coming up; and sent us straight back.'[65] These exemptions sometimes led to bitterness as farmers protected their sons by having them classified as essential workers.[66]

Classification did however protect some sections of the workforce, especially the skilled. By 1918 when the War Agricultural Executives were asked at county level to 'find' 30,000 men in England and Wales they were able to supply only half.[67] In this situation release of soldiers' labour was a key element, especially from the harvest of 1917 onwards. Initially many or even most of those released were farmworkers and some were asked for by name, particularly early in the war. At harvest 1916, of the 16,690 soldiers supplied by the army, nearly half had been asked for by name. As the war went on this became less and less the case and farmers increasingly had to rely simply on who was available. A Shropshire farmer complained bitterly that 'one of the men

I got was a piano tuner; I could knock nothing into him.'[68] Yet most worked well enough. As A. G. Street writes.

> When harvest operations necessitated any extra men these were provided by the military, and although many of them knew nothing of farm work they all helped with a will . . . (as) they preferred to work at something other than learning the art of destruction that was war.[69]

When troops and women workers didn't suffice, boy and girl labour was released from schools. At its most informal it was little more than a 'nature walk', as the Rev. Reeve of Stondon Massey in Essex recorded in his diary. 'School Children are everywhere employed gathering the blackberries in School Hours under the control of their teachers. The fruit is packed in baskets provided of regulation size, and sent by rail to the Army jam factories'.[70]

Sixty miles further north, 'Taddy' Wright from Gimmingham in Norfolk, had his education cut short to work for a local blacksmith under the 1915 Board of Education circular which allowed exemption from school attendance for key work for part of the year. 'The Norfolk Education let us go you see, and I suppose he put in a grant for us . . . Then I went back to (school) after the War, and I might just have well stopped at home. They couldn't do anything with us . . . we'd learnt too much off the soldiers.'[71] Mont Abbot was also taken from school and, by the age of fifteen, had achieved the rank of carter, 'with two bwoy chaps and a grampy under me, and nine great cart horses rattling their bins for grub.'[72] The numbers involved are difficult to come by, but in 1917 H. A. L. Fisher claimed that 600,000 children had been released early from education during the first three years of war. Since agriculture was the major user of child labour the scale of the problem involved is clear.[73]

The near-successful German spring offensive of 1918 stretched the resources of the country and the countryside to the limit. The upper age limit for conscription was raised to 51 and sweeping changes were made to reduce the number of men who held exemption certificates issued earlier in the war on medical or other grounds. The County Executive Committees objected strongly, seeing their role as protecting agriculture. In Cheshire, for example, they were faced with a demand for 1,000 men and investigated 2,600 cases before they could fill their quota. Even so, they objected that this was done under pressure, since the men could not be spared 'from an agricultural point of view' but were only released 'in deference to the urgent requirements of the nation'.[74] W. H. Barrett, having been discharged from both the army in 1915 and the navy in 1916, was called up again in early 1918 and ordered to report to Cambridge although he still had not received his pension following his last discharge as unfit.

> I spent a lot of time composing a letter explaining how happy I should be to be found fit, for then I would want no blasted Tribunal, but as the King was so anxious for my services perhaps he would send a little on account as compensation for past services.[75]

About half the men demanded from agriculture had been found when the recruiting 'campaign' was abandoned in June 1918 with the start of harvest. However, once harvest was over, it seems the activity was resumed. In August, Sir Henry Rider Haggard's gardener received his call up, though he was 52 and the village blacksmith, also an 'elderly man', and was called for examination.[76] By then though the question was all but redundant. Although Sassoon on the Western Front was thinking of another winter and the 'Great Offensive of 1919' the German advance had been stopped and was about to turn into a headlong retreat. Similarly, at home, this seems to have gone almost unnoticed. The schoolchildren of Essex were still gathering berries for jam in September according to the Rev. Reeve and Haggard's trip to Wales in early October showed no signs of change. Yet, by 28 October, he wrote, 'there is a certain something in the air which seems to suggest that the end of the war is not far off.'[77]

Armistice Day, 11 November, was greeted, initially at least, with mixed emotions. The news did not reach many rural areas until late in the day and most who worked the land were dealing with the cold and thankless tasks which agriculture produced for November.

> It were fine but raw on 11 November. We was tatering in Turnpike, with eighteen women, several of them war-widows, picking taters, and a little lad of three years sqwarking miserable because he were cold . . . Seemed he was crying for all of us, up to our necks in mud and war, sick to death of the waste of lives and the want of men . . . I dubbed him 'Little Tater' and carted

> across the baulks to his backaching Mam. We'd just decided to yet our dinner out of the field . . . when we spotted Postmaster Adams sailing down the road form Charlbury . . . 'It's over, they called it awf, 'leven o'clock this morning' . . . Little Tater . . . started to bawl again. I swung him up . . . 'All better! ALL better!' until at last he gave a smile. But his Mam warn't smiling. For her, and for thousands of others, it 'ud never be 'all better'.[78]

For most people such bitterness and doubt soon passed, even if they were to return to it in later years. In Norwich, Haggard wrote in his diary that, by evening 'the guns and maroons are firing and I hear the cheers of victory'.[79] The news took some time to reach the Rev. Reeve in Stondon.

> Some in Stondon heard the distant bells at Brentwood. But it was not till the afternoon that definite tidings reached the villages then it filtered through chiefly in the form of private messages . . . As soon as I had official intelligence the Stondon Church Bells were chimed . . . Distant rockets and other tokens of joy were heard around us as the evening advanced.[80]

The bells were also rung at Enstone, Mont Abbot's village in Oxfordshire although, because the real ringers were either away in the forces or had been killed, a 'scratch' team was got together. 'Thee never heerd such a pandemonium in you life. More like ringing a new scare in than ringing the old war out.'[81] Nor were later celebrations much better and the Bacchanalia reported from the urban areas found little echo in the villages. Beer had been short at harvest, leading to strikes in parts of Suffolk and Norfolk, and there doesn't seem to have been much more available to celebrate the peace. Mont Abbot and his fellow ringers walked five miles to Chipping Norton in search of fabled beer to find 'no beer; and the lamps was all out – no paraffin.'[82]

It was a bleak ending to four years which many thought had changed their worlds for ever. Yet, in most respects the war did little more than speed up changes which were already taking place. Even those things which seemed totally new, like a national Wages Board and guaranteed wheat prices had been mooted before the war. Deeper transformations, like the sale of land by the old elite were also clearly visible before the war although, as we shall see in the final chapter, these did increase after 1919. Other changes turned out to be temporary. The turn back to wheat didn't last and the move to a more varied agriculture continued in the postwar world. Similarly, what seemed like earth-shattering changes in women's position turned out, in the short run at least, to be meaningless. But in 1918 if anybody thought about those things in rural England they were quickly overwhelmed by the simple relief that 'it was all over'.

NOTES

1 Hall, op. cit., pp. 431–2.
2 L. Margaret Barrett, *English Food Policy During the First World War*, [London, 1985], p. 3.
3 Jonathan Brown, *Agriculture in England. A Survey of Farming. 1870–1947*, [Manchester, 1987], p. 10.
4 Barrett, op. cit., Ch. 1, *passim*.
5 Barbara Tuchmann. *The Proud Tower*, [London, 1966], p. xiv.
6 Groves, op. cit., pp. 144–9.
7 Street, *Gentleman*, op. cit., p. 135.
8 Siegfried Sassoon, *The Weald of Youth*, [London, 1942],, p. 207.
9 Street, op. cit..
10 P. Dewey, *British Agriculture in the First World War*, [London, 1989], p. 79.
11 Quoted in Barrett, op. cit., p. 17.
12 Dewey, op. cit., p. 79.
13 ibid., p. 61.
14 Barrett, op. cit., p. 4 and pp. 27–8.
15 For much of what follows see Barrett, op. cit., Ch. 2 and Dewey, op. cit., Ch. 3.
16 Barrett, op. cit., p. 44.
17 Street, *Gentleman*, op. cit., p. 137.
18 NRO Woods MS, op. .cit.
19 Dewey, op. cit., Ch. 4, *passim*.
20 ibid., p. 47.
21 W. H. Barrett, *A Fenmans Story*, [London, 1962], p. 32.
22 Angela Hewins (ed), *The Dillen. Memoirs of a Man of Stratford-on-Avon*, [London, 1981], p. 132.
23 Sheila Stewart, *Lifting the Latch. A Life on the Land*, [Oxford, 1987], pp. 73–4.
24 Siegfried Sassoon, *The War Poems*, Arranged and edited by Rupert Hart Davies, [London, 1983], p. 76.
25 Peter Simkins, *Kitchener's Army. The making of the New Armies 1914–1916*. [Manchester, 1988], p. 174.
26 *EWP*, 19th September 1914.
27 Hewins, op. cit., p. 138.

28 Simkins, op. cit., pp. 107–12.
29 ibid., p. 187.
30 Hewins, op. cit., p. 137.
31 Quoted in Simkins, op. cit., p. 72.
32 Quoted in Carr, op. cit., p. 231.
33 C. F. G. Masterman, *England After the War*, [London n.d. but 1923] p. 31.
34 Thompson, *Landed Society*, op. cit., p. 328.
35 Pamela Horn, *Rural Life in England in the First World War*, [Dublin and New York, 1984] p. 40.
36 ibid.
37 Carr, op. cit., pp. 231–3.
38 Nina Slingsby Smith, *George, Memoirs of a Gentleman's Gentleman*, [London, pb edn, 1986], p. 167.
39 ibid., p. 166.
40 Stewart, op. cit., p. 83.
41 For much of what follows see Horn, *Rural Life*, op. cit., Ch. 6 *passim*, which is currently the only good account of women's employment on the land during the war.
42 Horn, op. cit., p. 114.
43 Stewart, op. cit, p. 73.
44 Dewey, op. cit, p. 52.
45 Horn, op. cit., pp. 118–20.
46 Dewey, op. cit., p. 53.
47 ibid., p. 51.
48 NRO Wood MS, op. cit..
49 Dewey, op. cit., p. 131.
50 *EWP*, 8th April 1916.
51 ibid., 15th April 1916.
52 Horn, op. cit., pp. 122–5.
53 Dewey, op. cit., p. 134.
54 Brown, op. cit., pp. 70–1.
55 Dewey, op. cit., p. 179.
56 ibid., p. 177.
57 Interview AJH/Charlie Barber, op. cit..
58 Dewey, op. cit., p. 100.
59 ibid., pp. 225–6.
60 Interview AJH/Jack Leeder, op. cit..
61 Groves, op. cit., p. 165.
62 Howkins, *Poor Labouring Men*, op. cit., pp. 120–9.
63 Street, *Gentleman*, op. cit., p. 172.
64 Stewart, op. cit., p. 79.
65 ibid., p. 75.
66 Horn, op. cit., pp. 81–2.
67 Dewey, op. cit., pp. 107–8.
68 ibid., pp. 118–19.
69 Street, *Gentleman*, p. 171.

70 Quoted in Horn, op. cit., Ch. 8 *passim*.
71 Interview AJH/'Taddy' Wright, Knapton, Norfolk, labourers. Tape in author's possession.
72 Stewart, op. cit., p. 65.
73 see Horn, op. cit., Ch. 8 *passim*.
74 Dewey, op. cit., p. 108.
75 W. H. Barrett, op. cit., p. 60.
76 *The Private Diaries of Sir Henry Rider Haggard*, (ed) D. S. Higgins, [London, 1980], p. 145.
77 ibid., p. 149.
78 Stewart, op. cit., pp. 77–8.
79 Haggard, *Diaries*, op. cit., p. 150.
80 Quoted in Horn, op. cit., p. 247.
81 Stewart, op. cit., p. 78.
82 ibid., p. 79.

11

Aftermath 1918–1925

To most countrymen in the war zones, the overwhelming desire once the fighting had ended was to get home – home to the promises of peace and the land fit for heroes. George Swinford, from West Oxfordshire, but at Ath in Belgium in 1918, found it difficult. 'You had to have a letter from your boss offering you a job. My wife was eager to get me home, and as Father was working at Filkins Hall he got Mr Groves to write for me . . . Thousands with no job to go to stayed on there'.[1] 'Billa' Dixon, like hundreds if not thousands of others, found 'mutiny' a good way of ensuring a quick passage home. He, again like many others, was destined, in late 1918, for the British Army in Germany.

> We got onto a boat, the boat was nearly loaded up and instead of going they shouted out different names had got to go back, their employer had sent for them. Well we wore them little chevrons for every year in France . . . Well a lot of them going back hadn't even one chevron . . . Well these Australians said 'Don't stick that Tommy' . . . so they pushed them off. Then this lot stopped the next lot as they come of the train said 'Don't you go across'. So they marched us back to Chelsea barracks and broke us up in fifties with the guards, NCOs and took us up to Wimbledon Common. We went up there and got discharged home. So I was home again in two days.[2]

The land to which they returned, if not 'fit for heroes', was prosperous although that prosperity was unevenly spread. Those who had done best were the farmers, especially the larger tenant farmers growing cereals. Farmers, writes Dewey, 'were able to raise their share of the income of the industry from about two-fifths before the war to almost two-thirds in 1917–18.' As a result, 'whether one judges by the rate of rise in net income, or the rate of return on capital employed, farmers as a whole were clearly substantially better off during the war than before it.'[3] Some of this found a reflection in lifestyle.

The better off larger tenant farmers began to own motor cars which took them and their wives to markets and county shows in place of the old 'two-hander'. Leisure also took on new forms. Tennis, very much the territory of the incomers or the gentry before the war, now spread downwards with the new prosperity. 'There had been tennis-parties throughout the summer', wrote Adrian Bell of Suffolk, in 1920. 'All the young married farmers of the district had tennis lawns.'[4] To the postwar generation in A. G. Street's Sutton Evias it was golf. 'They had money, and having spent four long years without much sport or pleasure, they were out to have their fill.'[5] Yet, as in all classes, there had been irreplaceable losses. In John Moore's *Portrait of Elmbury* there is an elegiac account of the farmers' sons of Gloucestershire, 'who went to the Great War with the Yeomanry, riding their own horses which they refused to leave behind.'

> Somebody decided that the time had come to 'exploit a break-through' and ordered the cavalry into the gap. But there hadn't been a breakthrough, and there wasn't a gap. They young men settled down in their saddles and rode as they would ride a Point-to-Point into the enemy lines. Both of Mr. Jeff's fine sons fell that day; and after four years, out of the twenty (that went) only seven came home.[6]

Although they suffered equally terrible losses, in the short term at least, the rural poor had gained too. Labourers' wages, which had stood at between 12s and £1 a week, depending on area, in 1914, topped at £2 5s a week in 1921. Although much of this was eroded by inflation, especially in food prices, it was real progress. There were other more subtle changes. Although romantics might regret the passing of payment in kind, wage bargaining by the piece, or harvest beer, and their replacement by wages board rates, few labourers would have agreed. A more stable income and set rates more than made up for a few pence gained here and there. In some districts even housing improved where Rural District Councils took advantage of the short-lived Addison housing schemes.

The 'land fit for heroes' though was remarkably short on 'land'. The prewar interest in 'back to the land' movements found limited but enthusiastic support during the war from governments intent on convincing Tommy Atkins that he was fighting for something worthwhile. However, high land prices and the rapid moves to de-control the economy after 1918 meant that few ex-servicemen got the 'peasant holding' promised. About 16,000 holdings were created and 24,000 ex-servicemen settled on them, but this hardly constituted the social revolution many had hoped for.[7]

For working class women in the rural areas, as elsewhere, what changes in economic opportunity the war had brought soon vanished. In agriculture itself comparisons are very difficult since in the 1921 census the categories were again changed and brought farmers' wives and daughters back in as an economically active group. Nevertheless, if we take the 1908 Census of Production figure, we find that at that date there were 157,000 women working in agriculture at all levels including family labour whereas at the 1921 census there were only 107,000. Even given that the 1908 figure may include numbers of 'domestic' servants there clearly was a real drop. As in male employment, regional patterns continued to dominate women's work. The 1921 census showed that women made up 36 per cent of the Northumberland agricultural labour force and 33 per cent of that of Durham. In the south and east, Middlesex and the Isle of Ely, 17 per cent and 14.3 per cent respectively testified to the importance of women's work in the 'new' areas of commercial fruit and vegetable production.[8] Additionally, most of the alternative employment for women which had become available during the war, especially in engineering, vanished with the return of the men. It is interesting that almost exactly the same number of women entered and remained in engineering and its related trades between 1901 and 1911 as did between 1911 and 1921.[9]

If rural women made a permanent gain at all as a result of the war it was the Women's Institutes.[10] These appeared in 1915 under the wing of the Agricultural Organisation Society. In September 1917 they were given government support via the Women's Branch of the Board of Agriculture and by 1919, when the Board handed power over to the WI's own National Federation, there were upwards of 1,200 Institutes. However, to see the WI simply as either 'jam and Jerusalem' or some kind of government plot, both views which had currency in the 1920s, fundamentally underestimates their importance. They provided a focus for village women to organize on vital issues such as education, rural housing and sanitation as well as broadening their concerns into organizations like the League of Nations Union. Above all though, they simply gave village women a space of their own. This was recognized by the Cotswold shepherd Mont Abbot, who called the WI the 'biggest revolution of all'.

> Most Institutes in the villages before the war had been clubs for working men. Women warnt supposed to club together on purpose. They'd congregate occasionally in the 'Bode of Love', the little kitchen at the back of the pub . . . But coming together on purpose, as a body, and calling themselves 'the WI' – well! . . . They was only doing what we men going to the pub had been doing for years.[11]

Despite objections and mockery from the men, and outright hostility from the trades unions, the WI remained and grew in importance throughout the interwar years, constituting for all of that period the largest women-only organization in England and probably in Europe.

In a way, the most far reaching effect of the war was on the landowners, although here again what happened was a continuation of prewar practice 'speeded up' rather than anything especially new. Rents had remained stable throughout the war but, with the onset of peace, and backed by the government's pledge to continue the Corn Production Act, agriculture was a booming industry and one whose future seemed secure. In this situation the price of agricultural land rocketed and the many landowners began to sell. There was additionally the grim reason of death. The country elite had probably suffered proportionally worse than any other group from the loss of sons. A military tradition, as we saw earlier, encouraged them to enlist and the particularly vulnerable position of the junior officer at the head of his men meant that their casualty rate was very high and many a 'son and heir' lay in the mud of Flanders. There were other reasons. Rents had remained low during the war but to increase them suddenly might well have made a landlord liable for higher taxation. After 1919 death duties made it more sensible to dispose of land in payment rather than selling other assets or using capital. On the positive side, demand for land meant that by sale a landowner could realize sufficient capital to pay off debts and still have a surplus to invest at 7 per cent or 8 per cent per annum as against the 3 per cent return expected from rents.[12]

These factors together meant that in the years immediately after 1918 great areas of England came up for sale. 'The avalanche came with the spring of 1919', writes F. M. L. Thompson, and by 'the end of March about 1,000 square miles or well over half a million acres was on the market'.[13] The sales continued in the following year and only began to decline with the onset of depression in 1921–22. The *Estates Gazette* concluded that by that date about a quarter of the land of England had changed hands, a figure which is supported by the estimates of Thompson.[14]

The most remarked-upon buyers were speculators and the 'men who had done well out of the war'. In novels like Street's, *Gentlemen of the Party* or Adrian Bell's *Silver Ley* or *Cherry Tree* these figures, often brought together into a 'syndicate' as in John Moore's *Brensham Village* or Bell's *Silver Ley*, are the villains of the piece. They come in from outside and buy over the heads of the sitting farmer tenants in order to raise rents which had usually been held down during the war. In *Silver Ley* such a 'syndicate', its evil power added to by its anonymity in a society where, in ideology at least, everybody knows everybody, come to buy a group of Suffolk farms.

> . . . the farm had been sold by the local landowner to a syndicate of boot manufacturers from the North, who were in their turn intending to blandish the farmers into buying the farms of which they were tenants at a profit to the syndicate.[15]

Certainly there were such speculators abroad but the permanent transfer of land was not to them, or to those 'who had done well out of the war' from urban areas but to the farmers themselves. In the four years after 1918 something in the order of 25 per cent of the agricultural land of England was transferred into the hands of those who farmed it. That the transfer was often at very high prices, that the mortgage became crippling in later years, and that the farmers often did not want to buy the land was neither here nor there and an unwilling and unwitting social revolution took place.

The basis of this was the shift in social and economic power away from the aristocracy and the gentry to the farmers. As Thompson puts it 'these transfers marked a startling social revolution in the countryside, nothing less than the dissolution of a large part of the great estate system and the formation of a new race of yeomen.'[16] These 'new yeomen', while they were, in national terms, usually 'small landowners' were, in local terms, masters of the parishes where they lived, perhaps more surely than those who had owned a parish only as one of many hundreds. The focus of power and deference finally shifted in these years from the landowners to the farmers. It was the beginning of change which was to lead ultimately to the situation in our own day so well described in Newby *et al's* study of modern farming *Property, Paternalism and Power* where 'the social, economic and political leadership of rural society has passed decisively into the hands of the farmers . . . rather than the traditional landed aristocracy.'[17] As in many other areas, these changes could be seen before the war but it was the war which speeded the process up and which was the visible cause of change – hence the war became the watershed in popular memory.

The aristocracy, despite contemporary fears, did not vanish. Rather they tended to concentrate their holdings by selling outlying land and adjusting their lifestyle while judiciously investing the profits of land sales elsewhere. As a result many of the great families survived. This was less the case with the landed gentry. Here, with little surplus land to sell, death duties and taxation fell hard. Some moved abroad, classically to 'white Africa', Kenya and Rhodesia, where land was cheap and the cost of living low, but many simply drifted down to the ranks of the farmers. Significantly, few could be found to replace them – a small estate was no longer a worthwhile investment and, while country life continued to carry prestige, few thought estate management a sensible price to pay for it.[18]

However, these boom conditions did not last. In the summer of 1920 foreign imports of wheat had resumed to such an extent to make it possible that the guaranteed prices offered to farmers under the continuation of the Corn Production Act (the Agriculture Act of 1920) could effectively become a subsidy which would keep English prices high. In the spring of 1921 that projection suddenly took on a new urgency when Sir Arthur Boscawen, the Minister of Agriculture, told the Cabinet that the fall in cereal prices would bring the minimum prices agreement into force and that this would cost the nation something in the region of £30 million in a single year, approximately 10 times the entire annual budget of his Ministry.[19] As a result, on 2 June 1921, Boscawen announced the repeal of those sections of the Agriculture Act which guaranteed prices, along with all powers to enforce cultivation. Additionally, Boscawen abolished the Wages Board and the county wage committees, effectively ending guaranteed national wages.

The end of guaranteed prices, which after all had never really been used, was not sufficient to cause the disastrous years that followed. The import of cereals was bound to resume after the war, but the possible effects of that resumption were concealed in 1919 and 1920. Continued shortage in those years meant that, as during the war, the other part of the Act, that which imposed a maximum price for wheat, had frequently been invoked. So the end of the Act, especially since it meant wages could be reduced, was welcomed by many farmers.

However, by 1921, the world market had changed decisively. On Norwich market, one of the most influential in England, the price of wheat fell from £4 11s 10d a quarter at harvest 1920 to £2 18s 6d a year later, a drop of about 37 per cent. The drop in the price of barley and oats was worse still.[20] Nor was it only cereal produce, although the depression of the 1920s, like that of the 1870s was an arable one. Wool prices fell by between a third and quarter between 1920 and 1921, while store cattle and sheep fell by at least 50 per cent.[21]

After 1921, prices stabilized, not to fall again until 1929–30, but this brought little comfort to many arable farmers. Those worst hit were often the 'new yeomen' who had bought their farms on high mortgages or tenants who had been forced to take their farms at high rents at the end of the war. A. G. Street rented his father's farm on his father's death in 1918 'at a hundred per cent increase in rental'. By 1925, with a high rent and debts incurred by buying stock and equipment at high rates in the early 1920s, he was virtually bankrupt.[22] Those who bought farms at the high prices of 1918–21 were the worst hit. Saddled with high mortgage or bank loan repayments, the stabilizing of prices in the mid-1920s meant little to them since they had borrowed on the assumption that prices would remain high. These were the most bitter, and those who, with justification blamed the repeal of the Agriculture Act for their misfortunes. 'Grievance? I reckon I've got a just grievance', said one of Street's farming friends, 'on the strength of the

Corn Production Act I bought my own farm . . . I've been let down'.[23]

Suffering is a difficult concept to quantify but in the end it was probably the labourer, as always, who suffered most. Even at the height of postwar wages the farm labourers and craftsmen were still earning only 50 per cent of the national industrial wage. After the removal of the Wages Board, between 1921 and 1923, the 'minimum wage' fell from 45s to 25s, a reduction of nearly 40 per cent at a time when the cost of living index fell by less than 30 per cent.[24] Additionally, national recession increased unemployment in the market towns while from the winter of 1921 onwards farmers began laying off full-time workers and not using casuals, especially in the cereal areas. Since labourers were not included under the National Insurance Act we do not have even the inaccurate figures for the unemployed that this provides. However, in 1922–23, several Rural District Councils in East Anglia applied for, and were given, 'special status' as areas entitled to government assistance from the Unemployed Grants Committee.[25]

By the early spring of 1923 agriculture was perceived by those who were part of it to be in crisis and a delegation composed of the National Farmers Union, the County Landowners Association and the National Union of Agricultural Workers went to the Prime Minister. In a clear statement that neither the nation nor the Tory Party any longer believed agriculture to be 'special', or even to have a particular claim based on wartime needs for food, Bonar Law rejected their requests for agricultural subsidies. 'The question is, is agriculture to be self supporting or be supported by the State? I think the latter impossible.' He then went on to rub salt into their wounds, 'in every business you had to take the good with the bad. Farmers had had a good time during the war. That, no doubt, is taken into account now.'[26]

By March 1923 things had gone further down a different road. In January and February the farmers and farmworkers of Norfolk had been 'negotiating' a further drop in wages to 24s a week and an increase of three hours a week in summer.[27] These negotiations had a particular importance. Norfolk, as a predominantly arable county, had been badly hit by price falls and this was made worse by the fact that many Norfolk farmers were heavily in debt because of rent increases and farm purchases in 1918–21. More than that, both the Norfolk farmer and the Norfolk labourer were highly unionized. As negotiations broke down in March the whole of rural England watched and waited, for what happened in Norfolk would in some measure determine what happened elsewhere.

On 17 March the first men struck on the larger Norfolk farms, demanding no wage reductions and no increase in hours. On the 24th the union issued a strike call to all its Norfolk members, and by the following week over 7,000 men, about a quarter of the Norfolk workforce, were on strike. The strike was different in many ways from the disputes of the 1870s and 1890s. Firstly, the union was not isolated but part of a national labour movement which gave its support in myriad ways. Secondly, and more importantly, the strike took place in a context of changed relationships between master and man. There was no doubt in 1923 that it was a battle between the 'organized' farmers in the National Farmers Union and the Farmers Federation, and the organized labourer. The landlords had no part in it, let alone the important one they had in the 1870s. In this situation the 1923 strike in Norfolk was like the 1913 one in Lancashire, and took on a more straightforward class element. This was exacerbated by memories of the war. In many places the press noted men in old uniforms and the newly erected war memorials were often chosen as meeting places. 'Gathering from the various villages, they made the War Memorial . . . at Gaywood their rallying point, and like a regiment of soldiers they marched into the town.'

In some places it went further and violence often broke out. 'You have been soldiers; you know how to fight', said a speaker at one Norfolk meeting, while another striker shouted at a farmer's son working in a field, 'we fought for the land and we are going to have it.'[28] For most the feeling was simply one of ill-formed bitterness rather than political consciousness. A farm pupil called Eric Hockley who had been brought in to work on a large farm at Rougham in Norfolk was working with a team when a group of strikers came into the field and ordered him to unyoke the team.

> 'They swore at me and called us blacklegs, telling us we were taking bread out of their mouths. I undid the horses, and as

> I was bending down to do this, one of them hit with a stick across my back; another struck me a blow with his fist in my ear' . . . One of them asked Hockley, 'where were you in 1914?' He replied 'I am not 18 now.' One of the strikers then said, 'We have been through five years of war. You made your pile in the war and we are going to have it now.'[29]

All the feelings of the bitter years after 1921 are there: the memories of the war and the profiteering of the farmers who had done so well and, crucially, the intense dislike, even hatred, which sections of the labourers now felt for the rural elite.

The strike lasted until 23 April when most of the men returned after the intervention of Ramsay MacDonald had secured 25s a week for 50 hours plus guaranteed overtime rates. But not all returned. A week after the strike had ended over 2,000 men were still out because the farmers refused to take them back. Yet it was a victory. Norfolk had stopped wage reductions even if it had cost the Norfolk men dear. As 'Billa' Dixon, harvest striker in 1914, infantryman and soldier mutineer of 1918, and casual labourer through the bitter years after the war said,

> That was the turn of the tide, after that we went back . . . the farmers had had enough, they got chopped over the strike, we asked for another 5 shillings, and we got it, and went on . . . Then more went into the Union, and it got hold then up to where we are today. They were the start them days, getting the wages, and we had to do it on nothing.[30]

In 1923 a Labour government was elected, pledged to help the farmworker by 'the restoration of the National Wages Board and the County Wages Committees'.[31] In December 1924 the new county committees set minimum wage rates for the first time. In Norfolk it was set at 29s, while in most northern counties it was set at 36s for ordinary labourers. The strikers were vindicated.

The cereal harvests of 1923 and 1924 were good and prices stabilized again. Some farmers, like Street, responded by increasing the acreage under wheat and using artificial fertilizers. This worked for two or three years and gave a false sense of return to normal. 'You get good crops for a year or two. Then, for another year or so you get crops, which look good . . . Finally you get crops (whose) stems are too weak to carry the weight of the ear and . . . the crop "bruckels" over, and does not mature at all.'[32] Others, as in the 1870s, looked to new crops, like sugar beet, although this was really only practicable in East Anglia where there were processing plants.

In some areas a watered-down version of the prewar ruralist dream brought urban holidaymakers into the countryside and created a demand for bed and breakfast or rented accommodation which provided income via a wife and daughter's work. Farmhouse teas for cyclists and walkers became a common part of many a northern hill farm's income. Harold Hicks, whose father farmed 100 acres near the North Norfolk coast, remembered himself and his brothers being evicted from their bedrooms to sleep over the barn in the summer months while his mother 'took in' visitors.[33] In the West Country, a more popular area for rural holidays, the role of women, both in the diary and taking in visitors, saved many a Devon small farm from bankruptcy.[34]

In general though, at least until the mid-1920s, it was not so much another change in direction as a return to the farming patterns that were being established before the war, and which, in a sense, the war had disrupted by its artificially high demand for cereals. The slight improvement in fortunes around 1925 – as prices levelled out for most crops and livestock added to this trend. Any notion of 'back to the seventies' was clearly a temporary one.

In the mid-twenties then things seemed calm. Perhaps the worst was over, things 'stabilized', prices stopped falling and wages seemed to be improving again. It was as if the upheavals of nearly fifty years of depression and war had ended and a new system had come into being. In a way a new system had emerged, but it was to go through many more problems before it seemed safe and permanent, and the people of rural England were to find that there were many more traumas to be faced before prosperity and security, even for a minority, was to be the norm.

Looking back over the seventy-five years from 1925 there were, in rural England, both great continuities and substantial change. When S. L. Bensusan took his trip through the rural areas in 1927 in the steps of Hall, Haggard and Caird he still travelled, as we said at the beginning, through a diverse and regional economy with distinctive agricultural and social structures. Many of these had stood the test of time almost unaltered. England was still divided into upland and lowland zones – the north-west/south-east division which Caird had written about in 1851. In a way this was inevitable. Farming systems, which lie at the core of the social history of rural England, were not easily changed, especially in a period when artificial fertilizers and pesticides were unusual.

Within this great divide some areas retained further similarities. Norfolk, for example, according to Bensusan, was still dominated by the four-course rotation 'and it is very hard to get that system reconsidered by the rank and file of men who follow the rule of thumb.'[35] In Northumberland the memories of those who worked the farms as well as farm accounts show a similar conservatism in the arable areas. This was enforced in some cases by landlords insisting, even in the 1920s, on strict adherence to husbandry covenants dating from the 1860s.[36]

Social structures related to these regional agrarian divisions also showed a remarkable persistence. Bensusan's description of a Yorkshire Dales farmer of the mid-1920s could easily have come from an account of the 1850s or 1860s.

> In the first place he is a tremendous worker. His wife and children . . . help him; he has, in his devotion to the land, something that makes him akin to the French, Belgian and German small farmer . . . (He) gets a good many odd jobs; he seeks to find employment on other men's land at haysel and harvest, and he contrives to pay a good rent.[37]

Elsewhere in the north, in Lancashire and the north midlands, dairy and vegetable production, which would have been familiar in the 1880s and to Haggard and Hall, continued with a good deal of success. These areas remained prosperous through most of the interwar period, based on urban demand for milk, eggs and poultry.[38] However, these did mark a change as did the growth of market gardening around London. Here the adoption of alternative husbandry in response to depression was set to become a permanent change. No longer did wheat rule as the undisputed king of English agriculture. Vegetables, dairy products and even the despised chickens and, worst of all, flowers had entered the sphere of commercial and acceptable farming.

In other areas apparent continuity concealed important changes. In Northumberland, Castle Heaton Farm retained many structural features in 1925 which were there in the 1860s. However here, as elsewhere, changes within the system, especially of hiring, were making subtle alterations. Even in 1890, at the height of the depression, the farm's 'social system' based on living on the farm and family hiring with a large number of women workers remained firm. After the October hirings that year the farm employed, full and part time, twenty-seven workers of whom nine were women. Only four of them were not hired as part of a family. At the same point in 1925 the farm employed only seventeen workers of whom three were women. Six of them were not part of family hiring. A system which had stood up to depression and war was gradually collapsing. In the next twenty years it disappeared almost totally.[39] Similarly, in the West Country, Bouquet's work, which we have already mentioned, shows how increasing market demand for dairy produce took this sphere out of women's control and placed it with the males of the household. In its place, women in her Devon parish 'took in visitors', an increasingly vital part of the family income, yet one which was concealed behind bland agricultural statistics which saw this area of Devon as 'still' as much a dairy area in the 1920s as it had been earlier.[40]

These changes in hiring, along with a shift to different and more diverse farming systems, had a curiously contradictory effect. Nationally, hiring practices tended to become more and more uniform, especially after the 1890–1900s, with regional variations disappearing, particularly under the impact of machinery. On the other hand the growth of alternative husbandry produced a new set of productive relationships around quite different hiring practices.

The biggest change of all is at one level the most obvious, yet its real importance somehow remains obscured. At the beginning of the period covered by this book agriculture accounted for 20 per cent of the national income and 21 per cent of the employed population. At the end of our period, in 1924, it made up 4 per cent of national income and employed about 7 per cent of the population. This process of economic marginalization, in which agriculture was reduced from being the greatest 'interest' in the state in Caird's day to a mere 'sector' in Bonar Law's, is clearly of fundamental importance to economic history. Yet it goes much further than that. Rural 'Land' retained an almost mystic importance in English national culture, yet lost much of its real power in an economic sense. With this decline came the end of the 'agricultural interest' as a 'special' part of the nation. This is what the NFU delegation to Bonar Law found in 1923 when they were told that they were merely representatives of one not very important or efficient industry, whining to an impoverished government.

There were other areas of change, often not obvious in the short term or at local level. The long-term trend to owner-occupancy was of fundamental importance in shaping the social relations of the village and farm community not because of the 'break-up' of great estates, although that played a part, but because of the disappearance of the vulnerable 'gentry', the smaller landowners, who played a central role as a lieutenant faction. The 'squire', the wealthy and charitable parson, and the 'lady of the house', were vital in the paternalist model which, as we saw, was a creation of the thirty years after 1850. In the years after 1880, under the impact of depression and war, their position was undermined. The great landowners, on the other hand, showed a remarkable tenacity, but they had often been separate from 'their' communities, and the new owner/farmers, especially in the hard years of the 1920s, had little time or inclination for *noblesse oblige*. These changes, added to those in local government and the Poor Law tended, in the medium term, to undermine the power of the old village elites. No longer could a great landlord control settlement patterns, indeed he had little interest in so doing since the Poor Law was less and less meaningful as an agency of either welfare or control. As a result ideas like 'open' and 'close' which had dominated the discussion of rural social structures for over a century were now redundant.

Similarly the power of the Church, and for that matter the chapel, became less and less pervasive and relevant. After a period of relative success the religious institutions of the rural areas started a slow decline in the years just before the war which was not to be reversed. Anglicanism found itself simply another denomination in the years after 1918, although it retained a special place in the Remembrance Sunday services which were so important in the 1920s and 1930s, and in the consecration of village war memorials. Indeed, many in the Church hoped that the war would reunite the villages and the Church. The Bishop of Hereford wrote in 1920:

> I am persuaded that the Memorial Crosses, in the Churchyards, on the village greens, where the roads meet, will for many years

> to come cry eloquent but silent protest against all that divides and degrades village life.[41]

It was a faint hope. If the villages were to be united and better places the Church of England was to play only a slight part.

But it was not only the Church. As Gilbert says 'Chaplains (in the Great War) confronted with battalions which the *Church Times* called a "microcosm of the nation" were forced to face the reality of how little the religious culture of either Church or Chapel pervaded the wider secular culture.'[42] The wayside Bethel, which had provided so much for country working men and women in the 1870s and 1880s became less and less meaningful in an altered world. While nationally the Methodist connections moved to a 'non-political' stance, many of their working class members moved in the opposite direction. The new pietism which appeared before the war seems to have been increasingly irrelevant in the harsh postwar years.[43] Although the generation of village radicals born just before and during the Great War continued to hold an allegiance to chapel, they were to be the last.

In most of rural England the workforce continued to decline under the impact of depression and mechanization. The long-term trend, which began in the 1850s, continued after the war despite a slight decrease in the rate of depopulation in 1921. Tractors, a rarity even in 1918, became more and more common on large arable farms and because they speeded up many farming occupations allowed substantial reductions in the number of workers. Similarly reaper-binders, unusual before 1914, became the norm in the interwar years when taking harvest by hand vanished on all but the smallest farms. As a result of these changes the workforce on each farm grew smaller and relations between master and man grew closer again, although it was not until after the Second World War that this became obvious.

In parts of rural England this population loss was balanced by 'new' countrymen and women – urbanites and suburbanites – who sought a better life in the countryside. In some areas, especially the Home Counties, the outpourings of the towns created whole new communities on the outskirts of existing and formerly agricultural towns and villages. Ironically, as 'agriculture' declined as a part of the national economy so a mythologized version of its remnants became desirable to the urban elite. Guildford, Godalming,

Dorking, Beaconsfield, formerly market towns or villages, became the centres of a building boom, especially in the early 1930s, which transformed some of the poorest areas of rural England into some of the richest. Even in the 1920s though, these changes in the countryside had spread well outside the narrow belt around the metropolis. The move of the Bloomsbury Group *en masse* to the 'wilds' of Sussex in the 1920s was simply one example of what Bensusan saw in 1927. Worse still, as he saw it, was the growth of 'week-enders', 'folk who have acquired the property cheaply, or taken a long lease at a low rent.' In a bitter passage which speaks directly to the 1990s he says,

> Thirty years ago all these cottages belonged to the agricultural labourers, who paid from fifteen pence to two shillings a week rent; today, where they are rented, they fetch from £20 to £30 a year. Yet they are as much the property of the village folk as the old common lands that have been enclosed . . . Because they have been divorced from their proper ownership the young men and women of the village must emigrate or seek the slums.[44]

The rural areas of the south and east in particular also became more integrated into the national structure despite the persistence of regional forms and cultures. The retailing revolution may have given a new importance to market towns as we saw above but the products sold in the 'local' shops were increasingly the result of a national and international market and manufacturing system. Men and women were also less isolated from national trends as national newspapers replaced local and, from the mid-1920s, radio brought London into every home.

Sometimes directly and sometimes indirectly these changes altered or obliterated many locally-based institutions. We saw how Flora Thompson perceived her village to be culturally in a 'transitional' state in the 1880s. By the 1920s that process had gone much further. For example, we saw in Chapters 3 and 5 how important village friendly societies were to both the rural elite and the rural poor. In the years after 1870 they gradually disappeared, to be replaced by branches of the national 'orders' like the Foresters and the Oddfellows. Nevertheless, because they were branches, a local dimension was retained, especially local feasts and club days. The introduction of National Insurance removed the need for friendly societies in the urban areas, where their real strength lay, and so they gradually vanished from the rural districts, taking with them one small part of village identity and culture.

More subtly, the village community seems to have been 'respectablized'. Drunkenness and poaching, the two great rural crimes, both decreased substantially, the latter before the war, the former after. The rapid decrease in yearly hiring, even in the north, after the war reduced the size, importance and 'carnival' of the hiring fair. By the 1930s, even where yearly hiring and living-in persisted, bargains were usually made privately.

What these shifts added up to was a 'cultural' change which interpreted the marginalization of agricultural production we talked about above. Anthony Cohen sees a culture not as 'a coherent system of ideas' but as 'a way of doing things . . . a customary mode of thought and performance.' This culture relates to the everyday rather than to the exceptional. 'People thus become aware of their culture and experience their distinctiveness . . . through the evaluation of everyday practice.'[45] The same point was made over seventy years ago by George Bourne in his *Change in the Village*. Bourne saw this customary system under attack from a number of places. The customary world, like agricultural production itself, in national terms is rendered marginal and its values and structure, its 'way of doing things' becomes irrelevant. In his Surrey village, enclosure in the first half of the nineteenth century, followed by new farming practices and finally suburbanization, drove the labourers and small farmers into the position of what he calls 'the humiliated'. 'No longer are they a group whose peculiarities are respected while their qualities are esteemed. In their intercourse with the outer world they have become, as it were degraded, humiliated . . . '[46]

This is what Cohen and others identify as 'marginality'. Cohen argues, as this book has in its way, that this is not only or even mainly a spatial concept, it can equally be 'collective self images informing and informed by a community's perception of its inability to affect the course of events.'[48] This is precisely what happened in much of rural England in the years after the depression of the 1870s–1890s and especially after the Great War. The 'workers' of rural England, particularly the small farmers and labourers, became strangers in their own land. Their culture was tested against the urban, industrial and commercial and found wanting. The very basis of their livelihood and its representation was devalued and rendered, in the end, to some kind of 'heritage' which bore little resemblance either to their past or their present. How many now know the 'Five Alls' with its insistence on the primacy of agriculture and its total dismissal of all other forms of production?

> The Queen rules all
> The Parson prays for all
> The Soldier fights for all
> The Lawyer pleads for all
> The Ploughmen feeds all and pays for all.

All this was slow and complex. Cataclysm had little part to play although sudden falls in prices as at the end of the 1870s and 1921–22, and disasters like the flood summer of 1912 or the outbreaks of foot and mouth in Herefordshire in the early 1920s, seemed like that in the local world. But nor is the opposite extreme tenable. Rural England was not unchanging. There were no continuities going back unproblematically through some 'golden age' before 1914 or before 1880 or before 1850. Rural England was reshaped between 1850–1925 but in complex and varied ways, different in different regions and experienced differently by different classes and groups within it.

NOTES

1 Swinford, op. cit., p. 96.
2 Interview. Dixon, op. cit..
3 Dewey, op. cit., pp. 235–6.
4 Adrian Bell, *Corduroy*, [London, 1941], p. 228.
5 Street, *Gentleman*, op. cit., p. 179.
6 Moore, op. cit., p. 81.
7 Dennis Hardy and Colin Ward, *Arcadia for All*, [London, 1984], pp. 20–1.
8 *Census of Population 1921*, op. cit., p. 122.
9 Mitchell and Deane, op. cit., p. 60.
10 What follows is derived from the work of Maggie Morgan which is as yet unpublished but is the first scholarly study of the WI.
11 Stewart, op. cit., pp. 82–3.
12 Thompson, *Landed Society*, pp. 33–7.
13 ibid., p. 330.

14 ibid., p. 332.
15 Adrian Bell, *Silver Ley*, [London, 1932] p. 140.
16 Thompson, op. cit., p. 333.
17 Newby, Bell *et al.*, op. cit., p. 38.
18 Thompson, op. cit., pp. 342–3.
19 For what follows see Edith H. Whetham, *Agrarian History*, op. cit., pp. 141–71, and Howkins, *Great Momentous Time*, op. cit. Ch. 8. *passim*.
20 Howkins, ibid., p. 224.
21 Whetham, op. cit., pp. 143–8.
22 Street, *Farmer's Glory*, op. cit., pp. 219–33.
23 ibid., p. 230.
24 *British Labour Statistics. Historical Abstract 1866–1968*, [London, 1971], p. 166.
25 See Howkins, op. cit., pp. 224–31.
26 *Times*, 19th March 1923.
27 For the following see Howkins, *Poor Labouring Men*, op. cit., Ch 8 *passim*.
28 *MLE*, 9th April 1923.
29 *NN*, 7th April 1923.
30 Interview AJH/Dixon, op. cit..
31 *The Labour Party and the Countryside. A statement of policy with regard to agriculture and rural life* [London, 1922], p. 5.
32 Street, *Farmer's Glory*, op. cit., p. 237.
33 Interview AJH/Harold Hicks, Trunch Norfolk, farmer. Tape in author's possession.
34 For an important discussion of this see Mary-Rose Bouquet, *Family, Servants and Visitors, the Farm Household in Nineteenth and Twentieth Century Devon*, [Norwich, 1985].
35 Bensusan, op. cit., p. 50.
36 NRO T 34, op. cit..
37 Bensusan, op. cit..
38 ibid., Chaps XV and XIX.
39 NRO Woods MS, op. cit..
40 Bouquet, op. cit., pp. 56–65.
41 Alan Wilkinson, *The Church of England and the First World War*, [London, 1978], p. 291.
42 Gilbert, op. cit., p. 203.
43 Moore, op. cit., pp. 199–229.
44 Bensusan, op. cit., pp. 39–40.
45 Cohen, op. cit., pp. 5–6.
46 George Bourne (Sturt), *Change in the Village*, (1912), [pb. ed, Harmondsworth, 1984], p. 93.
47 Cohen, op. cit., p. 6.

Further Reading

Detailed references and materials can be followed through the notes to each chapter. This merely seeks to indicate some of the main works cited which are readily available for further consultation. It must be stressed this is only a small selection.

There are no histories of rural England which cover this period exactly. J. D. Chambers and G. E. Mingay, *The Agricultural Revolution 1750–1880*, covers the early part of the period essentially from an economic history viewpoint. G. E. Mingay, *Rural Life in Victorian England*, covers a longer period but is uneven in its treatment, although it contains the only easily available material on the rural professional and middle classes. *The Victorian Countryside*, two volumes edited by G. E. Mingay, presents a range of essays which are a bit like the curate's egg – 'good in parts'. Pamela Horn has produced several books on the period, including *The Changing Countryside* which covers much of this period as well as more specific works, of which *The Victorian Country Child* and *Rural Life in England in the First World War* are the most interesting. Howard Newby, *Country Life* is good on interpretation. For the early part of the period two outstanding specialist works cover general topics. These are K. D. M. Snell, *Annals of the Labouring Poor*, and L. Davidoff and C. Hall, *Family Fortunes*. For the later part of the period Edith Whetham's *The Agrarian History of England and Wales, Volume VIII, 1914–1939* is a good starting point.

On specific groups within the countryside there are many studies. For the elite I still think F. M. L. Thompson, *English Landed Society in the Nineteenth Century*, is the place to start although this is now supplemented by J. C. Beckett, *The Aristocracy in England 1660–1914*. There is no good study of the farmers as a group though there are accounts in Mingay's *Rural Life in Victorian England* and *The Victorian Countryside*. The farm labourers have been the subject of a recent study, Alan Armstrong, *Farmworkers*, and the historical sections of Howard Newby, *The Deferential Worker*, are excellent. This is also a key interpretive text. There are no full-length studies of women workers in the rural areas but Jennie Kitteringham's article in R. Samuel (ed) *Village Life and Labour* is a good starting point. This book is generally very important especially on the poorest sections of rural England. More work is now being done of the position of women in rural society.

On the physical and spatial nature of rural England, Christopher Taylor, *Village and Farmstead. A History of Rural Settlement in England*, is an excellent and challenging starting point. Dennis R. Mills, *Lord and Peasant in Nineteenth Century Britain*, puts the discussion about social structure and village type into perspective although many of his arguments have been criticised. Detailed references are to be found in the main text of this book. For those interested in anthropological ideas of community, Anthony P. Cohen (ed), *Symbolising Boundaries* and *Belonging* are both excellent accounts in the form of collections of essays.

For specific topics like crime, trades unions, the Church and so on readers should refer to the notes in each chapter. However, it is worth pointing to some contemporary materials and sources which are generally available and which are well worth consulting. The first of these are the British Parliamentary Papers. These are an essential source for the social history of the nineteenth century and a considerable part of the most interesting ones were reprinted some years ago by the Irish University Press. This reprint is available in many university and polytechnic libraries and some public libraries.

More accessible are nineteenth and twentieth century autobiographies and diaries, of which there are a huge number. Some are outstanding. Any list is bound to be a personal one but a selection of interesting and worthwhile titles would include some of the following: George Baldry, *Rabbitskin Cap* (Suffolk); W. H. Barrett, *A Fenmans Story* (Cambridgeshire); John Buckby *A Village Politician* (Bucks); H. St G. Cramp, *A Yeoman Farmer's Son* (Leicestershire); Sybil Marshall, *Fenland Chronicle* (Cambridgeshire); Fred Kitchen, *Brother to the Ox* (Nottinghamshire); James Hawker, *A Victorian Poacher* (Northants); 'The King of the Norfolk Poachers', *I Walked by Night* (Norfolk); A. Hewins, *The Dillen* (Warwicks); G. Swinford, *Jubilee Boy* (Oxon). There are many others referred to in the notes.

Finally there are four rural 'journeys' which provide convenient contemporary accounts through the period. These are James Caird, *English Agriculture in 1850–51*, (1852); Henry Rider Haggard, *Rural England* 2 vols. (1902); A. D. Hall *A Pilgrimage of British Farming* (1913); and S. L. Bensusan, *Latter Day Rural England* (1927).

Index